IT TRANSFORMATION

with SOA

Trials, Techniques & Tribulations

IT TRANSFORMATION

with SOA

Trials, Techniques & Tribulations

Israel del Rio

Abstraction Publishing Co

www.abstraction.com

IT Transformation with SOA
Trials, Techniques & Tribulations

Abstraction Publishing Co

First Edition

ISBN: 1-46805-380-9

EAN-13: 978-1-4680-5380-7

Cover illustration by **Tania del Rio**

Table of Contents

Table of Contents _____ **v**

Acknowledgements _____ **ix**

Preface _____ **xi**

Section I _____ **1**

IT Transformation _____ **2**

The Need for Change _____ **5**

The Drivers for Transformation _____ **15**

Business Needs _____ 21

Emerging Technologies _____ 23

Competition _____ 27

Assessing Your Organization's View of Technology _____ 28

Assessing the Future _____ **33**

Technology Prognostication An Example _____ 40

Envisioning the Business Impact _____ 45

Justifying the Technology Transformation _____ 49

Musings about Innovation _____ 54

Section II _____ **59**

Defining the Scope _____ **60**

Requirements _____ 60

Taming Complexity _____ 65

The Technology Strategy _____ **69**

The Architecture as foundation for the Technology Solution ___ 73

The Architecture Process _____ 77

The Architecture Scope _____ 82

The Architecture Reference Model _____ 89

On the Creation of Tenets and Standards _____ 94

Chiseling the Stone: The Category I Tenets _____ 100

Category II Tenets _____ 106

Category III Tenets _____ 109

SOA as the Solution _____ **112**

SOA—What it really is _____ 113

The Advantages of the Service Oriented View _____ 117

The SOA Distributed Processing Pattern _____ 124

*Section III*_____ *131*

*The Technology Solution*_____ *131*

An SOA Taxonomy_____ **132**

The Services _____ **136**

Service Classes _____ 141

The Service Types_____ 144

Service Delivery Patterns _____ 146

A Sample view of services in a System _____ 148

On Service Granularity_____ 151

The Service Interfaces _____ 154

The SOA Framework _____ **157**

The Access Layer _____ 161

The Membrane as the Boundary Layer_____ 164

The Orchestrators _____ 167

ESB and the SOA Fabric _____ 170

The Data Sentinel_____ 174

SOA Approaches & Techniques _____ **177**

Taming the SOA Complexities _____ 178

State Keeping/State Avoidance_____ 181

Handling Transactional Services _____ 184

The Data Visibility Exceptions _____ 187

Data Matching and Integration Engines _____ 189

Data Mapping & Transformation _____ 191

Caching—SOA on Steroids_____ 196

Managing SOA _____ 199

The Control Layer _____ 199

Best Performance Practices _____ 200

Performance Planning with Modeling & Simulation _____ 203

Engineering with SOA: The Foundation _____ **208**

The Role of Engineering_____ 208

System Availability & Reliability _____ 211

Security & Continuance _____ 216

SOA Systems Management _____ 219

   The Systems Management Stack _____ 221

   Dashboards and Centralized Logging _____ 224

Section IV _____ 227

Execution: Getting It Done _____ 227

Getting it Done: Managing the Transformation _____ 228

Governance and organization _____ 231

   The Product Management Team _____ 235

   The Architecture Team _____ 238

   The SOA Group _____ 241

Transitioning the Team _____ 244

   Filling the Skill Gaps: Contracting, Outsourcing and Off Shoring
_____ 250

On Leadership _____ 255

   The Leadership Style _____ 255

   The Leadership Team _____ 259

   Culture, Style & Pushback _____ 261

   The Office Politics _____ 264

The Relationships _____ 269

   Relationship between Technology and the Line of Business _ 269

   Engaging vendors_____ 274

The Execution & Implementation Steps _____ 279

   Milestone Based Project Management _____ 279

   On Tools & Methodologies _____ 284

   On Documentation _____ 288

   The Art of SOA Testing_____ 291

   Notes on Training _____ 297

   Migration _____ 300

IT Transformation Lifecycle. A Wrap Up. _____ 315

Y2K and the Fuzzy Nature of Success _____ 319

Section V _____ 323

The Future _____ 323

Emerging Business Models in IT _____ **324**

    Software as a Service (SaaS) _____ 328

    Data, Taxonomies, and the Road to Wisdom _____ 332

    Information Distillers & Aggregators_____ 338

    And in the End . . . _____ 342

Appendix A Examples of Tenets & Standards _____ *347*

    General Tenets_____ 348

    Data Tenets _____ 349

    Services tenets _____ 350

    Foundational Tenets _____ 351

    Presentation Tenets_____ 352

    The Standards_____ 353

Bibliography _____ *355*

Index _____ *359*

ACKNOWLEDGEMENTS

I have been privileged to enjoy a more than thirty year career working in IT, both as a technologist and as an executive—a career that has allowed me to witness many of the transformation cycles that have occurred in information systems. My career has involved working in industries that rely on technology for their most mission-critical needs and that, in the process, often stretch the design limits of 'state-of-the-art'.

In addition to working for a major IT vendor (IBM, if you must know), I've worked for two major airline reservation companies whose IT reservation systems are the paragon of high transaction environments (Computer Reservation Systems process on the order of 20,000 transactions per second!). I've also worked for two large hotel chains that, while supporting large volumes of globally generated transactions, also wanted to present compelling hotel content and services in support of their guests.

This book is a compendium of a series of blogs I have posted at http://www.soa-transform.com/ and it represents the accumulated knowledge and experience I've gained from the many professionals I've had the pleasure of working with throughout my career.

I am particularly grateful to Harwell Thrasher and Victor Grund for their insightful feedback on my book draft.

Harwell is a connoisseur of all things IT, founder of MakingITClear Inc. and writer of the highly recommended book, "Boiling the IT Frog". (Check out his excellent blog at http://blog.makingitclear.com/)

Victor is an extremely knowledgeable and attuned technology executive at IBM. In addition to potentially being a future IBM CEO (if he has his way), he is one of the key reasons why this book is better than it would be otherwise.

My lovingly wife, Rita, valiantly performed copy-writing on this book, turning my draft-level babbling into something that is hopefully easier to read. Also, I am incredibly blessed to have access to the great graphic design talents of my daughter, Tania, who nicely designed the book's cover (check Tania's artistic portfolio at http://taniadelrio.com/portfolio/). To them and to my other children, my deepest love and thanks.

Needless to say (but I am saying it, anyway), all mistakes and faults in this book are entirely my responsibility. Reader comments and/or corrections are welcome. Feel free to drop me a line at israel.delrio@abstraction.com.

PREFACE

Some time ago, during a television interview, a politician with whom I often disagreed, expressed a legitimate view on a controversial subject. I mumbled something about the fact that even a broken watch marks the correct time twice a day. My teenage son, Alex, overhearing my snide remark commented with the characteristic perspective of someone born in the computer age, "Not if the watch is digital!"

Information technology is in the midst of a revolutionary revamp. Many of the information systems that were deployed during the past two decades have now become fully depreciated and obtuse and too inflexible to respond to new business demands. As a result, legacy systems cannot easily leverage the extraordinary facilities brought forth by emergent technologies such as Cloud technology, Social Media and the like.

According to industry watchdogs such as Abeerden Group, Fortune 500 companies, which include banks and insurance companies, are sitting on over five hundred billion lines of COBOL (yes, COBOL, the computer language invented by the late Grace Hooper a year before John F. Kennedy became president). As recently as the year 2000, approximately 70% of all mission critical applications were still running on legacy technologies. This, despite the fact, as stated by Gartner, that systems using SOA (Service Oriented Architecture) for mission critical purposes had increased from 50% to 70% in less than a decade.

What these statistics show is that we are smack in the middle of an accelerated technology transformation. Commercial computer systems have now been around for more than sixty years and, with each succeeding technology generation, the number of legacy technologies that must be supported has increased. These are technologies that, under the law of diminishing returns, are becoming less and less capable of matching the speed of business.

The advent of IT practices and concepts such as Service Oriented Architecture (SOA), Software as a Service (SaaS), the Cloud and Open Systems, combined with the globalization of the IT workforce, have revolutionized the IT landscape. Whereas traditional IT processes were established over several decades to mirror a mainframe-centric view of data processing, new IT approaches better mirror and support modern businesses.

For many, although they may not yet be aware of it, the turning point at which it makes sense to completely transform IT systems has been reached. The question facing many organizations these days is whether it makes better sense to undertake a radical transformation program or plow along with tactical solutions via incremental upgrades. The answer is not always clear. Radical transformation requires a serious long-term commitment and, frankly, can represent a significant risk. Gradual improvements, on the other hand, can solve short-term issues, but this comes at the expense of digging a deeper hole for inefficient IT operations in the years to come.

Compounding the challenge, as I write this, we still find ourselves experiencing the aftermath of one of the deepest worldwide financial and economic crises since the Great Depression.

There will be, no doubt, those who suggest that this time of economic hardship is hardly the best time to begin work on IT transformation. However, if history has taught us anything, it is that the companies and ventures that emerged unscathed during previous downturns were precisely those that continued investing. Daring players took advantage of the hidden benefits of a crisis and exploited the new business opportunities arising from unsettled macro-economic environments. Remember, it took a truly catastrophic event—a ten mile wide asteroid striking the earth—to wipe out the dinosaurs. Dinosaurs had been around for more than two-hundred million years, but this cataclysm cleared the path for the eventual supremacy of mammals. Little furry animals that had lived a very-contented rodent-like existence prior to the asteroid strike thrived precisely by adapting to change. They are our multi-generational ancestors.

Speaking of generations. . . I often wonder why the creators of large, generational projects such as the Great Wall of China or the Great Pyramids chose to initiate these efforts knowing they would most likely not see them finalized within their own lifetimes. What inspired them?

I suppose they had the ability to imagine the completed work as transcendent. As long as they knew the project would eventually be completed, it little mattered to them that they themselves would not be around to witness the culmination of their ideas. Deep down they knew the real goal was to leave a lasting legacy. Now, I am not suggesting that transformation projects are equivalent to the building of the Great Wall of China (even though many times they do feel that way!), but compared to the fast-paced rhythm of business in the twenty-first century, any project requiring a three or four year commitment could very well be considered a generational effort.

This book is about transforming mission-critical IT environments. A transformation occurs when you move from a legacy system to a modern one. A legacy system could be a mainframe based environment using old COBOL code, or one based on Novell servers being used as file servers, or even a manual process. In fact, a "legacy" system may well be a non-existent system—a brand new IT implementation can also be viewed as a transformation program. Regardless of what you are transforming from, I will admit to this clear bias (call it a pre-condition): Today's sensible IT transformation projects' destination must follow a Service Oriented Architecture (SOA). It matters not where you are coming from, but rather where you are heading.

SOA enables technology transformation in much the same way air travel enabled globalization, or the way Internet enabled on-line shopping. Consider this: Internet-based B2C (Business to

Consumer) business grew by $70 billion from 1997 to 2002 even in the midst of the dot-com bubble burst. By 2004, B2C business was up by almost $1 trillion from "only" $56 billion in 1999[1].

If anything, pursuing SOA as a part of an IT transformation solution should remove the need for yet-another technology transformation effort in the future. If done properly, SOA establishes a foundation that can evolve a system via more graceful pathways.

Here's a childhood joke: "How do you put five elephants inside a Volkswagen Beetle?" Answer: "Two in the front, and three in the back." The joke may not be all that funny (even though it usually elicits a chuckle), but it is representative of the idea that complex, seemly impossible tasks, can be accomplished by approaching them with a degree of common sense.

A serious IT transformation project is similar to the task of putting five elephants inside a Volkswagen Beetle. By its very nature, technology transformation is a complex process and one that's sure to place strenuous demands on a variety of disciplinary competencies. It's also bound to involve nearly all segments of the enterprise, from top-level executives and strategic vendors, to every single employee in the organization. Add to it the challenges and resistance sure to be presented by the typical cadre of corporate opportunists and bureaucrats, and It transformation becomes even more complex.

Technology transformation is a holistic endeavor; one that touches basically every aspect of your enterprise. Because of this, IT transformation is bound to be an arduous journey spanning a period of several years and is the type of effort that demands a lifecycle and multidisciplinary perspective.

There are excellent books covering many of the areas that I will touch upon: management books, books about project

---

[1] "The Singularity is Near"—Ray Kurzweil

management, treatises on testing and quality assurance, "how-to" manuals on system management, and books directly focused on the emerging field of Service Oriented Architecture. This book differs from these others in so far as I will be focusing on the entire lifecycle of IT transformation; with SOA as the key technical enabler.

I will start by attempting to answer the very basic question of whether technology transformation is needed in your enterprise, and if so, how to create a supporting business case for it, as well as how to secure needed funding. Next I will cover the solution definition stages (again, using SOA), and how to successfully manage the execution and deployment of the new system.

This book is not intended to be a treatise on the different subject matters, but rather a narrative linking each discipline as we visit the various stages of the transformative project lifecycle. My hope is to provide a holistic view of the transformation stages, including a few of the actual trials and tribulations experienced by this author and others when attempting this type of project.

In addition, I will cover topics seldom mentioned in most IT books, including how to deal with office politics and how best to handle stagnant staff and uncooperative cultures. This type of awareness is necessary given the fact that the majority of complex projects fail not because of problems with technology, but because of economic and human factors. No matter how well the target system is designed or how well the chosen methodologies are followed, in the end, success or failure is going to come down to people. The landscape of failed projects is populated by the results of a lack of focus, commitment, discipline or courage. Poor execution by disarticulated teams or impediments due to the lack of suitable skills and unrealistic goals are but some examples of elements that are often neglected in the long and winding road presented by complex projects.

Given my background in travel and hospitality, many of the examples I give are based on the types of situations faced by these particular industries. Still, the challenges, methodologies, and solutions discussed in this book do not deviate very much from other industries. The financial and banking sectors, for example, share many attributes with the transportation and hospitality industries. They all need to provide very large transaction rates with mission critical availability; while providing bespoke functions to customers. The same is true for any industry dependent on highly available information systems, such as commerce and retail.

The audience of this book is the CIO, CTO or IT executive tasked with evaluating and driving a major technology transformation effort, and who oversees the management of IT resources and technology.

It is my hope that this book will provide a down-to-earth perspective on what is needed to successfully transform the information systems in your enterprise and effectively tame the inherent complexities of SOA when applied to large, mission-critical systems. Successful IT transformation is more than successful technology design. It is also about understanding the reasons for change and the environment under which this change is to take place.

Although not everything will be directly applicable to your particular situation, I am confident that you will find that it generally applies to the challenges you are likely to encounter. Because of this pragmatic focus, I realize my comments may come across as cynical at times. Even as I attempt to identify some of the barriers and individuals you will likely have to deal with, and the resistance you may encounter, I would rather do so in a light hearted manner.

The fact is that it is common to see transformation projects go through a series of different managers and teams.

A true transformation project has a lifecycle of its own—one that spans several years and presents different challenges at various points. I have structured this book in sections to mirror this lifecycle:

1. **Making the Case for Transformation**. Regardless of the perennial debate as to whether business or technology is the true driver of change, the truth is that not much is going to happen if there is not a real (or at least perceived) business driver that can serve as a basis for cost-justifying a technology initiative. Whether the driver for transformation is new technology or a challenge from a competitor, there is a fundamental need to frame the transformation exercise in economic cost-benefit terms to ensure it receives the necessary funding.

2. **Planning and Strategy**. This step binds the business drivers to high-level technology decisions. Key choices are made during this step, including the strategy and phasing approach. It is during this stage that most key decisions are made by the CIO and the CTO.

3. **Design of Technology Solution**. This section covers the various SOA design aspects. It is perhaps the most technical. If you find it overly detailed for your purpose, you may want to turn it over to your enterprise architects instead, inviting them to pay heed to the design concepts and techniques discussed. The advice and suggested SOA approaches in this section represent a distilled summary of hard-earned, how-to SOA experiences in the field.

4. **Execution: Putting Transformation to Work**. In this section I cover the organization, management, and also, political and cultural elements necessary to ensure the successful execution of a project, including navigating the dangerous waters of migration.

As a reader, you may choose to read this book from beginning to end, in which case I hope you will enjoy the narrative that touches on the key-decisions and issues facing those involved in a major transformation initiative. Alternatively, you may find yourself the inheritor of an ongoing initiative already in execution phase. You might then benefit by jumping ahead to the section on 'Execution'. Or, if you are assigned to participate in the strategy definition of a project that has already been approved, diving directly into the 'Planning and Strategy' section might be appropriate. Clearly, if you are in the pioneering stage and are evaluating whether a full-fledged technology transformation initiative is appropriate for you, the first section should prove the most useful.

Finally, I've added an additional section in which I discuss some general thoughts and trends regarding the future. There will always be a need to adapt technology to keep it current with the times. Having at least a general conception of what the future can be invaluable in helping to define a longer-lasting, more flexible and serviceable technology platform today.

Hopefully, future IT executive generations won't have to deal with the perils, trials and tribulations that you are certain to face during your technology transformation. If you succeed in laying the proper groundwork, you should come to feel just as proud of your legacy as those who designed the great cathedrals of the past!

SECTION I

Making the Case for Transformation

"If everything seems under control, you're just not going fast enough."
Mario Andretti—Race Car Driver

Trials

What is IT transformation? ✦ Should you even attempt it? ✦ Does your company need it? ✦ Can you afford it? ✦ What is your IT strategy?

Techniques

Understanding your current IT environment ✦ Figuring out how technology is perceived in your company ✦ Identifying which technology elements are essential to your business ✦ Establishing the drivers for change ✦ Aligning the line of business and obtaining their support for the technology approach ✦ Moving on with the business case; what technologies are to be used and how to implement them.

Tribulations

Securing required funding? ✦ Convincing the powers that be that technology is critical to the success of the company ✦ Getting your CFO's support by preparing and delivering a compelling business case ✦ Committing to an enticing, yet realistic return on investment.

IT TRANSFORMATION

For the purpose of this book, technology is defined in the context of information systems technology. This includes the system's hardware and software, the manner in which the system is architected, and how the data is structured and accessed. This definition also includes the algorithms, the IT command and control governance (including IT people), and the actual and potential functionality supported by the system.

As companies become increasingly aware that technology can be used to leverage competitive strengths (and the future belongs to those who use technology most effectively), technology becomes a keystone of the overall business strategy.

The scope of this book deals with how to transform technology at its very core. For example, while IT Transformation encompasses the investment strategies and tactics needed to leverage modern technologies by refreshing the old with the new, it shouldn't be confused with Business Process Reengineering (BPR). Yes, BPR may well be either a driver or a consequence of IT transformation, but IT transformation is not simply an exercise in reengineering. Replacing something old with something new, such as by adding a newer version of a module, does not a transformation project make. Even a larger effort, such as switching a database vendor, while important, is not a transformational undertaking.

Lastly, transforming basic administrative chores that are similar to those found in millions of other companies is certainly worthy of respect, but this type of effort is not IT Transformation. Thinking about deploying a new Enterprise Resource Planning (ERP) system in your company? You would probably be better off hiring an ERP vendor, or a qualified third party to deal with this transformation. My point is this: not every technology project, regardless of its size, is an IT Transformation project.

What then is an IT transformation project?

IT Transformation is more than mere optimization or modification of engineering components. Rather, it is a *holistic revamp of the existing base (processes and technologies) used to support the company's mission-critical business.* IT Transformation is not about change for the sake of change, but about better aligning the IT system to the needs of the business. Indeed, based on the results obtained from an April 2000 conference held at MIT, 90% of the attendees agreed that matching IT to strategic corporate requirements was the most important factor in a technology strategy; 80% believed that decreasing time to market for new products to be another major factor, and 70% felt managing IT with constrained resources was the driver.[2] This is a key point: IT transformation should ultimately be aligned with the strategic business view.

Because it deals with core business processes (by core, I mean revenue generating), technology transformation is intrinsically both complex and risky. A failure to properly introduce this type of technology is not the kind of failure one can sweep under the rug. If you are faint of heart you may want to reconsider attempting it.

Software projects are often difficult and, by definition, IT Transformation does include a large software element at its core. Multiple studies done to measure the success rates of software projects reveal numbers that give pause. For example, the Standish Group has found that only about one-sixth of all projects were completed on time and on budget (and I suspect this figure includes many projects that are not at very complex); that nearly one third of all projects were canceled outright, and well over half

---

[2] Enterprise Architecture and Next Generation Information Systems—Dimitris N. Chorafas

were considered "challenged." Also, the average challenged or canceled project was on average 189 percent over budget, 222% behind schedule, and contained only 61 percent of the originally specified features.[3]

In other words, IT transformation is serious business and is reminiscent of those prescription medicine advertisements shown on TV. They should come with a similar disclaimer.

Warning: *Technology transformation may cause financial hemorrhaging in badly managed companies, resource bloating when done without professional supervision, and abnormal levels of bad media. Other symptoms might include executive insomnia, board irritability, aggression, growth suppression and Tourette's syndrome associated with project delays and budgetary overruns. Consult expert advice prior to embracing this solution.*

---

[3] Major Causes of Software Project Failures-- Lorin J. May. This reference can be found at http://www.stsc.hill.af.mil/crosstalk/1998/07/causes.asp and it goes on to cover reasons for project failures.

THE NEED FOR CHANGE

Change is a curious word and one that often makes for clichéd slogans, political or otherwise. It is certainly one of the PowerPoint generation's most overused words. However, the fact remains that the need for change is real. Change happens— whether we like it or not.   In the end, staying the same in business, as in technology, is a surefire way to be left behind. Transformation happens all the time, right before our very eyes; often without us even being aware of it. Look around any major modern city and make a quick survey of the kinds of cars you see on the road. Now compare that view with a flashback of the types of cars that you saw back in the seventies. Yes, some cars today are pure vintage, thanks to hobbyists, but a look at the landscape today versus twenty or thirty years ago easily demonstrates that car styles have been updated dynamically in a steady process of sun-setting and replacement. Indeed, the median age for cars in the US is about eight years (creeping up to ten years as people are deferring new car purchases due to the recession).

Now look at the same city landscape and observe its buildings. If you are in the downtown area, chances are you will find a number of classic buildings, renovated if the city has gone through a downtown revival, decrepit if the city's economic center has shifted to the suburbs. Alas, IT systems have become more like the buildings than the cars. Wouldn't it be great if we were able to shift this paradigm and get to the point where IT systems can be revamped the way car models are every few years?

The advent of the Internet, combined with the globalization of the economy has created tremendous changes in the IT landscape. Unfortunately, as it turns out, most legacy systems cannot easily be adapted to support the type of services and capabilities that the twenty-first century economy demands. The World Wide Web has been a gamer changer. Its full impact is still undetermined, but it is certainly forcing us to take a closer look at original IT architecture.

The original IT systems were conceptually simple, based upon well tested, centrally located mainframes, and were able to be kept 'kind-of-current' by piling new technologies upon them year after year. However, these mainframe-centric systems cannot mirror and provide the flexibility needed by today's businesses unless given a fundamental design change.

Legacy systems were designed around less agile service and maintenance models. Back in the days when it was fashionable to hate IBM (before it was fashionable to hate Microsoft and then Google), centralized mainframe environments were closely controlled by the glass-house priesthood of centralized IT organizations. As a result, user requirements usually took several weeks to be acted upon. These systems, while technically simple, forced processes that presented serviceability bottlenecks and made it difficult to satisfy user demands.

The need to overcome existing system deficiencies is not new. In fact, addressing ongoing customer demands has been the lifeline of IT organizations for decades. There has always been a need to transform the original systems, and there has always been the desire to replace the legacy with any available emerging technology. However, legacy technologies were not, and are not, easily replaceable, and the truth is that, in every successive generation, as new systems are incorporated, the old systems are never actually retired.

The Gartner group has cleverly identified the typical lifecycle followed by new technologies: emerging technologies go through a phase of hype and excitement, followed by disillusionment, until they are finally appreciated and utilized in a realistic fashion (this is similar to the same lifecycle, you probably followed when meeting your couple!).

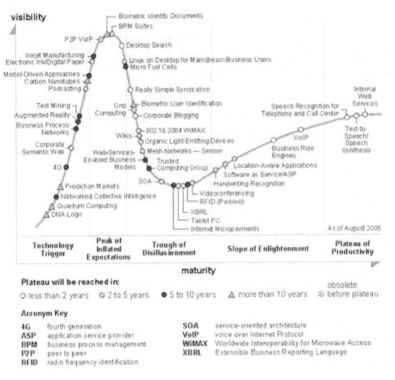

visibility

Biometric Identity Documents
BPM Suites
P2P VoIP
Desktop Search
Inkjet Manufacturing
Electronic Ink/Digital Paper
Linux on Desktop for Mainstream Business Users
Micro Fuel Cells
Model-Driven Approaches
Carbon Nanotubes
Podcasting
Really Simple Syndication
Internal Web Services
Text Mining
Biometric User Identification
Grid Computing
Speech Recognition for Telephony and Call Center
Augmented Reality
Corporate Blogging
Business Process Networks
802.16 2004 WiMAX
Text-to-Speech/ Speech Synthesis
Corporate Semantic Web
Wikis
Organic Light-Emitting Devices
VoIP
Web Services-Enabled Business Models
Mesh Networks — Sensor
Business Rule Engines
4G
Trusted Computing Group
Location-Aware Applications
Software as Service/ASP
SOA
Handwriting Recognition
Prediction Markets
Videoconferencing
Networked Collective Intelligence
RFID (Passive)
Quantum Computing
XBRL
DNA Logic
Tablet PC
Internet Micropayments

As of August 2005

| Technology Trigger | Peak of Inflated Expectations | Trough of Disillusionment | Slope of Enlightenment | Plateau of Productivity |

maturity

Plateau will be reached in:
obsolete
◯ less than 2 years ◐ 2 to 5 years ● 5 to 10 years △ more than 10 years ⊗ before plateau

Acronym Key

4G	fourth generation	SOA	service-oriented architecture
ASP	application service provider	VoIP	voice over Internet Protocol
BPM	business process management	WiMAX	Worldwide Interoperability for Microwave Access
P2P	peer to peer	XBRL	Extensible Business Reporting Language
RFID	radio frequency identification		

Depending upon the motivations of your business, and in particular the motivations of the business and technology executives who made past technology decisions, your company was at any given time an early adopter or a late adopter of various technology cycles. The way these technology decisions were shaped (aggressively or conservatively) was influenced by the particular level in the hierarchy of needs your company experienced at a particular juncture. In good times, the company might have introduced a state of the art automated system that gave it plenty of bragging rights, if not necessarily a significant return-on-investment (ROI). Regardless of whether your company was a typical early adopter, it is sure to have introduced emerging technologies that never moved past the hype-stage. How quickly your company attempted these transformations in the past depended primarily on the drive of the company's IT executives making those decisions at the time. And if your company is like most, chances are that some of those past

7

decision makers ended up introducing technologies that never moved through the Gartner's disillusionment phase in the now famous Gartner's Hype Cycle Chart[4]. Author Ray Kurzweil labels these technologies "False Pretenders"[5], and considers them a stepping stone in a technology lifecycle that looks similar to Gartner's. Mr. Kurzweil specifically mentions the audiotape as an example, but we can also mention the transatlantic blimp (like the Led Zeppelin), Quadraphonic sound systems, the original Apple Newton PDA, and so-called Voice recognition systems[6].

Alternatively (and perhaps, most likely) your company's heritage is the result of years of stagnation remedied by a string of tactical Rube Goldberg solutions needed to just get by.

The term "palimpsest" describes a manuscript page that has been effaced and then reused (in medieval times, paper was so rare that monks transcribing books were forced to erase previous text and reuse the paper). Indeed, a palimpsest is the word that comes to mind when describing the state of many an IT infrastructure today.

A second driver for adopting new technologies is real or perceived economics; economics that is the direct or indirect consequence of Moore's Law— the amazingly accurate dictum that predicts the speed at which technology costs half every two years.

---

[4] Source: Gartner (August 2005)
http://www.gartner.com/DisplayDocument?doc_cd=130115

[5] The Singularity is Near—Ray Kurzweil

[6] Let's call a spade a spade, Interactive Voice recognition (IVR) today does not work, and its intended use as a full communication interface for call centers is a disgrace.

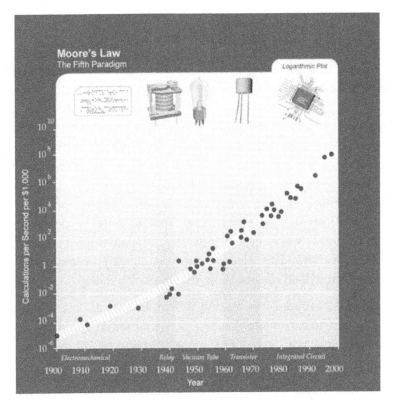

Image from Wikipedia Commons

It is misguided to assume that all mainframe systems are, by definition, legacy. Regardless, companies have been trying for years either to eliminate or to minimize the use of mainframes.

In the seventies, when minicomputers from vendors like Hewlett-Packard, DEC, Prime, and Philips came onto the scene, everyone assumed it would only be a matter of time before all those Big Blue mainframes disappeared into the sunset. Ironically, it was a majority of those minicomputers that went the way of disco dancing! While minicomputers did find a reasonable size niche in smaller businesses that were unable to afford one of the more expensive Big Blue machines, they did not come to depose the mainframe.

In the 80's a second revolutionary wave deposited millions of low cost microcomputers onto the world's workplaces, and once again the chatter in town was about how the mainframe was finally going to be replaced.

Along with the success of the IBM PC and the emergence of local area networks and file servers, such as those by Novell, distributed microcomputer environments sprouted up in corporations like fungus in a humid garden. The first users were sophisticated and required little support. Indeed, the last thing these departmental users wanted was to be bothered by corporate support groups. But as personal computer deployments gained penetration and began to reach unsophisticated computer users, maintenance and support organizations were faced with the challenge of supporting thousands of dispersed computers, with hundreds of unconnected databases; without the necessary tools.

The distributed processing environment of the eighties resulted in an extremely chaotic environment that was difficult to manage and that generated higher total cost of ownership; despite the lower cost of hardware.

Arguably, the Internet, and the resulting World Wide Web, came to the rescue by swinging the pendulum back and re-introducing a more centralized model via a "thin' device—the Web Browser.

Why I am telling you all this? First of all, because this brief history helps explain the current situation found in most data centers today, and secondly, because I want to establish that SOA, unlike the previous "distributed-processing" epochs, is not a false pretender technology, but the real thing. Now that real industry standards have finally taken hold; and technology costs have dropped significantly, it actually makes sense to sacrifice computing efficiency in favor of improved usability. As you re-architect new systems, focus can be placed on making them more enduring and flexible.

Still, a key step of the initial IT transformation process is for you to decipher and understand the true state of your IT system today. This understanding will give the basis for defining the areas that must be transformed first, the impact of the transformation, and the focus needed for the planning stage.

You can deconstruct your current IT system just as a seasoned archeologist can determine how different civilizations emerged by analyzing the earth's strata and digging up past artifacts. The big difference is that while the archeologist's analysis will reveal the clues of long extinct tools and civilizations, your analysis of the current system will reveal that nothing really has been laid to rest—IT data centers are all like the town of Macondo in Garcia Marquez's novel, 'A Hundred Years of Solitude', in that everything remains; the spirits of the past never go away. The fact is that most companies today, particularly those that have been around for more than ten years, have to deal with IT environments that represent the various strata layers of technologies that were fashionable in the past.

There is a traditional pattern to any current large company's information system. This pattern will most likely include some form of mainframe system still faithfully executing relic languages like COBOL or RPG; programs that can only be gingerly maintained by a dwindling group of developers with a correspondingly dwindling knowledge of these outdated computer languages[7].

Located next to that mainframe, you are likely to find a cluster of mini-computers serving some obscure network protocol translation. They are perhaps validating and parsing logic that serves no clear purpose, but that everyone is fearful to remove, lest the entire system collapse. Yes, as you dig deeper into your eight-year old plus system's documentation (partially updated recently thanks to your company's internship program), you will

---

[7] Actually, remembering a language is easy, what's hard is keeping current the tools used to develop and compile the programs under that particular language.

find a cluster of PC's still emulating dumb terminals and, in a topsy-turvy fashion, a few dumb terminals emulating PCs.

Unbeknownst to most, these very critical business intelligence reports are not being produced by that I/O intensive data mining OLAP system deployed by those very expensive consultants prior to your entry into the company. No, they are being produced by a series of spreadsheets, generated from a PC with MS Access, and scripted by a programmer-wannabe in the accounting department.

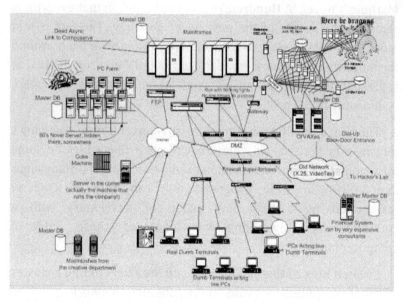

The illustration above is a bit over the top, I admit, but what's particularly worrisome is how closely it resembles many typical information systems of today.

How could it be otherwise? Despite many years of "best practices", information systems are usually implemented according to their own rules and pressures. Remember code reuse, modularization, CASE, and object orientation? These trends have come (and sometimes gone), leaving behind scattered indications of their presence. They represent snapshots of times gone-by when technical decisions were made to apply a particular technology to solve a problem at hand. Combined with the need to deliver something quickly and cheaply, it resulted in a brand new sub-system, one that has to be maintained, forever.

This reality brings me back to the principal purpose of this section: *Why to Transform?*

IT investments have shifted throughout the years from hardware, to networks, to security, to software, and finally to applications and services. Even within a particular segment, investment trends vary from year to year. Initially, the bulk of hardware investment took place in the provision of processing power, whether by leasing large mainframes or by purchasing large multi-processor systems. However, as processing costs plummeted, the focus shifted to investment in mass storage. According to Mr. Chorafas[8], Storage Area Networks have gone from 46% of hardware investment in 2000 to 75% in 2005. No wonder, according to U.C. Berkeley, the entire world's print and electronic media produces about 1.5 exabytes[9] worth of data per year (i.e. 500 billion U.S. photocopies, 610 billion e-mails, 7.5 quadrillion minutes of phone conversations, etc.). Every word spoken by all humans throughout the history of the world could be stored in around 5 Exabytes[10]. And these statistics were compiled prior to the Web 2.0. Taking advantage of the social-networking explosion and low data storage costs, today's

---

[8] Enterprise Architecture and New Generation Information Systems—Dimitris N. Chorafas

[9] An Exabyte being equivalent to 1000 petabytes. A petabye being equivalent to 1000 terabyes. A terabyte being equivalent to 1000 Gigabytes, which is about what you can get with two external disk drives for less than $200

[10] "How much information?"—Hal Varian and Peter Lyman. http://www2.sims.berkeley.edu/research/projects/how-much-info/print.html

companies are expected to exploit knowledge of every nuance, preference, detail, and characteristic of a customer, would-be-customer, partner, or business event. Ultimately, the IT revolution is becoming a revolution in how best to master and exploit this thing called "Information" by those who are better positioned to survive the very treacherous times imposed by the global economic fallout we now face.

Utilizing and accessing this monstrous volume of information with legacy systems is a non-starter proposition. This is not due to constrains in the mainframe technology, or even in the storage capabilities inherited from distributed file server solutions. It is due to the haphazard way legacy architecture construction led to an unstructured and heterogeneous mix of systems and databases.

Compare the prior diagram with that of a modular system that is capable of evolving gracefully while meeting present and emerging business demands via incremental investments only—the kind of system that can be developed with the new capabilities provided by the advent of Service Oriented Architecture (SOA), Rapid Application Development, Open Source Solutions, the Internet and global standards; the kind of system that truly allows seamless remote development and efficient reuse of off-the-shelf toolkits, libraries, and services.

The technology field is becoming an area filled with opportunities. The decision to solve each business requirement on a case-by-case basis, while continuing to defer the much needed cleansing and rationalization of the IT environment, must be made consciously—with eyes wide open. Continuing the inertial quick-fix response to new business requirements is a recipe for failure.

It is no longer feasible to indefinitely procrastinate the assessment of whether a transformation strategy is needed.

THE DRIVERS FOR TRANSFORMATION

Yes, everything deployed turns into a legacy pretty much the moment it goes into production. Think about it. In the history of civilization, technology's path of least resistance has been that of change. Systems deteriorate or eventually become obsolete due to their inability to any longer meet their objectives. Why? Well, the world changes, new problems emerge, new discoveries are made, disaster strikes, people are mortal and new generations, bearing new ideas and fresh visions, take over. Whether or not things were better in the past is really a philosophical debate, driven by the particular, subjective individual beliefs. In the end, there can be no doubt that in recent years computer systems have taken over the process and management of procedural chores that constitute the engine of modern civilization.

But this still leaves the open question: What precisely is it that should be changed?

Technology's impact on business and business's impact on technology are dialectic in nature. Many times business drives technology by demanding new technology solutions (The 1960's NASA Moon-shot is an example), but sometimes it is technology that drives business by opening previously untapped revenue-generating areas. Take the video-game industry. It is a direct result of the invention of the micro-processor, but the micro-processor was originally invented to meet the requirements of an electronic calculator manufacturer and is an example of technology opening new business realms.

Even so, it is difficult to clearly categorize technology's impact because feedback-noise often quickly develops with the introduction of new technology, blurring the difference between cause and effect. For example, new satellite communication technology encouraged globalization. International broadcasts of

15

sporting events have become common, so that people in Brazil can now watch the same soccer match as people in England[11]. On the other hand, globalization of communications also drove the need for significantly higher bandwidth and for reduced propagation delays than those experienced by satellite communications. Enter the deployment of more bandwidth capable fiber-optic based communications, which led to new uses of that bandwidth, and... well, you get the picture.

Again, transformation is primarily driven by the natural dynamics of business, but at times technology innovations generate the transformation of business processes. The best example: the manner in which the Internet, and in particular the advent of the World Wide Web, as a technology driver, opened a vast number of new businesses, revolutionized the major traditional business processes, and opened a multi-billion dollar online market. Business and Technology are but two of the key transformation drivers. I suggest that Competition and the internal dynamics of your company are two more. An evaluation of the elements for transformation in your company should include an assessment of each of the possible drivers for change shown next.

---

[11] One that Brazil will most likely win!

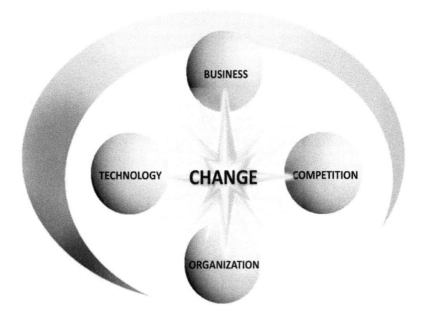

Business Needs. Ultimately, if you are going to justify a new project to remedy problems with an aging infrastructure, or have a need to introduce a new reporting system, or, frankly, anything that requires a purchase order, you are going to have to justify the results in business terms. Rarely will the business directly request you to change the technology. Do not expect your CEO to come up to you and say, "Hey Joe, here's a budget to move us to SOA", or give you the freedom to begin the transformative process on a whim. The truth of the matter is that you will be asked to deliver a specific set of business functionalities and capabilities, and you will then be expected to do so with a much reduced budget and tightened timeframes ("need this by yesterday"). Your challenge, should you decide to accept it, is to explain why satisfaction of these requirements merits the necessary funding and patience to launch an IT transformation effort. Just don't forget that when it comes to business satisfaction, the actual value of technology occurs at the presentation and application layers; not in the infrastructure.

Technology. So, often, it's not business requirements that drive change, but rather the basic fact that new technologies emerge with breakthrough functionalities, lower costs or novel usages. Your refusal to adopt them would rightly place you and your company in the nomination awards list of the International Cyborg Luddites (forget about Googling them; they don't have a Website). The driver is technology alone (not the competition and not the business). It is usually wise to introduce the change in line with normal replacement lifecycles. Take for instance the recent popularity of flat screen monitors. At first, executives drove their consumption (status-symbols are business drivers after all, right?), then the artist-types demanded them with a legitimate request to work in a flicker-free world. Shortly after, the senior technical staff acquired them (how come those folks in graphic design have those monitors and we don't?), until they eventually became cheap and prevalent enough to be the natural replacement technology for everyone with an outdated CRT monitor.

There are times when the transformation, driven solely by technology, is actually one of immediate and true value. When Visicalc first broke into the market as an accessory application for the famed IBM PC, it quickly became a success; the "killer-application" helping to justify the purchase of expensive PCs inside skeptical business environments. Indeed, the product's electronic spreadsheet metaphor was so powerful and revolutionary that its inherent value was apparent from the start.

Ignore the forces presented by technology drivers at your own peril. Failure to change with the advent of transformational technologies is perhaps one of the biggest reasons that previously secure companies have precipitously tumbled. The list of examples can be quite long, but suffice it to say that Polaroid's misread of digital technology, and Wang's failure to realize the ability of the PC to be used as a word processor, demonstrate the serious need to understand the impact of new technologies on business.

Competition. The world would be a much better place without those damn competitors. Alas, they exist, and they sometimes introduce products and services that challenge your business. Back in the earlier 60s, American Airlines revolutionized the way travel was booked by allowing travel agencies direct access to its central reservations system (SABRE). Competing airlines had no choice but to react, and to react quickly or face the prospect of a quick and painful death. After all, travel agencies using the SABRE system were more likely to book flights with American Airlines than with a competitor[12]. Being the first to use automated travel reservations gave AA a tremendous boost in market share and reduced distribution costs. As proven by millions of years of Darwinian evolution, competition is ultimately the biggest driver for change out there.

Your Organization. That is: *you* and your organization. *You* are the competitor who is first to introduce a new feature or capability. Someone from

---

[12] Several reasons: Initially these CRS systems were biased to favor the airline owing them. AA enjoyed this early competitive advantage until the Federal Government finally introduced regulation to prevent this, plus in addition agents could improve their commissions by having better and agile knowledge of flight availability and easier bookings.

your R&D group may come up with that one game-changing idea that truly deserves support. A new business process is identified that cries out for use within your system to effectively reduce costs now and in the future. Perhaps your company has acquired another concern, or there's been a merger or perhaps process and control inefficiencies are preventing scaling up of the system.

Let's now delve into each of these drivers in further detail.

BUSINESS NEEDS

What are some examples of specific business driven needs you are likely to encounter? Other than the normal business pressure to further automates in order to reduce operational costs, most major business driven transformation initiatives are the result of at least one of the following factors:

Globalization. Neither the electronic marketplace nor the emerging mobile communication technologies know borders. Technology is rapidly erasing the meaning of frontier. While there is still a great need for national-oriented products and services, the traditional market segmentation based on territories no longer applies.

Demand for New Services. The furious pace of today's businesses and the accelerated rate of introducing new products and services have accustomed the consumer to expect an ever-enhanced set of capabilities and functions at reduced cost. This is best exemplified by the expectation that new appliances or commodity electronics will continue to plummet in price while providing greater reliability and functionality.

Industry Realignment. Vertical industries are being redefined and becoming more narrowly specialized, while the impact on horizontal markets is becoming more quantitative rather that qualitative. As technology advances, more horizontal enablers are created, more standards are used, and the level of uniqueness in each vertical layer is reduced.

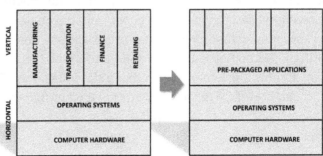

Admittedly, the above diagram is somewhat oversimplified. In reality, vertical markets are realigning more like plate tectonics, gradually intruding upon adjacent areas while creating market spaces full of commercial stresses and extruding emerging overlaps, which we now identify as convergence. In this sense, convergence is a symptom of the emerging economy; not a cause. The redefinition of vertical spaces is what creates emerging market overlaps and collisions.

The trend then is for the "vertical slices" to become thinner and the horizontal layers to become thicker. That is, every passing day more business elements are serviced by generic products. Horizontal players are bubbling up in order to provide infrastructure and packaged solutions that had previously been offered only by niche industries. This is also the space occupied by new business constructs such as Software as a Service (SaaS) providers. If we project this trend to its logical conclusion, we can expect to see more shrink-wrap applications and more software-as-a-service options available to varied industries. Moreover, as convergence with HDTV and cable-level bandwidth continues (you can now download Netflix movies and watch them on your 55" LED TV), many of these software applications can become easily accessible via the combo provided by the TV and the Internet. Imagine the future business possibilities this convergence could provide: on demand advertising with the capability to purchase a product as you view your favorite TV show. For example, consumers tuning-in to a James Bond movie could inquire about the rates offered by the hotel where Mr. Bond is staying while in pursuit of "Dr. No" and negotiate travel fares and accommodations, or even pre-packaged tours, to that featured destination—all from the comfort of their couch and using nothing more complicated that a state-of-the art TV remote, which might well be the next generation iPod or Blackberry.

EMERGING TECHNOLOGIES

Traditionally, new technologies referred primarily to information technologies such as micro-processors, system architectures, memory and networking. However, these days it helps to maintain a broader scope. When we think of video-games, consumer electronics, and wireless and mobility technology in the application of new software advances such as genetic algorithms and fuzzy logic, the impact on open source systems needs to be considered. Technology drivers are emerging from the integration of all these elements. This resulting convergence will impact commerce and your business.

Regardless of the specifics, new technologies share a number of attributes that make them influential in the way the market works. The emerging technologies of the eighties and nineties were influential because they provided the following key attributes:

Convergence. The world is about "convergence". Convergence of technology, markets, products and services is indeed taking place on many different levels. The problem is that the term is quickly becoming a catch-all phrase together with "paradigm-shift", "re-engineering", "disintermediation" and the like. Before the word becomes diluted from over-use, let's analyze the specific changes taking place and then properly define "convergence". I use the term in many different contexts, but hopefully I can properly clarify those cases where "convergence" is a cause of change and those in which it is a result of change.

In the context of technology, industries that were previously separated are now merging under a common market place[13]. As everything becomes digital, there is a clear drive to combine differing technologies. The "Negroponte Switch"[14] states that

---

[13] Gary Hamel, C. K. Prahalad. "Competing for the Future".

[14] Nicolas Negroponte. "Being Digital".

23

everything that was initially wireless is now becoming wired (e.g. TVs using Cable), and technologies that started as wired are now becoming wireless (e.g. the telephone). The move to shared digital links encourages such things as the convergence of television and computers. These two devices are now merging due to the advent of high definition screen resolutions and the high bandwidth potential of optical fiber to the home. The most apparent conclusion of this type of convergence is that the distribution channels (TV, Internet) will become commodities and the main source of riches will deal with content.

Customization. New technology is most cost effective when deployed on a global scale. Fortunately, since not all markets are global, when there is the need to provide local level content, technology enables a high degree of customization. Customization-ability entails flexibility. Only technologies that are conceived and designed with the intent to support various configurations can be adequately deployed in these current times.

Leveling. Here's some common advice: "If you are a small business, try to appear as a large business; if you are a large business, try to appear as a small business". Electronic distribution venues like the Internet have made it easy for home-based and small businesses to deploy virtual storefronts that appear similar to those of a Fortune 100 company. Large companies, on the other hand, can provide personalized services under the guise of small boutique brands. Furthermore, the global market reach for all sizes of companies is the same. We truly have a level-playing field.

Low Cost. New technology is low cost. As mentioned earlier, the phenomena of on-going reduction of computer costs—better known as Moore's Law—has driven computer costs to the point that historically every 10 years the power of the computer increases by a factor of 1000. Futurist, Michiu Kaku[15] now predicts the one-penny-computer. At this price, Mr. Kaku predicts a future with computers one million times as powerful as today's desktops.

Standardization. The most important core enabling technologies are no longer vendor specific. Technology standards are quickly being consolidated around successful solutions tried out in the Internet realm. Network protocols, utilities and interfaces are now standardized, and better still, available as open source code that can be freely downloaded[16].

Availability as Commodity. As a result of standardization, infrastructure technologies that previously required custom implementation are now becoming commodities. There is also an on-going industry push to "commoditize" well known application services. These application-specific services can be bundled and reused with ease. Another benefit is that commoditization breeds new products, such as hardware appliances, that can do the work previously done only in the upper layers.

Web 2.0-Social Interactions. Thanks to broad technology availability, anyone can create videos and display them on the Web with the reasonable expectation that they will be watched by thousands, if not millions of people. Millions more have blogs where they post ratings, reviews and comments that are often more appreciated than those of seasoned professionals. Then there is the emergence of virtual communities that attract individuals with shared interests. Add to this the emergence of E-Bay, Amazon.com, and other electronic marketplace sites and the sheer volume of usage (over 1.4B people used the Internet in

---

[15] Michiu Kaku. "Visions; How Science Will Revolutionize the 21st Century".

[16] It's worth noting that Open Source is NOT free. Once you become hooked on it, you'll have to pay ever-increasing maintenance fees to obtain the required support for its use!

2008, four times more than in 2000[17]), means that there is a true shift of commerce to a style that is very different from the way it was as recently as ten years ago. It's difficult to imagine any modern business not being impacted by this type of change.

---

[17] Internet World Stats—
http://www.internetworldstats.com/stats.htm

COMPETITION

New Competitors. Changes in technology, coupled with Internet-driven electronic marketplace revenue streams, are encouraging new business entrants into untraditional areas. Think of Microsoft which entered the electronic travel distribution space when it founded Expedia. Apple got into music distribution, and Google is now delving into the wireless space with their Android technology and into content with their acquisition of YouTube. We will likely continue to see companies that traditionally covered one particular business segment move into new competitive spaces. Your company may be comfortably leading the market, but you should keep an eye out for potential emergent players.

Value Chain Realignment. The main effect of new technologies, such as the Internet, is that they encourage direct contact between the supplier and the end-consumer. This direct contact is driving the establishment of virtual marketplaces. Traditional service intermediaries are now faced with the need to realign their role in the value chain in order to survive.

ASSESSING YOUR ORGANIZATION'S VIEW OF TECHNOLOGY

Some people view their automobile merely as a utility—a means of transportation to get them from point A to point B. Others view it as a strategic enabler: "This Porsche is sure to get me more dates!"

A corporation's view of technology is no different. The trick is to find out whether your company views IT as a sports car or merely a dependable truck.

First, let's agree there are two types of information system technologies: those needed to support the running of your business, and those that are core to your business. The former include applications such as accounting and payroll systems as well as Intranets. Indeed, the patterns associated with these services have made it easier for major vendors to offer customizable packages under the umbrella of ERP (Enterprise Resource Planning) that can be configured to meet a company's specific business needs. The latter usually consists of applications and systems formed under more proprietary circumstances and that support the actual business operations: point of sale, promotions, customer relationship management, guest facing sales and marketing (including Web portals and campaign management), product distribution and tracking, reservation systems (such as those used by airlines and hotels), etc.

In principle, ERP systems are needed by all industries, but transformational projects for back office systems can only be truly justified when there's a need to respond to a big business event such as a merger or an acquisition. Also, ERP investments are rarely justifiable on the basis of competitive advantage— arguments for cost saving or administrative agility advantages notwithstanding. Instead, large ERP projects are usually approved because they tend to serve the operational governance of the CFO, who ultimately is the person with the budgetary approval power.

Justifying technology transformation projects that can deliver a direct business benefit is another matter. Their value is often not appreciated because of their high costs. Ironically, because ERP projects typically require proprietary vendor architectures and high-consulting support to customize the solution, they often end up costing much more than IT projects that deliver competitive features. That's why there's always the question of how to position these core projects in light of the company's view of technology as a competitive weapon.

Given that IT systems designed to support the core business usually require some costly proprietary development, it has long been a chimera of some businesses to make their core support systems behave the way ERP is viewed today—as a commodity. This view sees technology not as a strategic asset but as a mere utility needed to "get-the-work-done". Basically, this view of IT is akin to the way most of us view electric or gas services—stuff we can't live without and what we expect to always work.

Organizations that view IT technology needs as a utility are typically organizations with cultures not predisposed to accept change. You'll recognize them when you hear statements such as, "Sure, the business could use this new function, but we don't want to bother with changing things when we can just patch a quick solution for now," or: "Yes, this new technology will solve many issues, but we can save money by hanging on to what we have for a little longer." My particular favorite, overhead from an out-of-touch CEO in the midst of the dot-com explosion of the late nineties: "Nah, if it grows like a weed, it must be a weed. This Internet thing is nothing but a fad!"

Let's face it. To the executives with this limited perspective, IT is just the geeky intern that shows up whenever there's a need to "fix" the laptop or "get email going". This is a view predicated on a strict utilitarian view of IT as a service organization and nothing more. In this case, your first challenge is to educate the executive brass on the true extent and governance of the IT organization. However, even with all the education in the world, if your company is in an industry that traditionally does not rely on or receive obvious benefits from modern technology, chances are that your attempt to justify that big transformation project is going to fall on deaf ears unless, that is, you're able to position your message in line with the company's culture.

Then there are those companies that consider technology to be a strategic asset. Frankly, these companies may also suffer from an equally insidious problem of overusing technology. They cling to the belief that technology and only technology will pull the company out of the ditch and increase profitability. It's safe to assume that a large percentage of the failed IT projects providing fodder for the Harvard Review's case studies came from the realm of extremely high and unrealistic expectations.

So, there you have it. Understanding the view of technology within your company and your industry is a good starting point towards the understanding of the feasibility, scope and value of your IT transformation effort.

What then are the considerations for assessing your company's positioning vis-à-vis technology?

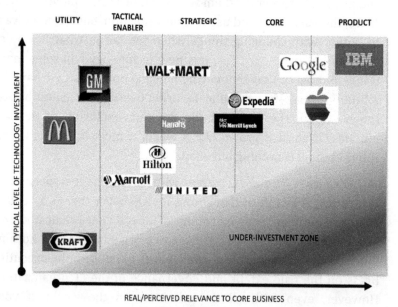

In the previous diagram, you find a general assessment of how various well-known companies *might* value technology. (Note: my sample assessment is somewhat subjective, and you have every right to disagree with the way I positioned some of these companies.) The vertical axis represents the typical level of IT investment as a proportion of the company's revenue, while the horizontal axis shows the real or self-perceived value of technology by the company. For example, a company whose actual product is technology related but that has a low percentage of investment in IT would fall in the under-investment zone in the bottom right. Your case for transformation should be easier in this situation. The upper-left shows technology over-investments. GM (who was on the verge of bankruptcy) was typically a heavy investor in technology, even though it did not traditionally position itself as a technology company, but rather as a car company—a big car company (Hummer or Yukon, anyone?). In fact, EDS was spun off from GM after one executive concluded that providing DP services was not a business for GM to be in.

More importantly, I suggest you do the exercise of placing your own company in the diagram. Where would it fit?

For example, the two brands to the left are representative companies that might well see technology as a utility. They do depend on technology, mind you, but chances are they want it as cheaply as possible, so they can focus on their actual lines of business: selling of food products. These are companies who view technology only as a tactical enabler. Still, just because a company requires technology only as a tactical enabler does not mean that IT can't be leveraged against the competition. Even in this scenario there might be contributions IT can make to the core business (e.g. automated ordering kiosks in retail, use of loyalty systems and CRM.)

In the middle of the horizontal axis, there lies the Twilight Zone of technology funding. Technology becomes truly strategic when the end product would not exist if technology did not operate with excellence and efficiency. In this area you'll find companies that have typically leveraged the power of technology to their competitive advantage. Two examples are Sabre, with its powerful computer reservations environment for airlines, and the financial institution, Merrill Lynch[18], leveraging on-line financial services.

In the upper right of the chart are those companies whose life blood depends on maintaining a leading hand in technology. These are companies whose technology *is* the actual product. Even though it might be easier to make the case for technology in these companies, don't be surprised if you get push-back resulting from stale thinking or stunted vision. "Why should we invest in that Internet thing?" someone at Novell might have asked back in the late eighties or, "Why do we need those PCs?" from DEC's Olsen.

Ultimately, there can be no question that the further to the right you find a company, the easier it should be to make a case for technology transformation. However, in this scenario the execution of technology transformation will be the most difficult because you will be touching the actual lifeblood of the business!

---

[18] Merrill Lynch was just saved from bankruptcy as a result of the 2008 financial meltdown thanks to its acquisition by Bank of America. I left it in this example just to remind us how business events can and do trump any other consideration.

ASSESSING THE FUTURE

Technology strategy should not only align with the view of technology in your organization but also with its view of the future. After all, if we lack vision defining the direction of our transformation, we are no better than the proverbial drunken man searching only under a lamppost for his lost keys because "that's where it's illuminated". Now, before you say, "Hogwash! No one can predict the future," I'm not suggesting you engage in an exercise of mindless divination but rather in one of informed assessment. There's a method to the madness. After all, there are differing degrees of confidence among forecasting, predicting, prognosticating, and prophesying—the former being more worthy of respect than the latter.

While the financial folks project into the future by forecasting (estimating or extrapolating known variables), domain experts can predict the future, in the sense that *to predict* is to state or make known in advance, specifically on the basis of specialized knowledge, about what should be expected to occur. Your stockbroker is (or should be) in the business of predicting the market. Most experts make their living by their presumed ability to make predictions based on their subject matter knowledge—a doctor can predict the progression of a disease, given a certain treatment. An experienced manager ought to be able to predict whether a project is likely to succeed or fail depending upon how resources and plans are laid out (she might on occasion be wrong, but chances are that she will be wrong far less often than someone without the same level of experience in project development). Still, although predicting is great, far more intriguing is the field of prognostication.

The palm reader in the hippie district performs divination, and the mystic interprets dreams as prophecy, but I'm not suggesting you plan your business's future based on these techniques.

Instead, most of us can prognosticate the future given the right methodology. Prognostication is prediction with a bit less certainty, but it is still based upon informed opinion. There are those industry experts who are valued in the publishing world, or on the lecture circuit, because of their seemly uncanny ability to prognosticate the future[19].

We can all prognosticate according to present indications or signs. If we keep our senses open, we can all foretell what may happen. There is no reason why informed assessments of the future should not yield valid predictions and prognostications.

No black magic is needed to prognosticate. Prognostication's first technique involves the **identification of the various technology trends whose trajectories can combine in novel ways**. In hindsight (and isn't everything easier in hindsight!), most major technology events are the result of a novel synergistic convergence or of an evolutionary technology development. The revolution that comes about as a result of a single unexpected scientific discovery, such as the mastery of fire, the invention of the wheel, or the invention of writing, is a rarity. The chances of serendipitous transformation in a world blanketed by thousands of scientists who are engaged in all forms of structured research are low; so most of tomorrow's developments are likely to be the result of elements that are well understood today. In hindsight, the "invention" of the Internet should have been easily prognosticated [20]. Think of the following small list of transformational technologies invented during the past fifty years:

- **1950's**: Single purpose-computing
- **1960's**: Multiple purpose business computing (360 Mainframes)

---

[19] Michio Kaku's excellent books on the future are an example

[20] To be fair, legendary MIT professor Michael L. Dertouzos is on record as having predicted the WWW as early as the late seventies.

- **1970's**: Mini-computers (DEC, Prime, HP)

- **1980's**: PCs (Commodore, Radio Shack, IBM, Apple), LANs

- **1990's**: World Wide Web

- **2000's**: Social Media takes off

- **2010's**: Mobility and Geo-location Technologies

Place a computer on every desk, coupled with higher communication bandwidths and available for a reasonable price, a properly designed switching network with true worldwide standards, and most importantly, an easy to use presentation standard that allows flexible use, and voila—you have the Internet!

A second technique for prognosticating the future is to **extrapolate what is known and imagine what would happen if a known element were to become pervasive;** regardless of how outlandish the extrapolation might appear at first. This is where the Western Union committee chartered with evaluating the telephone invention from a certain Alexander Graham Bell got it wrong when they concluded: *"Bell's proposal to place his instrument in almost every home and business is fantastic. The central exchange alone would represent a huge outlay in real estate and buildings, to say nothing of the electrical equipment. In conclusion, the committee feels that it must advise against any investment in Bell's scheme. We do not doubt that it will find uses in special circumstances, but any development of the kind and scale which Bell so fondly imagines is utterly out of the question."*

Consider this: the electric engine was invented in the 19th century. If back then you had told people that, in the future, people would be using not one, not two, but literally hundreds of engines in the course of their daily lives and in a completely transparent manner, you would have been considered insane. Yet, here we are today. Electric motors are everywhere and are core to our everyday existence. Do this experiment: count the number of electric motors you use throughout your day, including the electric fans inside your computers, the motors spinning your

CDs, the motor moving the coolant through your refrigerator, the fans in your microwave oven, the vibrating motors in your videogame joysticks, etc.

Extrapolate this technique to computers. You may have heard of the now famously wrong prediction made in 1943 by IBM's then CEO, Mr. Watson, stating that *the world market for computers is around five*? Computers are now everywhere, including your car. Indeed, the genius of Bill Gates, encapsulated by his original motto, *"A computer on every desk"*, was his ability to rightfully prognosticate the PC revolution despite how outlandish his vision seemed at the time. Contrast Gates' view with that of Ken Olsen's (DEC CEO). In a 1977 statement, he said, *"There is no reason for any individual to have a computer in his home."* And what happened to DEC? Bill Gates applied the principle of pervasiveness; Mr. Olson did not. As a result of his failure to respond proactively to the advent of PCs and open networking, DEC faltered until it was ultimately acquired by Compaq; which in turn was acquired by HP. Last I checked, Microsoft is still going strong despite the emergence of new challengers, so good prognostication is undoubtedly essential to the future success of a company.

A third technique of prognostication is to not under-estimate the importance of this statement: don't ignore the value of **second generations. "New and improved" matters**. Let me explain. Let's say an invention comes along and becomes popular. The smart investor knows that something even better is going show up before to long. Remember the Atari videogame console? Many at the time thought the videogame market was saturated and that it had no further room to grow. Even the people at Atari thought so. They basically gave up on a business which today exceeds the movie and music businesses combined! The terms often applied to these outcomes are "disruptive technologies" or "game-changers". Think about it, Apple, aware of the success of Napster, correctly read the tea leaves and took on the challenge of creating the service that is now known as ITunes. There wasn't anything specifically unique about ITunes. Rather, it was how Apple was able to combine disparaged elements to create a unified whole: delivery platform for Online Music, device to render download (iPod), basic commercial agreements with music label companies, etc.

I plead guilty to believing back in the late 90's that the market for Internet search engines was saturated and done for. After all, wasn't Yahoo the perfect indexing tool? And weren't there very capable search engines out there such as Altavista and Excite, among others? Good thing, our friends at Google didn't agree with my limited point of view! So, look around for first generation ideas with the potential to really stir things up with the development of a newer and improved version.

A fourth prognostication technique is to **define a likely frame of reference with assumptions bound by bracketed extremes.** For example, when trying to prognosticate the future of our planet, one can assume that it will fall somewhere in between the following possible extremes:

FUTURE THAT CAN RUIN YOUR RETIREMENT PLANS	FUTURE THAT WOULD MAKE THE JETSONS JEALOUS
• *World economy continues into a protracted recession that collapses civilization into "Mad Max" territory*	• *World Peace via global social awareness*
• *Nuclear terrorism tilts civilization towards a new dark age*	• *Environment is managed*
• *Yellowstone eruption wipes out Earth*	• *World hunger is conquered thanks to artificially produced food*
• *Plagues: Ebola virus mutates to produce air-borne contagion, Avian Flu*	• *Water is made available to all people*
• *Asteroid crashes into planet*	• *Hypersonic flying makes global travel even more practical*
• *Global warming continues unabated. Polar caps melt, flooding major coastal areas*	• *Humanity takes to space: space tourism becomes common*
• *Energy crisis. Total oil depletion*	• *Telepresence*
	• *Transparent Computing*
	• *Personal interplanetary probes*
	• *Genetic therapies cure diseases*
	• *Genetic regeneration. Grow body parts*

Chances are that the future will turn out to be a Goldilocks' type choice somewhere between these two extremes—not all good, but hopefully not all bad. It's the job of technology leaders to assess changes in terms of probability and of the impact they could have on the business. Your IT strategy should match this assessment. Look again at the good and the bad prognosticates listed above. It doesn't take a genius to realize that climate change and energy supply issues will surely be at the forefront over the next several decades. Of the items listed on the right, which ones could be driven by those listed on the left? Look closely and you can see that every major bad news risk could drive advances on the good news list. There is something to the cliché that says, 'for every problem there is an opportunity':

Nuclear Risks → *Additional focus on defense and safety technology spending*

Plagues → *Greater focus on genetic research*

Climate Change → *Increased research and development of low carbon emission energy sources*

Observations determine that an asteroid will be headed our way in the near future? [21] You can be sure that investments in space technologies will be the top priority. Then again, this is probably one challenge we don't ever want to have to deal with.

That's it. If a crystal ball is used it will be just for effect and nothing more. In the next section I'll suggest how to apply these techniques to prognosticate a specific future opportunity.

---

[21] 400-meter Asteroid 99942 Apophis is predicted to have a close encounter with Earth in 2029. During this pass, there is a small, but non zero probability that it go through a gravitational keyhole (a half-mile wide region of space) causing it to modify its future trajectory just enough to ensure it will impact Earth on its next pass: April 13/2036. Thought you would like to know!

TECHNOLOGY PROGNOSTICATION
AN EXAMPLE

Let's play around a bit with the techniques covered in the previous section. My most recent experience is with the travel and hospitality industry. It's my believe that this industry is on the verge of major tectonic shifts due to changes in travel patterns caused by rising energy costs, economic restructuring and, yes, technology. For example, when travel costs rise and the economy tightens, people change their leisure travel habits, and there is a reduction in business travel as more business is conducted by telephone, via emerging online meeting sites or through old-style videoconferencing.

Still, anyone who has ever tried to hold a productive meeting via a 25 inch TV screen knows how hard it is to detect nuances in facial expressions or to read the body language of other attendees—aspects of human interaction that are often underrated. The quality of such business meetings usually turns out to be less than satisfactory. Good business communication is about sensing mood, detecting reactions, and establishing the kind of warm rapport that only seamless proximity can provide.

Could there be room for an emerging technology in this area? I suggest we can try to answer this question by following the prognostication techniques I've covered earlier:

- Reinterpret the past and don't ignore the value of second generations
- Extrapolate what is known and imagine what would happen if a known element were to become pervasive
- Identify the various technology trends whose trajectories can combine in novel ways
- Define a likely frame of reference with assumptions bound by bracketed extremes

Original videoconferencing can be considered a first generation technology; just as Atari was for videogames. However, the technology has advanced to the point where it has overcome some of its original limitations thanks to the use of larger high definition screens and better control of the interaction. Clearly, companies like CISCO and HP have already identified enhanced teleconferencing as an area of great opportunity for the future. However, even though both companies refer to their enhanced teleconferencing products as "Telepresence", what would happen if an economic and effective form of actual 3-Dimensional Telepresence were to be developed? What I have in mind is something more like the effect portrayed in the latest Star Wars movies—something I will refer to as "Virtual Presence".

Just like in the important meeting between Ki-Adi-Mundi, Yoda, and Mace Windu,[22], wouldn't it be great to use Virtual Presence to avoid having to fly from LA to New York to attend a two hour meeting?

---

[22] Okay, as Star War fans we forgive the movies' scientific inaccuracies such as sound being generated in the vacuum of space, just as we shall ignore the manner in which the teleconference is riddled with static more closely associated with analogue transmissions rather than digital!

If Virtual Presence were to become ubiquitous, efficient and economical, it could definitely become a transformational technology. The real question is this: How close are we to developing it?

Economically speaking, if past trends are any indication, chances are the initial engine for introduction of this type of capability will come from the so-called adult entertainment industry—especially if Virtual Presence can be complemented with technologies that can enhance sensory experience. There could be the addition of gloves with actuators to simulate the sense of touch, and . . . well, you get the idea. Smirk all you want, but economics wouldn't be a problem in this area!

What will happen next? Just as travel led applications in the early Internet days, its avoidance will surely drive Virtual Presence technology. After all, business travel takes time, money and energy (in a world that's becoming more aware of energy consumption, this is not a trivial issue). Also, let's be frank: business trips are often not as fun or as effective as we would like them to be.

I once attended a conference in which I was a member of a panel answering questions related to the aftermath of 9/11. One of the questions dealt with my recommendations as to how companies could reduce travel. Being a representative of the hospitality industry, my answer was simple and sincere: "Please don't cut travel, just stay at one my company's hotels!"

Clearly, business travel avoidance is not a good thing if you happen to be in the travel and hospitality business. Now, I know some of you may argue that travel avoidance is precisely the goal of original videoconferencing, but I'm not talking here about outdated NTSC TV screen resolutions. Virtual Presence is about truly replicating the experience of being in the same room with someone who is many miles away. After all, existing videoconferencing systems are a "false-pretender" type of technology.

To create Virtual presence, we will need a 3D scanner—perhaps a laser-based system that can rapidly trace each participant; digitizing the contour of their bodies and faces in real-time.

Next, we'll need an extremely fast network to transfer the digitized information generated by the scanner. We will certainly need a very fast pipe to transfer, even after compression, terabytes of scanned data. Also, in order to rapidly compress this information, we're going to need a very fast computer. After all, we won't be able to exceed the speed of light, and there's a practical limit to the amount of information that can be transferred on a sub-second basis.

We will need fast computers on the receiving end to decode the scanned images and 3D holographic technology to project the resulting image to an area in the virtual conference room.

Do we now have the technologies that can make this happen? Well, not quite yet, but we may be very close...

- Huge bandwidth: The shift from analogue to digital has spearheaded novel uses by the telecommunication networks. It was only as recently as 1997 that telephones first began to carry more digital than voice conversation data over its wires. A mere 7 years later, only 3% of all the data transmitted across telephone networks consisted of voice.[23]

  In 1999, Bell Labs was able to transmit 1.65 gigabits of information across a single fiber optic line in one second. This is equivalent to transmitting the entire contents of the Library of Congress in about six seconds.[24] Five years later, in 2004, at the spring 2004

---

[23] As the Future Catches You—Juan Enriquez

[24] Ibid

Internet2 Conference, a new record was reached with the transmission of over nearly 11,000 kilometers of data at an average speed of 6.25 gigabits per second. In 2007 the record was up to 9.08 gigabits per second

- Moore's Law to the max: Hardware costs continue to be driven down.

- 3D holographic display technology is currently being tested in labs.

- Basic 3D scanners are now on the market and their prices are dropping.

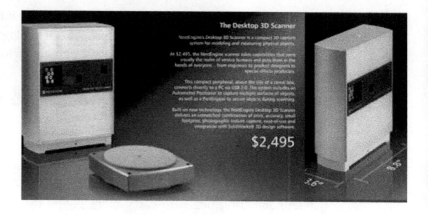

In terms of timing, Virtual Presence could very well be just around the corner. In my prognosticating opinion, we should expect real, albeit expensive, applications no later than 2015 (remember, 50" plasma TVs cost $100K at first). So the main questions are these: When will economics allow for its broad deployment? More importantly: What is the likely business impact of such a technological development?

ENVISIONING THE BUSINESS IMPACT

"This 'telephone' has too many shortcomings to be seriously considered as a means of communication. The device is inherently of no value to us." **Western Union internal memo, 1876**

It happens all the time. . . Too often, the industry leader invariably misses the chance to grab onto an emerging business. Wells Fargo failed to get into the railway business, Western Union didn't become involved in the telephone industry, and the Rail Companies, lords of transportation in the nineteen century, missed out on the chance to capture the automobile industry.

One can prognosticate the future of technology by maintaining a proactive effort in monitoring new developments coming from the world's R&D labs. The challenge is to understand the transformative impact these technologies could potentially have on business. Discerning a business's future will always be more of a divination-based exercise.

Even today, it's difficult to predict, let alone prognosticate, the ultimate future business impact from the emergence of such Web 2.0 services as Youtube.com, Facebook.com, or Twitter.com. This is not to say that techniques used to prognosticate technology cannot also be used in imagining "what-if" scenarios for business. However, the ability to prognosticate with sound information and well-founded assumptions is at the core of what it means to be a true visionary. Most resumes today include some form of, "I am a visionary", claim as opposed to, "I am a prognosticator" claim because it just doesn't sound as legit.

Envisioning the future of business is as intriguingly fun as it is difficult. If this weren't the case, there would be far more billionaires roaming the face of the earth. Look at how

Amazon has transformed the book industry (and continues to do so with its e-reader, the Kindle), or the way Apple has taken the music industry by storm by combining a number of differing technologies and creating a viable online music distribution business model (a business that no one from the traditional music industry had the foresight to invent, perhaps because they were too focused on fighting Napster rather than riding the winds of change!).

Granted, although the Virtual Presence example may be a bit obvious, there can be no question that a formally established Virtual Presence would seriously impact the travel and hospitality businesses; not to mention the possible impact on industries such as entertainment, education, and healthcare.

True, worrying about this impact might be, well . . . a bit premature, but nevertheless, visualizing possible outcomes can help to position your business as a leading entrant. It can't hurt to be prepared should it develop more quickly than expected.

We can envision that the initial versions of Virtual Presence will be so expensive that it will have to be leased from large, well-established Virtual Presence providers. This service can be viewed as the start of a potential transformative development in the future, but whether hotels will be the natural focus area for this type of service is still unclear.

As the cost of technology drops, its availability becomes the realm of opportunistic service providers. Witness the emergence of Internet Cafes; still popular in countries where home-based Internet access is still not prevalent. This brings to mind a childhood recollection of mine when owning a TV was considered a luxury and I had to pay twenty cents to watch every episode of The Lone Ranger at my neighbors.

As the cost of technology becomes affordable by the masses, you begin to see a gradual segmentation of services based on quality of service. Most of us can use Internet based video-conferencing using "free" tools like Skype but, for more professional Videoconferencing, you would utilize professional office support businesses such as those from Kinkos. Also, for large employee teleconferencing gatherings, you could lease the services of movie theater operators who offer this service.

In our example, when trying to understand the implications of this emerging technology on your hospitality business, you would do well to evaluate whether there is a business model that combines a future Virtual Presence capability with meeting room facilities. For example, you could estimate additional food and beverage revenues, plus sleeping room accommodations, for people arriving from regional locations to attend this Virtual Presence event.

Then again, although Virtual Presence technology does not yet exist, this should not stop you from imagining its eventual advent and deciding whether it makes sense to position your system by entering the present Teleconference business. For example, notice today's placement of high-end Telepresence services like Marriott's and HP's announcement[25] to enable the use of HP's Halo Telepresence Technology from Marriott's conference room facilities. Clearly, Marriot is forward looking in this area.

In any case, this prognostication/envisioning exercise showcases the importance of continuous technology monitoring, defining your very own R&D roadmap, and

---

[25] HP and Marriott International Form Alliance to Open "Public Access" Halo Telepresence Rooms.
http://www.telepresenceoptions.com/2008/03/hp_and_marriott_international/

assessing the impact technology can have on the business. While you should avoid becoming an order-taker when it comes to articulating the IT Transformation plans, you should never forget that ultimately everything revolves around the business.

At the core of any prognostication and envisioning exercise is how to match your transformation direction with the business strategy. If your hotel company (in this example) is typically focused on leisure travel, for example, then the idea to push for investments in Telepresence technology will likely not be well received. That is, unless you can find an angle that leverages the use of teleconferencing by vacationing guests, in which case you might end up with a powerful competitive differentiator.

Regardless, in the end, you will need to business-justify the investment in technology transformation if you are to make it happen.

JUSTIFYING THE TECHNOLOGY TRANSFORMATION

This is the recipe: Slice and dice your company's view of technology, add a pinch of prognostication, sweeten the core issues faced by your legacy technology; then bake this mixture together with your business requirements. You can then serve up a fully cooked technology strategy.

Clearly, the key ingredient missing in this recipe is your actual budget. Even if there is a commitment to invest in IT, you should be able to prove that it is worth the investment to undertake a transformation project rather than simply ride the legacy bandwagon for a little longer. If you do decide on the latter approach, you might want to put this book back on the shelf for now and revisit it in a year. However, if you believe there's a legitimate need to invest, you'll have to figure out how to go about convincing the CEO and CFO, and any other executive holding the purse strings, to open the company wallet.

All this is just my roundabout way of saying that, no-matter-what, you are going to need to develop a business case that shows the benefits of transformation in terms of dollars and cents; not just in qualitatively ethereal terms. You have to be able to determine the benefits of return on investment that the transformed IT will deliver.

In addition to the identified direct returns from the business team requesting the functionality, the ROI should include the monetized benefits derived from future time to market opportunities, reduced operational expenses (including cost avoidance), and if possible, estimated additional revenue resulting from functionality and features that would otherwise not be feasible with the legacy system. Nowadays expectations on technology returns are actually more aggressive, and it's not unusual to see ROI expectations ranging from 6 to 9 months.

How do you go about doing a business-oriented justification? Studies show that, in a typical IT budget, 80% is spent on system maintenance and the remainder 20% on strategic efforts[26]. Indeed, as IT budgets suffer from pressures caused by the global economic meltdown, there is little room to maneuver when faced with the allocation of ever diminishing monies to the maintenance of systems that must remain operational.

Ultimately, funding a transformation initiative can only come from a mixture of savings in day-to-day maintenance costs, supplemented with the injection of capital from business driven initiatives. In the end, the business case should be framed in terms of a combination of the following benefits:

- Future cost savings due to the avoidance of maintenance expenses resulting from the use of newer technology. These savings can come from leveraging external operation services, removing dependencies on single vendors, opening the door to competitive pricing, and using lower cost commodity hardware and open source code. (Caveat emptor: Open Systems are usually cheaper, but not always! Check the fine print of those support license agreements.)

- Incremental revenues due to the higher effectiveness of the new technology. For example, fewer customer losses due to better service, better accounting and auditing information, reduction or elimination of maintenance outage windows, better business intelligence, and so forth. For good measure you should also include estimated development cost savings associated with the use of modern technologies and functionality enhancements.

---

[26] Enterprise Architecture and New Generation Information Systems—Dimitris N. Chorafas

- Added revenue generated by new business opportunities, or competitive advantage enabled or supported by the new technology. The ability for the business to quickly implement a new promotion or define dynamic pricing based on more sophisticated customer intelligence, or more targeted and flexible up-sell and cross-sell capabilities. Scaling up to rapidly adsorb an acquisition, and the ability to quickly connect to new partners via B2B services, are among the types of benefits you will need to quantify and elaborate upon.

You can try to reduce current operational and maintenance costs to help fund the initial investment for IT transformation but, needless to say, this might be extremely tricky to accomplish. Ironically, were you to accomplish this feat, you would also be playing with a doubled-edged sword. The company might simply pocket the recouped funds rather than proceed with the transformation.

Obviously, if there is money to be saved from conventional cost saving measures (renegotiating maintenance fees, reducing marginal staff, deferring expenses, etc.) you should do these as a matter of normal business. However, you would do well to identify those short-term savings resulting from the commitment to a strategic transformation direction. For instance, if the company commits to the technology transformation effort, you might be able to nominally reduce service-level agreements for non-critical parts of the current environment. However, with the expectation that such an SLA reduction is a short term risk to be remediated by earlier new project deliverables. Additionally, you might be in a better position to re-negotiate deals with your current vendors with the promise that they will be considered as potential suppliers for future strategic work. As part of the short term cost reduction, you might agree to initiate a short-term outsourcing of legacy operations, especially if your long term plan is to also outsource operations of the strategic system.

Be aware that it is at this early stage of justification that the seeds of large project failures are often buried. The challenge always comes down to this: If one is careful to include all possible costs and risks in the request for funding, you risk scaring off support for the project. After all, executives by their very nature are generally risk-adverse and wary of accepting cost estimates that, while realistic, may command a significant level of investment.

The temptation then may be to sugar-coat the request for investment by presenting best-case, diminished cost estimates, and over-promising on results.

Please don't do it.

A better approach is to make a request that clearly delineates benefits and costs for a series of deliverable phases. This way the executive decision-makers can make informed strategic decisions as to the level of investment to which they are willing to commit. By limiting the scope of what's being promised, you lower the initial funding request; yet you can indicate that you expect to ask for additional funding in the future as the project succeeds and proves it worth. Ideally, you will be able to define a first phase that produces benefits but also points to subsequent phases that provide increasing returns with less and less additional investment. However, never propose a phase that consists simply of "infrastructure" positioning as this lacks a clear business case (see my rant below about the idea of business-justifying SOA on its own).

Most importantly, be wary of over-promising results in order to secure support for the new project. Remember, you will to have to deliver on that promise! In the end, over-promising will only come back to haunt you and is not a productive strategy. Seek at all times to follow this one wise dictum: under-promise and over-deliver.

<rant>

Given that you will likely use a Service Oriented Architecture (SOA) as the backbone for IT transformation, you might feel tempted to justify the endeavor on this basis alone. Don't. There is no way you can make a business case for SOA. SOA is part of IT strategy; not a business strategy. SOA is about "how" you will implement technology transformation; not "why".

Developing a business case to justify SOA and then getting your CEO to sign a multi-million dollar check to implement it is not doable. Believe me; I've tried! I once made a presentation to the CEO of my company naively asking for a gazillion dollars to implement this thing called SOA. He was a gracious CEO and I'm glad he didn't kick me out of the room when I made this request. Instead, he politely asked me to go back and make a business case for my proposal. Good luck with that! It doesn't matter that SOA just happens to be the most exciting thing to come out of IT since the invention of Red Bull, or that it truly empowers a business by aligning its IT structure to business processes and goals, or that it does all this with cost-saving open-source technology that can freely inter-operate via services, or that (write in-your-promise-here). What does matter is that your company will only fund initiatives that are framed around business benefits, and these initiatives are those that deal with "why", and not "how", the company does things. Only after the project has been approved does SOA become relevant as the solution's approach.

</rant>

MUSINGS ABOUT INNOVATION

Thus far I have focused primarily on aspects related to the corporate culture, business requirements, and funding considerations that serve as a foundation for an IT Transformation initiative. Shortly I will delve into the more technically focused steps required to provide the strategic technology framework for this transformation, such as the gathering of specific requirements, setting the program scope and defining the high level architecture and technology transformation tenets. However, before I proceed with this technical nitty-gritty, I want to highlight one important element that I believe to be at the core of any IT transformation initiative: *innovation*.

Surely, one of the sweetest and most rewarding outcomes of a renovation program is the introduction of innovative features, technologies and processes. A transformation program that results in more of the same tired, old solutions, is not going to excite anyone and is less likely to meet emerging requirements.   Without Innovation, IT Transformation would be like pimping a Ford Pinto with velvet seats and a "La Cucaracha" horn.

Innovation can and should take place at each step of the transformation, from the identification of business processes suitable for improvement, to the manner in which you lay down the technology strategy, to the methods and processes you follow and, most certainly, to the specific elements and inventions of the solution.

Then again, this may be easier said than done. The creation of innovation is not the sort of thing that can be written down in a plan. Innovation is about the *"how"* we solve problems and not about the *"what"*. There are plenty of white papers that attempt formalize innovation processes. It's as if innovation were something that can be created by simply following a recipe: "Put processes here, structure this, add water, and bingo! Invention will happen!" Forgive my skepticism. It just doesn't work this way.

After all, the genesis of innovation is perhaps one of the most intriguing aspects of all human endeavors, and its appearance can often only be explained as the result of the combination of the right circumstances and a little bit of luck. Innovation is more about atmospherics than about process. Why? I don't believe an innovation process can be formalized with the same kind of structure as that used in methodology-rich disciplines such as auditing or quality assurance.

The truth of the matter is that the one proven way to foster innovation is to secure resources with the smarts and ability to generate ideas; all the while ensuring them an environment that supports and encourages the emergence of their ideas. Even then, new ideas may not occur, depending upon the presence or absence of a third element: serendipity.

Serendipity matters. Think of the invention and use of the wheel. Depictions of Sumerian carriages pulled by horses confirm that the wheel was first invented at least 5,000 years ago. On the other hand, look at the Americas. The Aztecs never used the wheel for transportation, even though they had invented it and used it in children toys. Why? The most common explanation is that the wheel was impractical to them because they lacked horses, oxen or any other animal capable of pulling a carriage. Fair enough, as far as explanations go this is not a bad one. It's just that I don't buy it. Even though the Aztecs did not have horses or oxen, they did have access to readily available beasts of burden: enemy prisoners and slaves. Given that human rights was not high on that society's agenda, one would imagine that instead of extracting the hearts of thousands-upon-thousands of their war prisoners, the Aztecs could have put some of those folks to a more practical use by having them pull wheeled carriages. No, a simpler explanation is this: the idea to use carts with wheels as a form of transportation simply did not occur to them! In fact, it's just possible that the one individual that might have come up with the revolutionary idea to use the wheel for transportation was one of the unlucky fellows whose heart was yanked out for the benefit of the gods! With their pervasive human-sacrifice program, the Aztecs definitely failed to provide the right innovation-fostering environment.

Now, before you begin to argue that perhaps the Aztecs were just not all that smart, think of wheeled-luggage. Why was the idea to attach wheels to luggage not conceptualized much earlier?

I'm amused every time I watch a fifties movie showing people lugging around immense traveling trunks. Most of us old enough to have used vinyl records remember going through airports, train and bus stations hauling heavy luggage. And yet something so seemly obvious and technologically viable, such as attaching wheels to luggage, did not occur until very recently!

Again, why is this?

It wasn't that the technology to attach wheels to luggage didn't exist, or that train stations lacked even terrain, or that travelers of yore had bigger muscles, but quite simply that the idea had not occurred to anyone!

A caveat regarding innovation is this: beware of the gimmick. Gimmicks are to innovation what margarine is to butter. They only give the appearance of innovation but fail to provide real value and benefits. They shimmer with the glow of vanity that hides their ultimate banality. They quickly become anchors that usually add cost and obfuscation to the deliverables. Remember that annoying Windows paper clip "assistant"? Gimmicks often occur when there is an artificial pressure to innovate; to come up with "new stuff" regardless. The potential for their embarrassing existence is another good reason to avoid the establishment of inane innovation quotas.

You don't need gimmicks. Perhaps it's true that the best ideas are often the simplest ones—like the wheel. However, if you plan to develop a new system that includes a fair share of innovation, you should do more than simply hope for the best. A good environment for innovation is made by constructing appropriate facilities (offices, labs, and equipment), providing individual and team recognition, establishing open communications, instigating flexibility and, most importantly, ensuring the team is fully aware of the shared objectives and is passionately committed to success.

Then again, a little bit of luck doesn't hurt.

Serendipity awaits.

SECTION II

Strategy, Architecture & Planning

"Would you tell me which way I ought to go from here?" asked Alice.
"That depends a good deal on where you want to get," said the Cat.
"I really don't care where" replied Alice.
"Then it doesn't much matter which way you go," said the Cat.

Lewis Carroll, Alice's Adventures in Wonderland (1865)

Trials

How does one define a system from scratch? ✦ How to define an all-encompassing technology strategy that assumes a ground-up effort? ✦ What should be built? How will it be built? Who will be the vendor?

Techniques

Gathering requirements ✦ Getting the line of business involved early on ✦ Defining the enterprise IT strategy, architecture, and logical roadmap ✦ Validating approach against business priorities and funding ✦ Creating a system architecture that has the right scope and level of detail and adopting the tenets and standards.

Tribulations

When the strategy document becomes just another nicely bound book, collecting dust on the coffee table ✦ urge to rush into implementation before the plan is fully defined ✦ Avoiding tactical requirement "distractions" ✦ Dealing with scope creep.

DEFINING THE SCOPE

REQUIREMENTS

The Strategy and Planning for the IT Transformation effort must emanate from the definition of scope and the understanding of the requirements that will be targeted by the initiative. Many compromises must be made in the process, and these compromises will become both cause and effect of the ultimate strategic direction.

The compromises deal with the interplay of these parameters for each requirement:

- *Quality*: The solidity of the deliverable

- *Cost*: The amount of money available for delivery

- *Schedule*: The expected delivery timelines

- *Scope*: The functionality that is being delivered

These variables are known as QCSS attributes (Quality, Cost, Schedule, Scope), taken from the initials of each. As accurately pointed out by Mr. Harwell Thrasher[27], the business requirements can only reasonably specify three of these factors. The fourth factor will be a result of the project's dynamics. For example, if the business wants a project done within certain cost restraints, under a specific timeline, and with a specific scope, the quality of the project will be in question.

---

[27] "Boiling the IT Frog" by Harwell Thrasher

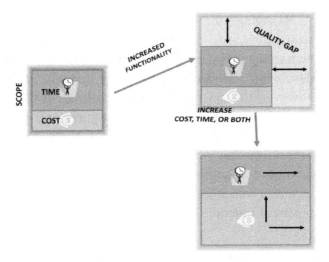

In this diagram, Functionality is represented by the surface area of the square. The Cost necessary to meet the Functionality is shown in light grey, and the Schedule (timeline) is in dark grey. Quality is the percentage of the Functionality surface that is being covered by the Cost and Schedule squares. The diagram shows that if the Functionality scope is increased (larger surface), you will either have to increase the Cost, the Schedule, or both to match the new requirements; if not, Quality will suffer.

This "Thrasher Law" applies to all projects and to any combination of attributes. Furthermore, imagine the QCSS variables as knobs on a control panel, each influencing the other[28]. The more money available for a given project, the more potential resources that can be committed; thereby enabling faster delivery and/or more extended functionality. With less funding, chances are the scope will have to be reduced if timelines are to be maintained.

---

[28] Microsoft article "A short course in project management" in http://office.microsoft.com/en-us/project/HA102354821033.aspx also has an excellent explanation of the QCSS concept

Managing the project budget and timelines is a straightforward, project management function. Project Management disciplines that effectively do this have been developed and can be applied in a systemic way. In truth; however, the most complicated challenge of this stage is to properly manage the number of requirements you are likely to receive from business. Let's face it, this is an IT Transformation project that, very likely, has been sold as the mother-of-all-solutions and that will, no doubt, have the business salivating like a kid in a candy store with all the potential functions they have been deprived of for so many years.

The impact of requirements tends to follow Pareto's 80-20 rule. That is, typically 20% of the requirements provide 80% of the value, and the remaining 80% only add a 20% value. Now, going to the business with the message that you will only implement 20% of their requirements is probably not a good idea. First, the Pareto principle is just that—a principle; not a law. It might be that in your case 40% of your requirements represent 70% of the value. Secondly, who knows with precision what's the 20% of most value? In any case, extra business value can always be attained by delivering as many additional requirements as possible. Who knows what might be the difference between having a highly competitive solution or an also-ran.

What you first need to do is identify the 20% to 40% of requirements that everyone agrees are a must, and then proceed to carefully analyze and prioritize the remaining requirements in light of their diminishing returns. My own philosophy is to do as much as possible with the money and time allocated (in essence, establish first the cost and schedule surfaces), and then draw a line in terms of what requirements are to be met during that first phase. You can place the unfulfilled requirements in a subsequent phase that might or might not be funded on their merits. If you can do so without eliciting the wrath of the business team, then you have succeeded!

As you can see, managing the overall scope is an activity best handled by the project leader and is not to be delegated to line project managers. It requires finesse and political skill in dealing with business customers.

<rant>

> More often than not, you'll be obliged to forget the chimerical goal of getting clear requirements from the business. Fact is that the "handoff" of requirements from business to technology is the widest chasm in a transformation. The truth is that oftentimes the business group won't be able to produce requirements for the simple reason that they aren't exactly sure what it is they want. To be fair, they might know the desired outcome when thinking in terms of results. "I want to be better able to track customer preferences." But then just try to pin them down on the details. "What kind of preferences?" "What kind of customers?" "What particular reports will you need first?" You'll soon find your head spinning.

> In the end, the Business Analyst (and by this I mean YOUR Business Analyst, the one under your supervision!) will generally find he has the responsibility of "guessing" the set of requirements that best respond to the stated goals. The problem is that this is a hit- and-miss process that can quickly become very costly. It can also become a political mine-field, especially when you deliver requirements that the business team can easily disown down the road. I'm not sure I have a perfect answer for this conundrum, but an approach that has worked less-badly is to have the BA literally extract and derive the requirements from the business experts via a series of direct interviews ("interrogations" could be a more appropriate term, but please don't use water-boarding!). Make sure to gather,

synthesize and escalate to the business leaders the ultimate key decisions they'll have to make regarding the requirements: final scope, priorities, timeline commitments, resources they put on the table for testing and accepting deliverables, governance of deployment, etc. Regardless, you should to have them sign the documented requirements thus produced. Good luck with that!

</rant>

TAMING COMPLEXITY

A second dimension that is often left unexamined during the requirements phase is the need to assess the project complexity and define the strategy of how to manage this complexity. By this, I mean how to determine what to automate versus what to leave as a manual processes.

The complexity of a project is an intrinsic variable ultimately determined by the business processes. Keeping in mind the key dictum that a technology solution can never be of lesser complexity than the underlying problem it hopes to solve, you should first ensure that, before any attempt to automate them, the business processes are as optimized[29] as possible. Many technology projects end up being unyieldingly complex because they try to tackle what is in essence a mash up of chaotic business rules.

Having said this, there is no reason why the technology solution should be more complex than necessary. For instance, poor technical decisions or the use of inappropriate software tools can add unnecessary complexity to a project.

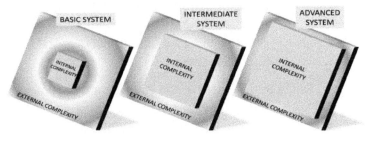

Recognizing that a project has an intrinsic complexity framed by the business requirements, your challenge is to

---

[29] In fact, one of the intrinsic benefits of IT Transformation is that, just as the act of smiling can make people feel happier via backward neural influence, this transformation can also serve as a trigger for much-needed business transformation.

efficiently tame this complexity within the realm of technology and budget available to you. Here we have the "Law of Preservation of Complexity": *N = S + U; where N is the total complexity of the solution (as determined by the complexity of the business problem), S is the technology system complexity, and U is the complexity that the user faces when interacting with the system. Given that the intrinsic complexity of a project is "N", it is your decision how to apportion the complexity between the system and the user.*

When you think about it, the simpler the user interface, the more complex the technology backend that supports that iteration is bound to be. I'm fairly certain that the underlying software supporting the Apple iPhone is quite complex, given that it is a device universally recognized as providing a very intuitive interface. Alternatively, simple technology implementations tend to deliver solutions that are more manual in nature and hence more complex for the user (remember all those MS/DOS commands?). A complex solution that delivers an easy-to-use implementation is bound to cost more to develop, but its operational costs, due to reduced support and training costs will be lower. A simple solution that places the burden of complexity on the user can typically be developed more rapidly and at lesser expense, but its operational cost will be higher.

Taken to the extreme, the simplest automation solution is one in which automation ceases to exist and all business processes are manual. The most complex automation solution will probably involve the use of a sophisticated, artificial-intelligence system that is able to take on all automation burdens[30]. This capability, however, has yet to be invented.

---

[30] As I write this, I've come across the announcement that IBM is starting a project funded by DARPA to build a new type of computer that simulates the way the brain operates. A multi-disciplinary working team that includes Neuroscientists and other disciplines will work on

In the end, it behooves you as technology leader to ensure that no unneeded technical complexity is introduced into your projects (watch out for that young bright, software maverick who pushes for that "cool", dynamic rules engine to do the payroll!). Always keep in mind that the most important independent variables in apportioning complexity are the understanding of the key business priorities and the true capabilities of technology.

The trick is to strike the proper balance in the deliverable. A good technical delivery will endeavor to place the bulk of complexity inside the solution black-box, making the interaction with the software simpler and more user friendly, but not at the cost of creating a solution that can't be implemented.

---

this project. I doubt this type of approach will work (the airplane was finally invented when men stopped trying to emulate the way birds fly), but who knows?

<rant>

Many people confuse complexity with over-automation. If the complexity of the technology solution does not ultimately simplify the interaction with the user then you are not improving things. A personal peeve of mine is the recent "popularity" of so-called voice-response systems. If they were used only for simple voice driven selections, then there would be no problem. The issue arises when these interactive-voice-response (IVR) applications are made to carry out more complex interactions. The fact is that technology is not yet at the point where it can support these interactions in a seamless manner. In the end, the only purpose these "voice-recognition" systems accomplish is to weed out customers' access to the support staff, at the price of lowered service levels and heightened customer dissatisfaction. The manner in which companies use these systems is a typical example of adding complexity for the wrong reason.

</rant>

THE TECHNOLOGY STRATEGY

So far so good, the business strategy is understood, the requirements are known within a reasonable degree of certainty and, by now, you have framed the relevant scope and priorities of your company (are you in a business that requires a view of technology as a competitive weapon or as a utility?). To boot, you have also apportioned how you will deal with complexity. It is finally time to develop *the overall technology strategy that most clearly matches the technology plan of your business.*

At its simplest, the technology strategy should provide a digest of the technical *"Whats"* and *"Whens"* mapping the key business needs. These are the technical approaches; described in terms that business folks can understand. Here are some examples:

What: "We will replace the entire system with new technology components via gradual investments."

> **When**: "Over a two-year period, starting with a Phase 1 deliverable that will support new customer analysis tools."

What: "We will buy a new ERP from vendor XYZ and outsource all new development to India."

> **When**: "We will hold off until next year. In the meantime we will research outsourcing partners and develop an RFP."

What: "We will continue to use the operating system 'as is', but we will use new technologies to develop any new business systems."

> **When**: "We will do so on an on-going basis as new business systems become approved."

If you've ever watched a group of children playing a casual game of soccer, you may have been amused at how they wildly chase after the ball as a pack (believe me, this happens whenever children are let loose with a soccer ball!) There is no structure to the way they play and, as a result, their efforts are usually for naught as they comically interfere with each other. The children know the "*What*": to play soccer; they also know the "*When*": right-now. What they lack is knowledge of the "*How*".

Just as the "*What*" and the "*When*" should have emerged from the definition of the agreed transformation previously discussed, the "*How*" is the essence, the secret-sauce, of the technology strategy. The "*Whats*", the "*Whens*" and the comprehensive explanation of the "*Hows*", represent the detailed strategy that is to serve as the blueprint for the multi-year IT transformation plan. This technology strategy blueprint is depicted in the diagram below: the core technical solution, including the overall technical approach, the high level architecture, and the standards and tenets you will adopt.

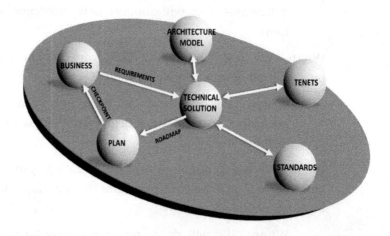

The technical strategy is not meant to be a photograph—something static—but rather an evolving movie. To become a living, breathing strategy, it must be continuously cross-checked with the changing business requirements. If adjustments are needed, you should ensure the solution continues to conform to the business requirements, and that any resulting changes to the architecture and standards only occur on an as-needed basis and not as a result of a whim or sudden change in direction driven by dictates of fashion or politics. You will need to implement a governance to oversee the evolution of the strategy, as well as to manage the change control processes. This is in order to avoid the dangers that so-often plague many large projects: scope diffusion, runaway requirements, or irrelevance of the solution.

One of the key roles of the strategic governance is to ensure the strategy is communicated and understood at all levels of the organization. The whole technical staff, from the most junior programmer to the most senior manager, should be intimately familiar with all the elements of the technology strategy.

While your communication to the technical staff will most likely emphasize the *"How"* of the strategy, the message to less-technical constituencies, such as executives, will have to be framed in a easier-to- understand, 'elevator-chat' form dealing with the *"Whys"* and the *"Whats"* of the strategy.

In this simpler communication you can still speak about the core technical solution and the general principles regarding the transformation: Will you develop the solution internally? Will you rely entirely on the services of a third party vendor? Will you use a hybrid of internally developed modules available externally as a service? (Software-as-a-Service: SaaS). If you are going to build the solution internally, what role will the IT department play? Will you hire new developers or integrate third party augmentation services? Will you bring in temporary contractors for software development or will you off-shore development? If so, which components will you off-shore? Will you outsource the whole damn thing? What are the timeframes and general costs? What are the benefits? When will the benefits be realized? Which vendors do you consider strategic to your project?

Clearly, this (possibly long) elevator talk will not easily accommodate the explanation of the detailed architecture or standards, but you should at least be able to cover the general concepts, such as whether you plan to use open source software or whether the solution will be accessible via the web.

Now, why do we no longer have elevator operators? Remember the days when operating an elevator was considered to be such a specialized role that it required a, usually bored-looking attendant to press those buttons as a service to you? Come to think of it, you may want to mention to the CFO that you will be using something known as Service oriented Architecture...

THE ARCHITECTURE AS FOUNDATION FOR THE TECHNOLOGY SOLUTION

While your executives should be able to understand the *"What"* and the *"When"* defined by the technology strategy, it is in the *"How"* that the magic occurs. So, *"How"* are things done?

Defining the "How" is an art; not a science—an art expressed through the creation of the architecture. Still, you should always ensure that, if the architecture is to meet its goals, you keep an eye on the way the architecture supports the strategy. Think of how a building is constructed . . . If the business plan is "Promote Religion", your strategy could be "Build a Temple"; if your business is to "Enable Commerce", your strategy might be "Build a Mall". The architecture should match the strategy just as the strategy should match the business. How you architect a Catholic Church would be different from how you architect a Synagogue. There are in fact a set of patterns and principles that drive the design styles for each of these buildings.

Still, the fundamental question from the technology perspective remains: How do you design the temple or church? *"How"* do you build these structures?

What's the best architecture?

Well, 99% of the time the answer to any given question (architecture or otherwise) is that "It depends". You will not arrive at the correct architecture by blindly following a set methodology. If it were that easy to dissect and replicate an expert's judgment, most "thinking" jobs would have been taken over by computers long ago (do you remember all the hype about expert systems supposedly being able to capture and replicate domain-specific expertise?) No, defining and executing the *"How"* is what justifies your paycheck. Creating the architecture requires inner judgment, which is the inherent product of many years of experience, mixed with a healthy dose of common-sense.

This is how the federal government defines architecture[31].

An enterprise architecture is a strategic information asset base which defines the business, the information necessary to operate the business, the technologies necessary to support the business operations, and the transitional processes necessary for implementing new technologies in response to the changing needs of business. Stated differently, the enterprise architecture is a strategic asset repository, which consists of models that define the current and target architecture environments, and the transitional processes for evolving from the current to the target.

A bit of a mouthful, but what were you expectingt? Remember, this is a definition put out by the government. To put it more simply, a modern architecture must meet the following conditions:

1. Provide a unified, end-to-end systems approach to technical architecture and design. In other words, it should provide a Unified Architecture Reference Framework. This framework should converge, consolidate and functionally align the various technology elements in a coherent manner with that of the business.

2. Define the architecture patterns that the company will live and die by. At its apex, the architecture must follow what I call a broad theme. Here I suggest that if the architecture is to have the required flexibility to properly meet the

---

[31] http://cio.gov. Note that I chose to use this government framework, but I could have just as easily chosen other well-know architecture frameworks such as the Zachman framework. I believe that no one framework is superior to any other as long as you stick to the chosen model.

business objectives, the broad theme should be the use of the service oriented paradigm (SOA).

3. Incorporate principle-based evolution to move your company from its current state toward a target state. This includes a roadmap of development initiatives that incorporate the adopted strategic tenets and standards.

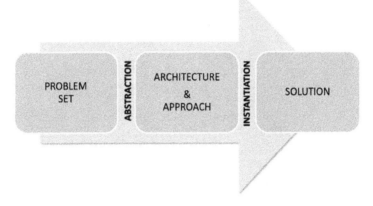

As shown in the diagram above, the process of architecture is ultimately a process of abstraction. Unfortunately, this is often confused with the idea that architectures are just a bunch of un-implementable constructs.

It is your mission to ensure that the architecture is viewed as a stepping stone to a process that will ultimately lead to concrete solutions. This process should have a top-down approach that progressively moves the architecture from a high level definition down through levels of finer detail:

- **Level I**, the highest conceptual level, contains standards, current architecture, architecture segments, sub architecture models, target architecture, strategic direction, transitional processes and external architecture drivers.

- **Level II** breaks down the current and target architecture models to cover specific business functions and technology.

- **Level III** further breaks down the technology architecture into data, systems, and infrastructure.

Next I will cover the specifics for each level in this process.

THE ARCHITECTURE PROCESS

The progression of the architecture definition process begins at stratospheric heights, moving back down to the earth in what is hopefully a smooth-landing implementation rather than an uncontrolled crash. All architecture definition processes should follow a top-down progression. As discussed earlier, this progression is grouped into levels: Level I which represents the most abstract steps and Level III which deals with the detailed design and engineering.

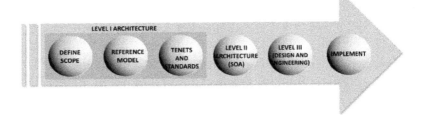

The objective of the Level I process is to develop a conceptual **architecture model** that properly mirrors the business process it is meant to solve. In order to be meaningful, this model must offer an end-to-end view of the defined scope; so the first Level I task is to **define the scope** of the architecture.

At this point in the process it's okay if the model is suitably high-level, otherwise you could trade-off coverage for specificity (to abuse the cliché: You could fail to see the forest for the trees). At this early stage you should resist the impulse to over-define the solution. I say this fully aware that a common criticism of architecture is that, due to its abstract nature, it can become too ethereal and impossible to implement. The alternative, however, is to fail to develop the most flexible solution in an attempt to tackle detailed implementation concerns such as performance or operability. Remember, God was allegedly able to create the universe in six days and then, so satisfied with the results, able to rest on the seventh day (I still contend He missed out on quality assurance). You on the other hand, have to take the more humble view that, in all likelihood, the solution you define will not initially be perfect. Your focus should be one of flexibility. Architectures defined under the pressure of parochial concerns often end up becoming the opposite: stilted and monolithic.

A composer represents the symphony in a musical score, and a building architect's vision is conveyed through the use of a mock-up. Likewise, a good IT architecture model should be fashioned in a manner that business people can relate to. As a high level construct, the architecture model need not depict all the elements necessary for a proper technology solution, but it should serve as the basis from which the detailed technology components will emanate. The visual representation of the architecture model is known as the **Architecture Reference Framework**. Creation of a powerful framework as a communications tool is a key ingredient towards the success of the architectural process.

Last on the Level I list, you will need to provide the bridge between the abstractness of the architecture model and the reality of the technology design. This bridge is provided by the definition of tenets and standards.

For example, the United States of America was formed as a federated republic with three independent powers to ensure checks-and-balances. This arrangement represents the architecture model created by America's founding fathers. The Constitution describes the standards that define the workings of this model, and the Bill of Rights represents the tenets.

Like the Constitution, which can be amended according to Article V, the standards can be further refined into a more detailed form as the architecture development steps are followed. Standards should not be seen as an inflexible mantra never to be deviated from, but they should provide a foundation against which to measure technology decisions.

Now, like the Constitution, which seems like a nuisance at times to politicians, architectures are sometimes seen as an expensive burden in terms of performance and practicality. The reason for this is tha,t oftentimes, people attempt to reify[32] the architecture as opposed to instantiating it[33]. Attempts to reify the architecture by trying to implement architectures in a too-literal a fashion will usually result in contrived, inflexible systems. Instead, the architecture model, tenets, and standards should be seen as a kind of Rosetta stone for the purpose of translating the more ethereal architecture concepts into more concrete, practical implementations.

I present the view that architecture processes should be driven from a Top-Down perspective. There is, amazingly, a school of thought out there that proposes the idea that a successful implementation can serve as a baseline pattern for a new architecture. This Bottom-Up view is most commonly espoused by extreme proponents of Agile methodologies who have forgotten that methodology's forte is in applying quick development and implementation processes; not in the creation of comprehensive, repeatable frameworks. A detailed implementation, no matter how well executed, cannot constitute a true architecture because it is an implementation; one that intrinsically lacks an appropriate level of abstraction.

---

[32] The Webster's Collegiate dictionary defines reification as, "to regard (something abstract) as a material thing." People who assume a flag "is" the country are reifying the abstract symbol of a flag. An Architecture that depicts a logical system as being completely modular should not be reified as an implementation that demands each module be run in its own computer.

[33] "To represent (an abstraction) by a concrete instance". Merrian-Webster.Online.

In the end, "architecture solutions" derived from trying to generalize a successful implementation end up being so narrowly defined that the best one can hope for is to use them as the proverbial hammer that turns everything into a nail.

Moving downwards from the Space Shuttle heights of Level I, the Commercial Jet, **Level II architecture** deals with the current and target architecture models that map to specific business functions.

Drum-roll here!

We have finally arrived at the technology level that ultimately corresponds to the domain of Service Oriented Architecture! In Level II we deal with the various methodologies and processes needed to define the services' ontology and the enterprise design for the entire SOA fabric. Later on, I will expand on this level (after all, we are dealing with IT Transformation ... **with SOA!**).

There's no arguing the fact that the architecture should ultimately deal with practical details. It's just that the mapping to reality is more of an engineering exercise; not an architectural one. Call it semantics, but **Level III** is actually a stage dealing with the engineering and detail designs in which the architecture principles are correlated with specific technology elements and pragmatic tenets; not to wash-out the principles, but to apply them. Practical trade-offs can be made here to ensure the system will perform under real-life situations. Engineering in Level III is when and where you can and should address all questions of performance, practical scalability, and operability; not before. Hopefully, your great work at defining flexible architecture principles during the Level I and II steps will make this engineering effort easier.

Engineering in this sense is the art of translating the architecture patterns into real world solutions that take into account well-known practical implementation constraints. As such, the definition of the Level III architecture is more about the practice of engineering .

Remember this key dictum:

Architect for Flexibility, Engineer for Performance.

The engineering and implementation processes are responsible for instantiating the abstract architecture into a concrete form. Level I and Level II Architecture may have defined the need for a glass ceiling in the structure, but the engineering process will decide the thickness and brand of that glass ceiling. The strategic engineering role will seek further reuse of common solutions (e.g. use the same glass manufacturer for all glass ceilings), without infringing on the overall architecture guidelines. Architecture is all about doing your best; engineering is all about doing what's best.

Next, let's define the Architecture Scope of Level I.

THE ARCHITECTURE SCOPE

Because architectures should strive for flexibility, there is always a danger that, if not scoped properly, you may end up with a pile of "architecture" documents that no one will ever read, let alone implement. When defining the architecture it is essential for you and your team to define the proper scope. Keeping it real means boiling the ocean is not a viable option. ("Let's boil the ocean to get rid of those German U2s. How you implement it is up to you.") When MS/Windows came out it was certainly a great improvement over the MS/DOS way of doing things. However, the fact that MS/Windows was not architected from the beginning to handle security concerns resulted in Microsoft having to spend untold millions to finally get it 'sort-of-right' with Windows/7.

For example, when defining the scope, ask yourself if you are trying to address only the customer-facing automation side of your business, or if you will also include the backend support systems[34]. If the latter, chances are you will need to consider integration to the ERP vendor. In any case, you'll need to define whether to take an end-to-end customer lifecycle perspective or to focus only on specific core business processes.

Should you support international environments? If your company is a conglomerate, will you cover multiple business units or just one particular division? Are you even empowered to define the backend architecture?

Answering these kinds of questions requires a candid, non-delusional understanding of whether you have the kind of organizational governance to define far-reaching enterprise architectures or are limited to specific areas under a

---

[34] As per my definition, a pure backend ERP project does not an IT Transformation project make, but there can be super-duper projects that require front-facing and backend integration.

narrower span of control. That subsidiary headquartered in Paris might not appreciate your efforts to dictate their technology!

Understanding your own limitations is essential. Clearly, it would be nice if the scope of the architecture encompassed as much of the "problem-space" as possible, but the fact is that real-life problem-spaces are highly irregular.

Were you to depict a typical problem space using a shape, chances are you would end up with a splattered blob like the one below:

THE PROBLEM SPACE

Non-withstanding your governance limitations, you could define the architecture with a scope so broad that it covers all possible areas of the problem space—like throwing a stick of dynamite into lake to catch fish. This 'solve-world-hunger' approach will involve a great deal of things that simply don't belong to your specific transformation initiative. While all-encompassing, this ambitious approach will most likely be very expensive and non implementable.

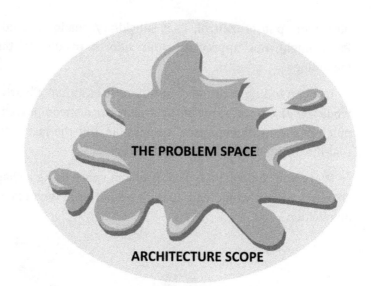

The next diagram depicts a more realistic approach. The architecture scope here represents a compromise between specifying the largest possible conjunction of common elements in the problem set; while ignoring the more "far-out" cases. It is this conjunction that forms the core of enterprise architecture—the main area of focus for the strategic architecture group.

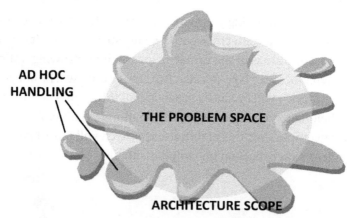

Areas of the problem space not covered by the core architecture can always be handled as exceptions on a case-by-case basis. How important is it that content integration with the three person art-department is through the use of an 8GB USB stick? And yes, you have to accept that the branch office in Namibia will enter their one daily purchase order on a typewriter and then fax the batched orders weekly on Friday nights. When the day comes that Internet connections there become cost-effective, you can bring them into the architecture fold.

Such pragmatic exceptions avoid the need to over-architect data bases or data exchange formats and help keep the architecture simpler. Of course, it is best to minimize these special cases as much as possible. If you set the scope in a too-narrow a fashion then nearly everything becomes an exception! In addition to assuring yourself hours of extra work that this fly-swatting approach to solving issues requires, you will also cost the company more money than necessary.

Even though the exceptions should be in the periphery of interest for your architecture team, you should at least be aware of their existence. Better yet, the architecture group should establish preferred guidelines on how to best admit exceptions so that the possibility of their future alignment with the core architecture is not compromised. For instance, establishing the use of a standardized Comma-Separated-Value (CSV) file for "non-traditional" data exchanges (including the art department's USB stick), or defining the product codes to be typed in the purchase orders from Namibia, at least ensures that exceptions can be better handled in the future.

It's also worth remembering that the fluid nature of a business requires the ability to append new problem space areas to the original space (imagine if a business merger or company reorganization occurs). Typically, these "out-of-space" problems will have to be first handled on a reactive basis following the rule that new features are always needed "by yesterday". However, you should have you team work on integrating these to the mainstream architecture as soon as practical. When this occurs, you will need to start the process of redefining the architecture scope anew.

But what does the term "Scope" means in practical terms? What is it precisely that your architecture team should define as being either inside or outside of scope?

The architecture scope should define the layers of technology to be used (off-the-shelf or homegrown). Also, the scope should detail the applicability of the architecture as it concerns your organization's structure, both horizontally (how many departmental functions and geographies it spans), and vertically (what level of detail will the architecture attain? Will you stop at the regional level or define the departmental elements?). In regard to timelines, your scope should be the long-term—there is no such a thing as a short-term architecture.

Perhaps you recall that back in the late eighties there was an Open Systems Interconnect standard (OSI) being pushed by the International Standards Organization. The specification reflected a design-by-committee approach that failed to take hold when faced with more effective de-facto standards such as TCP/IP. However, one of its most enduring legacies was the definition of the seven-layer interoperability stack. This stack divided the various system elements in accordance to the type of service provided by each layer.

This framework can be useful in showing how the IT industry has been traversing the OSI layers toward commoditization. In the early days of IT, much blood was shed in battles centered on which technologies were to be chosen for the networking layers. Architecture scopes had to deal, for example, with whether to use SNA or DECnet, or even whether to implement something proprietary (it so happened that one of my deliverables in a long ago project was for a proprietary communications protocol). Today it would be incomprehensible to debate against the use of TCP/IP as the protocol of choice, unless you are in a research organization testing the next big thing. The industry has converged to standards that moved the battleground upwards in the stack; toward OSI's highest layers.

The diagram below shows the OSI layers. Shown in the horizontal axis are the trends toward standardization. In consequence, these days the focus is on actual application and service specifications; not on the underlying networking layers that, for all practical purposes, are now completely commoditized.

00's	**Application**	Ad-Hoc	Services
90's	**Presentation**	ASN.1	HTML/XML
80's	**Session**	APPN, RPC	IIOP, HTTP
70's	**Transport**	SNA, NetBIOS, IPX...	TCP, SNA
	Network	SNA, DecNet...	IP, X.25
60's	**Link**	BSC, SLC...	Token Ring, Ethernet, Frame Relay
	Physical	Vendor specific wiring	RS-232C, RS422 8803.2, X21

Commoditization →

Standardization →

For all the criticisms leveled against it (the OSI specification truly became a boiling-the-ocean example[35]), it

---

[35] Ironically, the OSI standard is an example of an architecture scope run amok. Its broadness made it extremely difficult to implement. In fact, the standard became so bloated that various "implementation subsets" were defined. The irony of that compromise was that if you had Vendor A

at least served as a unifying schema. The problem is that the OSI Reference Model is now outliving its usefulness. Despite the industry trend toward standardization and commoditization, an area of "infrastructure" that remains to be standardized is the Service Distribution Fabric[36]. SOA is today in a state of maturity similar to that of the networking world back in the eighties. With the so-called Enterprise Service Bus (ESB) we have vendors resisting standardization measures in order to sell their own proprietary solutions and gain competitive advantage. As happened with TCP/IP, the world awaits a vendor independent, SOA standards specification.

While we wait for that to happen, your role will be to apply your know-how to best adapt the solutions that meet your specific needs from the range of available technologies and standards. Defining the scope of the architecture, even when "only" focusing on the highest layers of the OSI stack, remains a challenging and fundamental proposition.

---

implementing subset X, there were no guarantees this vendor could interoperate with Vendor B implementing subset Y. The whole point of having a standard to ensure vendor interoperability was lost!

[36] This is commonly referred to as Enterprise Service Bus, but since we are not yet at the point where vendors agree on what the ESB term actually encompasses, I prefer to use the more generic term: Service Distribution Fabric.

THE ARCHITECTURE REFERENCE MODEL

Let's say you're a clothing designer competing on an episode of Project Runway (I reluctantly confess to being a fan of this show), and are asked to design a man's suit. Chances are you will design it according to the desired needs and characteristics: winter or summer, business or black-tie, silk or wool fabric, etc. Also, you'll likely incorporate your own particular professional touches even as you utilize suit patterns to construct it.

For the most part, despite the range of variations that can be expected in the design, chances are that when creating a typical business suit you will end up with a pair of pants and a jacket; not a Scottish kilt or a clown outfit.

Fundamentally, architecture models are no different. When solving a similar business problem, most architecture models will end up looking similar regardless of the vertical industry to which they apply. For instance, the architecture model for a high transaction airline reservation system is going to be very similar to the architecture model for a high transaction banking system. Indeed, these verticals do in fact share many of the same technologies. The phenomenon of "convergent evolution" also applies to architectures. Whenever nature requires a solution to a specific problem, evolution tends to arrive at an analogous solution for survival challenges. For instance, it is known that the structure of the eye evolved independently of other animal species (the eyes of insects, octopi and humans are different) and the flight of bats is an independent result of the flight of birds.

But even if most architecture models will resemble each other, as the saying goes: "the devil is in the details." It will not suffice to copy a model from a textbook and brand it as the definitive model for your company. At a minimum, your model must meet these characteristics:

- It must be **Realistic**. No matter how abstract a model, it should ultimately be implementable. Also, the term "realistic" here means that the model should apply to the specifics of your company.
- It must be **Mutually Exclusive and Collectively Exhaustible**. This is a fancy way of saying that it should be complete, but also economical, in its definition— without overlaps and without gaps. Unlike actual implementation designs, which I believe should be slightly redundant and overlapping, reference models can strive for Platonic-like perfection.
- It will clearly describe its key areas as inter-related, decoupled modules. In today's terms this means that it should be **SOA-friendly.** Even though, we are still in Level I, and SOA will be formally introduced in Level II, it should be clear by now that unless you are architecting something very unique and with a very specialized domain (for example, software for biomedical devices or for games), SOA is the way to go.

The actual Architecture Model will probably be a brief reference document outlining in narrative form the key concepts of the model: components, key technologies, interaction maps, component inter-dependencies, etc. Remember, we are still in Level I, at the hundred-thousand foot level.

The next step is to represent the architecture model via a highly iconic diagram that incorporates all the key elements of the logical architecture as well as representation of the architecture mapping the business processes. I call this diagram the Architecture Reference Model (**ARM**). This diagram is destined to become the friendly-face of the Architecture Model you will document. The ARM is to become your banner in all subsequent architecture socialization efforts. It serves multiple purposes:

- **Synthesizes** in a single chart the key architecture elements and messages you wish to convey

- Serves as a **communications icon**, identifying the focus of your technology team.

- It becomes the **rallying flag** for all your technology design efforts. It gives a point of reference to help the project team place the various detailed efforts into context.

- It helps to communicate with vendors

The ARM should be not so detailed that it drowns in complexity; nor so high level and so generic that it could apply to any architecture reference model. If your ARM could apply to the coffeehouse across the street, it is likely generic. The ARM should include substantial content.

The ARM should be visually appealing and compelling. Enlist the services of a professional graphic designer, if necessary. Remember you're looking for the ultimate iconic point of reference to summarize all your technology design efforts.

Initially, expect the ARM to change fluidly as you receive feedback from the initial drafts, and as you become more assured of the specific architecture representations. After a few revisions, however, the ARM should become more stable. This is not to say that it will never change, but if you've developed a properly designed, architecture framework model diagram, adding elements to it should not require extreme changes to the core graphic.

The ARM shown below is based on an ARM designed for an innovative hospitality solutions company. It is reproduced here with their appreciated consent (AltiusPAR Hospitality Solutions—www.altiuspar.com). What should become immediately apparent is that, even though the diagram was initially created for a specific type of industry (Hospitality), it could just as easily be applied to other industries. Admittedly, I deliberately used generic terms (e.g. Customers instead of Guests), but tailoring and narrowing the specification of this diagram to other industries would be relatively easy.

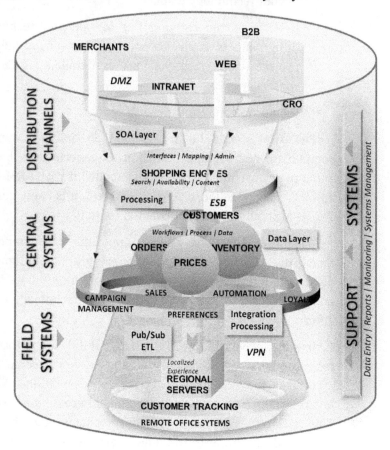

See how the ARM above visually highlights the following specific aspects of the proposed architecture model:

- External users (Merchants, Web, and Business-to-Business) will be handled via an external access layer.
- The Intranet and internal customer support systems will be placed inside the DMZ.
- All users access the SOA layer to obtain Shopping, Content, and other Services

- The Data Bases are "hidden" from the service users by the service layer.
- Subsystems such as Campaign Management, Sales Support, Loyalty, etc. must support the external and Intranet users and be accessible from regional systems (presented at the bottom of the cylinder)
- You will be providing Publish/Subscribe services to the field offices which will only be able to access the core system via VPN
- There will be support and management systems for all layers in the hierarchy

The list could go on and on. A good ARM is a little like a good painting in that, the more you inspect it, the more information you can gather from it. Don't underestimate the importance of achieving an ARM that can convey all key architecture model aspects in a single diagram. The intrinsic value it provides by focusing the transformation project framework is invaluable. Besides, it will make a great poster for your office wall!

ON THE CREATION OF TENETS AND STANDARDS

You have defined the technology strategy and the architecture scope. On the table sits a clear architecture model and on the wall is a poster detailing the architecture reference framework that will serve as a coherent beacon throughout the effort. What comes next?

Four decades ago, men set foot on the moon. The beginning of that incredible journey was promulgated in this mission statement by JFK: *"This nation should dedicate itself to achieving the goal, before this decade is out, of landing a man on the moon and returning him safely to Earth."*

This is one of the best examples of a mission statement that you will find anywhere. It is succinct, clear and comprehensive (I especially like the bit "...and returning him safely to Earth"—very thoughtful.) What was not clear was what would follow next. It wasn't obvious at first that NASA would be the agency responsible for the mission (the Air Force wanted the gig), and then there was the question of who would make a good astronaut (the idea to use circus performers, divers, and mountain climbers was first considered, but disposed of in favor of test pilots). Then there were the questions regarding the type of technology to be used and what the project governance should be (heavy use of contractors working under a common NASA governance was the one chosen). The number of decisions and choices that had to be made was staggering.

As with the moon mission, to reach the sky you must first touch the ground. Even at Level I, the architecture must move into the "where-the-wheels-touch-the-road" area. Work may start as abstract and conceptual, but eventually it has to reach the point where it is necessary to explicitly articulate the specific rules, tenets and preferred standards that will constitute "the practical canon" of the architecture. This canon will help clarify the preferred approach and will serve as a lighthouse for dispute resolution purposes. As covered earlier, the US Constitution is a perfect example of Tenets and Standards defined to make possible America's "mission" as represented by the Declaration of Independence (the part where we are all entitled to the pursuit of happiness?)

When applied to systems architecture, you'll need to start defining concrete approaches. For example, it's all very well to pursue a distributed processing model, but will you use the suite provided by a specific vendor? And if so, which one? Or, will you prefer to play the integration game and select amongst best-of-breed solutions. If so, which ones and under what criteria?

You'll need to define tenets.

The dictionary definition of tenet is this: *a principle, belief, or doctrine generally held to be true; especially one held in common by members of an organization, movement or profession.* In our context, the tenets should be mapped within the end-to-end architecture model and should represent a summary of the consensus and direction of specific strategic choices.

Tenets[37] should be documented in such a way as to provide broad exposure to the technology principles without being buried in dense documents. Tenets can be categorized and should be prioritized in the case (hopefully rare) where two tenets result in contradictory directions.

There are different types of tenets:

- **Category I** Tenets represent clear-cut best practices that apply to all projects. These are the tenets that are core to

---

[37] Tenets are also referred to as "Principles" by many. I prefer to reserve the term "Principles" for the meta-category of tenets about tenets.

the project and therefore the ones that you need to worry about first and foremost.

- **Category II** Tenets tend to revolve around the "technology context", or industry, and are usually a more detailed specification of process and technology choices.
- **Category III** Tenets represent choices made at a departmental level. Because these options have a narrower scope, their selections can be more a matter of individual or department preference. That is to say, given a set of feasible options, you simply choose those that you believe are the most appropriate for your company.

Just to state the obvious, Category II Tenets should not violate Category I Tenets, and Category III Tenets should conform to Category II Tenets.

The formulation of tenets is key to the entire transformation project. Think what went on during the framing of the US constitution. With tenets, you define the rules that will guide all future decisions. If you have not yet defined clear governance for an architecture group, you should do right away.

At this point in the process, the core architecture team should be relatively small; formed of a few senior individuals able to cover the span of knowledge needed for the transformation (systems, applications, data, SOA, etc.) Most importantly, this core team should be tasked to facilitate the elaboration of tenets and standards.

The next question is what specific role you and your architecture team will take vis-à-vis the tenet and standard decision-making. Here are some approaches:

1. **Moses Coming Down from the Mountain**. You and your architecture team go to a retreat, hash out the Category I Tenets and return wearing long white robes to announce your "commandments" to the rest of the technology areas.

In my experience, this style only makes sense in two scenarios:

- A project has been so delayed that any further debate or analysis-paralysis will place its success in jeopardy. A strong, "do now-ask questions later", stance is required.
- The great majority of the technology team is formed by external resources and therefore not emotionally committed to the project

Otherwise, I do not recommend following this approach. That is, unless you wish to disenfranchise the very people whose support you will need in the grueling months and years ahead. You would also risk losing the benefit gained from the insights and opinions of the rest of the technology team.

2. **Edicts from the Benevolent Dictator.** First of all, let me state that I believe the term "benevolent dictator" to be an oxymoron. The Benevolent Dictator is a less severe approach than that of Moses because it at least allows the voicing of the opinions of all key technical members through the means of a Technology Steering Board. All the opinions can be assessed and the chosen tenet decided upon. If this were truly an unbiased process and resulted in a decision that was properly based on the strength of favoring one tenet over another then this method would actually be ideal. In truth, it is almost impossible to remove the natural biases of the decision-makers. You risk alienating the rest of the technology members should they perceive the entire exercise as one of paying lip service.

3. **The Democratic Caucus.** Here you debate and ultimately decide the preferred tenet, based either on consensus or outright vote. Obviously, you will need to allocate extra time to allow for the very heated debates sure to follow (along with securing the assistance of HR and a good

therapist to deal with the aftermath of bruised egos!). In principle, this process may work under some circumstances, but it also has its issues if you have an organizational structure that is already fragmented into groups.

In Mexico, there is a language at risk of being lost forever. The language of Ayapaneco had been spoken by the Indians in that country for many centuries. Today, the language is spoken by only two elderly men: Manuel Segovia and Isidro Velazquez. They live half a mile away from each other in the village of Ayapa in Southern Mexico. The sad thing is that anthropologists are unable to capture their language in order to preserve it. The two men don't care for each other enough to converse!

Let's face it, the chances that you will get a consensus between mainframe people and those who dabble in Java is no greater than getting Manuel and Isidro to talk to each other!

4. **The Grass-Roots Convergence**. Why even bother with a process? Allow people to decide for themselves! After all the Internet emerged with approaches and standards that eventually replaced those of established vendors. I believe this approach is actually effective in small start-ups and in those situations where you have a highly involved and well-experienced base. I am afraid that it might not be quite as effective in the more cavernous world of large enterprises where the process can lead to anarchy if not well structured.

So which choice is best? My own view is that Category I Tenets should generally be chosen using the Benevolent Dictator approach, if only because of the wide span and strategic importance they represent. Also, Category I Tenets should closely adhere to the strategic objectives already defined for the project. You can't expect the entire technology base to have all the information needed to make well-informed decisions (perhaps only you are privy to information regarding a secret acquisition of a company that uses a certain technology, but which can't be shared). In any case, I advise against the Moses approach. You don't want to shut down the opportunity to gain valuable insights from the team.

My suggestion is that for Category II Tenets you try the Democratic Caucus approach, with the proviso that, if no clear decision is forthcoming after a healthy degree of debate, that you retain your Benevolent Dictator prerogative. This should ensure a fair amount of compromise as your team will surely want to be a part of the decision making!

If at all possible, to the extent that Category I or II tenets leave room for flexibility (as they well should), it is worth your while to allow the base team to recommend specific departmental Category III tenets. Obviously, you will need to oversee that the Category III decisions do not deviate from higher level tenets.

A final point: during this phase it would also be wise to establish the process and principles under which the tenets will be enforced and revised. Your entire team should be made aware that the establishment of tenets and standards is a serious matter, and that its ultimate outcome will be the reduction of stresses resulting from byzantine arguments and the focus gained by the shared understanding of the environment.

So, what exactly are these Category I, II, and III Tenets I have been talking about?

Chiseling the Stone: The Category I Tenets

Category I tenets must be able to withstand the passage of time and survive the challenging trials that a complex project presents. These tenets are not meant to vary over time; all the more reason for them to typically prescribe common-sense, best practices. In many ways these tenets are so common-sense that their 'motherhood and apple pie' appearance make them seem to be nothing more than a collection of distilled clichés. I suspect that when you read through the sample of Category I Tenets below, you're going to say, "Duh! These are so obvious, why bother to even mention them?"

Well, we live in a world where many believe we never really landed on the moon; where the so-called "birthers" refuse to acknowledge President Obama's birth certificate and where many believe 9/11 was a self-inflicted government conspiracy. Irrationality loves the vacuum. Even if you discount all irrational arguments, the fact remains that there are a surprising number of cases where rational counter-points can be made against what seems to be a solid, "clearly-uncontestable" tenet. Even "obvious" tenets should be stated explicitly. Otherwise, you could risk someone, somewhere along the line, taking the counterview based on the validity of an isolated exception to the rule, or on the strength of their single, forceful opinion.

Take for instance the tenet, *"Be Proactive; not Reactive"*. This statement seems obvious. There are those, however, who might argue that being reactive is a lower risk proposition, especially if agility in quickly playing catch-up with the competition can be maintained. To them, the tenet should read, "Be reactive, but also be quick to adapt to changing conditions". In this light, the former tenet doesn't sound so obvious anymore. Who knows, based on differing conditions it could well turn out that you transformation strategy should be reactive after all.

It's important to state the Category I tenets openly and unabashedly. Following are a few *sample* Type I Tenets, representative of the Category I Tenets you'll need to define. Even though I am quite certain these tenets will hold water under a large number of conditions, they were selected under specific situations that might differ from yours. Clearly my list is not exhaustive, and yes, my lawyer also advises to remind you that you should assess these tenets in the light of your own transformation effort and use alternate, or even opposing tenets as appropriate!

- *Functionality requirements must be driven by the business requirements.*

    This statement simply reinforces the need to ensure that business is involved from the start in defining the specific features and priorities. However, getting the attention of business for what is essentially a strategic initiative can be a difficult undertaking. Business folks are typically immersed in addressing short-term issues. More significantly, typical business executives rarely focus on strategic technology issues (actually, that's a good thing as this should be your responsibility; not theirs), so you will have to go the extra mile to extract and map the business requirements needed to create the technology plan.

- *Be Architecture Driven; Not Vendor Driven.*

    This is a Zen-like, "Be-the-Architecture". Remember, we are talking about the transformation of IT elements that provide key competitive differentiators to your business. ERP is sufficiently commoditized so that most companies should be happy to follow the lead of vendors in this area. And yes, if you buy into the SAP or PeopleSoft views of the world for these particular IT domains, you'll do just fine. Remember, however, that if you are to buy into the complete architecture view of a vendor for the development of your new core technology, you are making a generational commitment to that vendor—a commitment that ties your company to the vendor's future for eons to come. I can't tell you how many times I've come across companies that fully bought into a particular vendor's architecture only to see that vendor go the way of the Dodo (an extinct bird—check it out in Wikipedia). What this tenet says is: Design your architecture according to your company's needs. Make the architecture vendor-neutral and then, and only then, approach vendors to ask how they can help fulfill your vision.

- *Use of off-the-shelf industry standards and products is preferred for all commodity-level elements*

  I've seen my share of companies who've spent an inordinate amount of time and effort developing their "own version of network protocols" or their own "very cool, in-house version control system." Unless there's a clear cut reason for you to develop a commodity component in-house, you're better off having your team develop only those components that will create differentiating solutions. It's wiser to focus on providing value-added features not readily available on the open market; the kind of features that leverage your company's core competencies rather than divert resources to areas that can be easily met by a simple product purchase.

  Now, this tenet might be seen as possibly contradicting the prior one (Become Architecture Driven; Not Vendor Driven); so let's clarify: Defining a "proprietary" architecture is in no way wrong and is, in fact, advisable. A bespoke architecture, however, does not presume the use of proprietary components. In fact, an architecture that's well tailored to your needs will wisely identify the areas of focus for differentiated, value added development and the areas and manners for interfacing off-the-shelf components.

- *Architect from a Holistic Perspective*

Don't focus only on the needs of a particular business function or department. If the sales department requests a Prospect Tracking Tool, you could spend your time and energy defining the contact management tool requirements, designing the workflows and data bases involved, and defining a terrific prospect tracking tool. However, if you fail to think holistically by envisioning the synergies that can make the tool better, you will be de-meriting the solution. What if you could tie in this solution to a more generic customer data base? What if you could gather customer purchase history and tie in that information with the tracking tool? Say, you were to find out that for the past two years you spent X amount of hours wooing a customer who generated only a minimal amount of business, while another customer, who had been contacted only a few times, now represents 10% of your revenue? Wouldn't you like to design a system capable of managing such a broad view?

Before you accuse me of over-scoping with a, "what if all that's needed is a tracking tool; nothing fancy or expensive!", I am not suggesting that you actually implement this type of holistic design. I'm suggesting that you architect the solution so that, should you decide to implement it, it will take into account the potential interactions with the rest of your system.

- *Move to Service Oriented Architecture*

Enable an end-to-end, distributed service oriented framework that provides all necessary services independently of the underlying technical infrastructure. Arguably this is a Category II tenet, but given SOA's establishment as the de-facto architecture pattern for modern systems, I think this is now a tenet that has attained a chisel-in-stone status.

- *Minimize costs by driving reuse and convergence*

  This is like understanding the need for exercise, not smoking and avoiding fats—obvious advice that's rarely followed. Many choose time-to-market even with all the added costs this heterogeneous solution demands. "You want a new campaign management solution? No problem! Let's buy that super-expensive module from that company that invited us to the Ryder Cup last year! Later on, we'll figure out some way to tie their customer data base in with ours!"

- *Place automation of core business functionality in back-end systems*

  It is better to have the bulk of the capabilities served via back-end engines rather than designing a monolithic front-end that implements all functions. Many Web sites that have attained a large size organically are now suffering from limited scalability due to the failure of their designers to move the business logic to backend engines. The front end component should be limited to providing user interface capabilities such as interaction workflows and presentation level integration, and access the backend business processes via services.

- *Keep the number of programming languages (and redundant technologies) to a minimum.*

  I am old enough to remember FORTRAN, a language widely used in scientific work. COBOL was later invented by the great Grace Hopper as the language of choice for "business applications". Next came PL/I, an IBM specification that kind-of-combined COBOL with

FORTRAN. As if PL/I were not bloated enough for the US Federal Government; the Department of Defense invented ADA, which is probably gathering dust in some of those old computers running the country's nuclear silos (geek joke: "it's a good thing that ADA was a strongly typed language!"). Meanwhile, a host of other languages sprouted-up like weeds in an unkempt yard. We had Basic, LISP, Algol, Modula, Eiffel, and C, then C++, followed by Java which *is* "like C++ but with garbage collection and no pointers". Next came the wave of scripting languages that have come to look more and more like actual languages. Enter the Ruby vs Python debates.

I am certain that ten years from now, a similar passionate debate will be raging between followers of two as yet unknown languages (I don't envision the day when computers will be programmed in plain English). Call me a nerd, but why would we want to tell the computer to "Move money in the customer's savings account to his checking account" when a simple TransferMoney(From, To, Amount) will do?

Bottom line is that out there are now literally thousands of computer languages (compiled and interpreted).

This doesn't mean you have to use them all!

The trouble with languages is that they tend to become the object of emotional preferences. It's natural that programmers will gravitate toward their familiar language. Especially in large projects expect to be pressured to allow whatever programming languages your programmers' desire. If there is an area where the proverbial stake needs to be sharpened, polished and placed into the ground, it is on this one! It's important that early on you establish the tenet of using no more than two programming languages and no more than one scripting language.

This tenet should also extend to the use of any other redundant technology: keep the number of J2EE Platforms to a minimum; keep the number of RDBMs to a minimum . . . You get the idea.

Now, I am not saying, "Have only one RDBMs solution", or "Have only one Language". Strive for simplicity, but not to the point that you become simplistic!

Category II Tenets

These are the types of tenets you can laminate in plastic and frame on the office wall next to the water cooler. They don't often change, but change they sometimes do. These tenets usually define the current state of the industry preference for specific technologies. While usually applicable to current environments, there is no guarantee they won't eventually need to be revised. Take a trip down memory lane and imagine a return to the year 1969. Yes, Woodstock happened, and you probably don't remember it, either because you hadn't been born yet or because you were in fact there. After listening to Janis Joplin, Santana and Jimmy Hendrix, you show up to the office and are given the task of defining the tenets for a data processing application. You clear your mind and readjust to the fact that you are back at work. You define a tenet that states customer records shouldn't exceed 80 characters. Why? Because each record must fit on a punch card, and a punch card holds a maximum of 80 columns. Clearly, when there's a need to code for the year field, you'll opt for conciseness and drop the "superfluous" 19 from the year, etc. Another tenet might have been to make certain that all job submissions are hand-delivered to the "Batch Service" window with the user signing the log sheet.

Unlike Category I tenets that tend to be industry-agnostic, Category II tenets have a more focused applicability. Some of these tenets will be more appropriate for a particular industry segment, geography, or IT situation. If you are in a service industry, for example, you will have tenets that emphasize functionality over other attributes. If you are in the manufacturing industry, you will probably focus on tenets geared to reducing costs. And if you are in the videogame industry, your tenets will highlight usability and playability.

The list of Category II Tenets can therefore be extremely large. Below, I show some such tenets as examples. Again, when it comes to creating your own tenets, you'll need to assemble your team and map those tenets that best apply to your specific conditions and that contribute to meeting the Category I tenets previously defined:

- Move to a common development environment to maximize use of common support processes and tools within any of the deployed platforms.

- Object-oriented methodologies and approaches will be pursued whenever possible. Percentage of reused code will be a success factor. This reuse can be measured by how many common object classes are instantiated across programs and how many prior services are utilized and so forth.

- Use state-of-the-art programming tools and techniques to ensure maximum development productivity. Use Life Cycle and Service Studio components to facilitate service reuse. Optimize the development cycle by using design methodologies that permit analysis of the system under a business view and rapid prototyping for proof of concept. Use UML whenever possible.

- Ensure reliability through redundant clustering, either purchased or built. The strategy is to seek system level resilience via n-plus one redundancy with automatic fallback/recovery.

- Consider security requirements from the start. Establish security, logging and billing mechanisms based on service-oriented constructs.

- Message queuing is the strategic middleware standard. Mapping to other middleware will be supported as required, but the canonical service distribution protocol will be SOAP based.

- Unify connectivity protocols and communications interfaces end-to-end. Reduce the number of different access methods and protocols used inside the central complex. Use open, off-the-shelf protocols and systems. TCP/IP is the preferred connectivity protocol.

- Hide the complexity of the DBMS from the applications, users and processes that access the data, by encapsulating these database accesses with service oriented APIs.

- Enable distributed data access with connectivity to heterogeneous DBMS within one unit of work.

- Avoid DBMS access across the wide area network. Propagate remote data queries via a service-oriented approach.

- Portals will deal with user sessions and presentation and will orchestrate the user interaction, including content presentation, but the business services will be provided by backend engines and will not reside in the front end portals.

- All systems to be adapted, built, or bought must provide the following features:

  o Proactive and reactive monitoring capabilities

o Fault tolerant, load balancing, and fail-over capabilities

o Performance measurement, logging, and system health reporting

o Integration with system administration and management standards.

In addition, Category II Tenets are the natural realm for all SOA-related tenets. These tenets deal with desired levels of service-granularity, SOA governance, SOA management approaches, etc. Because the grand theme of IT Transformation is the use of SOA, I will cover these tenets in detail later.

Category III Tenets

These are the tenets that are defined at the departmental level. They describe naming conventions, documentation standards, reporting mechanisms, and pretty much anything dealing with the nitty-gritty of running a project. They are, therefore, just as important as the other categories. It's a good idea to keep a formalized track of how these tenets are defined, communicated and enforced.

A typical challenge is that, at times, tenets are created as Level III when in fact they ought to be vetted with a Level II scope. The opposite is also true. A sure sign of an organization trying to over-control a project is having Category II Tenets that should be left to a subsidiary unit. Remember that allowing a degree of departmental freedom in choosing tenets at this level is actually a good way to ensure fluid dynamics and engagement of the base in the overall standardization process. In the end, you may have something akin to British Common-Law whereby Level III Tenets become so widely adopted that in time they emerge as de-facto Level II Tenets!

In my experience, developers tend to converge around novel tools that, due to their emerging nature, have not yet come onto the radar of the corporate bigwigs. Sometimes this results in conflicting viewpoints between the directives driven from the top and the preferred technologies driven from the grassroots. When this occurs, it's time for you to open the floor to debate and get ready to make some compromises.

An example of this situation is the manner in which TCP/IP was adopted as the preferred networking protocol. It's a fact that TCP/IP emerged from the grassroots, even as corporate directions coming from the top were trying to enforce the OSI or SNA protocol stacks. The 'can-do-now' and 'can-do-cheaper' pragmatism espoused by departmental gurus won over the 'comprehensive' and 'structured' OSI dogma espoused by the architects.

Because the OSI standard was a camel (i.e. a horse designed by committee), it was nearly impossible to implement, and the grassroots' preference for TCP/IP did turn out to be the right choice. To be fair, there are examples where grassroots-driven adoptions ended up being counter-productive. Take the wildfire adoption of the distributed Novel servers in the latter part of the eighties that ultimately led to the organic emergence of extremely complex environments. These environments had such a high degree of data heterogeneity and processes that companies had a hard time moving away from them. Now, I'm not suggesting that the Novel corporation or its technology was at fault (after all, it was in fact a leading technology at the time). Rather, the issue was that much of the deployment of this technology happened pretty much 'under-the-radar'. Most companies ended up with duplicate data bases. These data bases lacked the necessary security, managed data badly, and in many instances, contained application code that was written for the very proprietary vendor environment and, therefore, could not be reused.

So what are examples of Category III Tenets? The list can become fairly detailed and nuanced. I suggest breaking down these particular tenets into logical groups so that you at least have a means to compare and contrast tenets coming from different groups. The following groupings are recommended:

Data Tenets. Specific to the data, these tenets would include naming conventions, partitioning approaches, etc.

Foundational Tenets. Tenets dealing with system infrastructure and management would go here. Network IP standards, server naming standards, etc. would also go here.

Presentation Tenets. These cover usability standards, use of presentation elements, navigation, etc.

SOA Tenets. XML tags, repository placement, service levels, etc.

General Tenets. Tenets dealing with general governance and project processes, including vender-selection strategies, evaluation and testing methods, etc..

Appendix A includes specific examples of Category III Tenets.

Also, if you can group the Category II Tenets along these lines, it would be an extremely useful way to ensure coherence between the Category III and Category II Tenet narratives.

That's it. . . If you are all "teneted-out", I don't blame you. It's time to dive into the Level II Architecture stage and, in particular, into SOA as the solution for that architecture level.

SOA AS THE SOLUTION

It's time to move on to the more detailed **Level II Architecture**. There are myriads of variations in Level II Architectures and most have probably been tried in the past. Every few years or so, you wake up to find new technologies that promise to solve all of your IT ailments: high level languages, structure programming, fourth generation programming, CASE Tools, Object Oriented Programming, and an ever-expanding list of software development methodologies. However, given that this is the dawn of a new millennium and we have over six decades of commercial computing under our belts, I would suggest that not planning to adopt SOA (Service oriented Architecture) for a new system would be like planning to build a house using straw and mud. Yes, there might be reasons behind the preference to build a primitive hut (as a part of a movie set, perhaps?), but in general I'd rather build a house using modern construction materials. Wouldn't you?

Defining a high level architecture these days is all about adapting SOA precepts to support the chosen architecture. Even though SOA can aid in simplifying the definition of the Level II Architecture, you and your team still have to make the key decisions related to SOA-specific choices. Remember, this is the stage where the architecture moves from abstract to more pragmatic levels. With Level II you will still be high enough up so that you don't need to worry about negotiating the ground level, but at thirty-thousand feet you have to keep a watch out for weather patterns. It is in this stage that you can better discern the horizon and where true innovation can be applied with unique solutions that can ultimately serve as key success differentiators in the ultimate deliverable.

SOA—WHAT IT REALLY IS

The first thing to keep in mind is that SOA is about simplifying the business process automation and not about introducing technology for technology's sake.

A friend of mine related this anecdote after attending a small Mexican town celebration of the activation of its first automated phone exchange. As the mayor gave a glowing discourse on how the town was finally "entering the 20th century", and people would now be able to automatically place calls simply by dialing the numbers on their phone, an elderly woman sitting next to him complained, "Automatic? This ain't automatic! Automatic was when I lifted the receiver and asked Maria, the switchboard lady, to connect me to my daughter!"

She had a point. From a user's perspective, all that matters is the ability to articulate a need in a simple way, and then have the need satisfied by the appropriate service. Alas, this woman will have to wait many years before she once again receives the same level of service she received from Maria. Maybe if she (or her grandkids) programmed her cell phone, she could once again connect to her daughter simply by speaking her name. However, if she wanted a connection by voicing something like, "Connect me to someone who can fix my stove", this would require the emergence of software that can truly understand natural-language and take intelligent action (don't get me started with the so-called Interactive Voice Recognition systems of today!).

The beauty of thinking in terms of services is that you can avoid getting bogged down by how the service is provided. The manner in which the service is provided should be, in the end, immaterial to the person requesting the service. What matters is having a well-defined interface to the service. If you order a meal in a language that is not understood by the waiter, then you can be assured the request either won't be met or that you will get served a dish full of proteins and fats of unknown origins (something like this actually happened to me while in Hong Kong, after erroneously assuming I had ordered chicken!)

How then do we define SOA? Simply stated, SOA deals with the ability to ask a system to do something (typically a coarse-grained business or system process) without having to tell it HOW to do it. Think about it. When you go to a restaurant and order a dish from the menu in the correct language, you are applying SOA principles. SOA is about abstracting the request so that the business need can be posed directly to the system via the use of a proper interface request.

In fact, SOA is nothing new. From my perspective, Service Oriented Architecture was actually invented more than ten thousand years ago with the advent of modern civilization. The SOA inventor is unknown, but most assuredly was some lazy bum trying his best (let's face it folks . . . it was a he!) to avoid work and pass on responsibilities to others. Specialization resulted in people becoming more competent in their chores and, in the process, the framework of rules and procedures needed to facilitate this delineation of responsibilities became part of the societal laws we have today. Back then you had a merchant asking a scribe to log a transaction, or a king requesting a priest to plead his case to the gods, or a man of commerce paying someone to carry his produce. Agriculture, war, religion, the construction of temples and edifices; all the core activities we associate with modern human endeavors, are the results of someone doing another's bidding along the concepts we now refer to as Service Oriented Architecture. Once SOA became firmly entrenched, there was no turning back. SOA became the paradigm of civilization. As it expanded, it created the specializations and professions we see in today's world.

So, why wasn't SOA used in IT systems from the very start?

Earlier generations of computer technology did not have enough "juice" to support SOA. RAM was too expensive, disks were too slow, and communication speeds were hilariously sluggish (300 bauds[38] was super-fast, and data at that speed would have taken you something like twenty-four hours to download just one song from, say, The Gabe Dixon band—one of my favorites). Still, information systems had to support business systems and business needed IT; so an implicit compromise was struck. When it came to IT, SOA was abandoned in favor of an approach that forced business to adapt to computers rather than the other way around. For example, computers did not have sufficient storage space to store dates; so only the last two digits of a year were stored. Computers didn't have the ability to present information in plain English. No problem, only abbreviated codes, upper-case text, and cryptic commands were used.

The result is that traditional IT quickly devolved into an assemblage of monolithic processes, inflexible data schemas and unfriendly interfaces. Eventually, as a consequence of Moore's Law, computers became more and more powerful and more capable of tackling increasingly complex tasks. We have now come full circle. Instead of having to adapt to the computer's limitations, it is the computers that are now expected to adjust to human ways of interaction and the need to handle high-level questions and processes. Computers can now provide natural interfaces, follow complex, heuristic-driven, reasoning logic and seamlessly tap large amounts of stored information; all in real-time. SOA is the natural way to architect systems. Its use in computer systems is the result of finally being able to effectively mirror business processes with technology thanks to the arrival of powerful computers, cheaper storage, and faster networks.

---

[38] In old modems this was equivalent to 300 bps.

Now, effectively doesn't mean efficiently. Applying SOA conveys a certain acceptance that we can afford to "waste" computer resources to achieve the flexibility and transparency advantages SOA provides (more on this later)— something similar to how we have accepted the performance impact of using a higher level language over machine language programming. Now, don't get me wrong, badly implemented SOA can result in major costly failures. Just because we can now afford computational power to better mirror business processes doesn't mean that resources are infinite, that budgets are boundless, and that the laws of physics can be suspended. In fact, SOA gives you flexibility, and we all know that with flexibility comes plenty more ways to screw up! SOA is not a panacea but, when properly applied, computer systems can become part of the SOA future, just as SOA has always been a part of our past.

THE ADVANTAGES OF THE SERVICE ORIENTED VIEW

So, if SOA is so "old" why do we still have all this excitement about service oriented architecture applied to IT? Isn't SOA the obvious choice? In fact, the history of computer science has always been about movement from the very complex to the obvious. While in the pioneering days of computing it took a John von Neumann to work out programming concepts, these days even an Alfred E. Neuman could easily write a decent program. The reason the "obvious" solution was not used in earlier decades was because "obvious" solutions required more advanced technologies. Think of the electronic spreadsheet which was invented in the early 80's (Visicalc). In hindsight this invention is something obvious. Why then wasn't the electronic spreadsheet invented even earlier? If we take a look at the character oriented, computer screens prevalent in the decade of the 70's, it's clear that a spreadsheet model would not have been adequate for the teletype-like devices of that era. It took cheaper, bit-mapped displays for the electronic spreadsheet idea to become viable.

What's obvious these days is that implementing systems with SOA can lead to better solutions as long as the inherent issues of SOA are tamed and appropriate service interfaces and service management governances are established. In this context, a service-oriented view provides many advantages:

1. Allows a **direct mapping to a business** perspective. SOA allows the implementation of solutions that can directly mirror the business processes. In the past, system designers had to translate business processes into computer driven structures. System implementations based on awkward mappings of business requirements did work. However, given that the most natural way to describe business processes and organizational flows is through a consumer view, and given the fact that older computers couldn't cope with these views,

the resulting IT systems almost always ended up being difficult to use.

In fact, SOA's facilitation of a direct mapping with the business supports the emergence of higher-layer business tools such as Business Process Modeling (BPM). BPM represents an even higher level of abstraction of automation which can still be used to dynamically generate software solutions. The capability to give the definition of business processes to actual business users, and then have these definitions used to generate actual applications, is only feasible when these processes can call predefined services.

Without SOA there is no BPM.

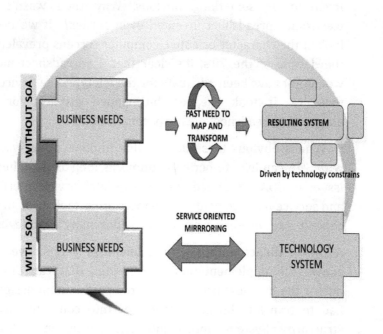

2. Enables **Reuse of well-defined logic blocks**. This is a Lego approach. Just as a building contractor assembles the skills needed to build a house, services can, in turn, call services. A general-purpose service can be re-used by several applications.

Admittedly, reuse is not a new concept. It has been the holy-grail of computer science for many years. For example, in the early days, code reuse was sought via definition of macros or subroutines—chunks of source code that could be embedded into the application.

While this approach had the advantage of reusing source code that provided generic functions ("Convert Data", "Hash a Table", etc.) it did have its issues. First of all, programmers would sometimes tweak the library code to better match their requirements; making the code non-reusable. Also, as new programming languages emerged, these libraries became outdated and could no longer be used. This is not to say that the use of macros is no longer valid. The use of macros or functions for repetitious snippets of code is still a recommended best practice, but only within the confines of a single application.

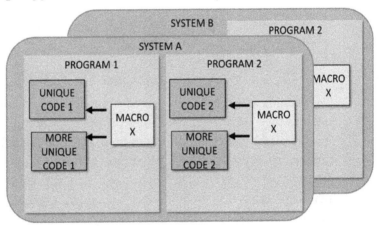

In time, other code reuse techniques emerged. The most important of these were the linkable libraries. Unlike macros, the programmer could use the library without having to know the source code; thus giving some degree of protection against improper changes. However, as with macros, these static libraries become embedded in the executable code, using more memory and ultimately forcing the updating of programs whenever the libraries changed.

Enter the Dynamic Libraries. The familiar Windows DLL (Dynamic Link Library) is basically a library that becomes dynamically linked to a program, pretty much on demand. However, dynamic libraries require the use of a specific running environment (i.e. MS/Windows) making them viable only when executed in the same system as the calling application.

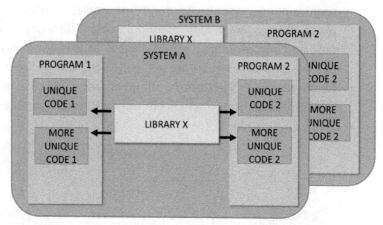

Dynamic Libraries represented a good step forward and, indeed, they have been extremely popular as commercially available add-ons for development tools such as Visual Basic and, more broadly, under MS/Windows frameworks. Still, what if you wanted to use a dynamic library from a different platform? What if you could place dynamic libraries into any system and be able to call them from any platform?

Enter the concept of Services!

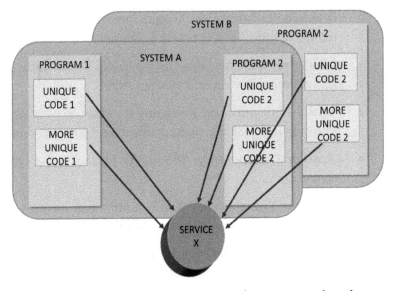

Just as with DLLs, you can acquire and use external tools and services, but more fundamentally, because of the loose coupling, you can run your service in a system completely different from your own. You can call a Linux service from a Windows application or call a service located somewhere in the Cloud.

SOA is all about transparency . . .

3. SOA is the foundation for **transparency**. If you call a help desk these days, chances are that the person at the other end of the line is based in a foreign country. Thanks to the lower communication costs and the benefits provided by educational standards and globalization, companies benefit by sourcing services wherever they are the most cost effective. Likewise, you can run services anywhere and have them accessed by any authorized user. SOA allows you to place a function where it makes the most sense. But, since what makes sense today may not make sense tomorrow, SOA is also about allowing change with a minimum of effort. We can finally decouple the way we logically partition functions from the way we deploy physical computer systems. Service

Oriented Architectures should provide as many of the following transparency tenets as possible:

- **Access Transparency.** Provide the ability to access the system from different devices and mechanisms.

- **Failure Transparency.** Designing the systems with automatic service failure fallback, without affecting the application.

- **Location Transparency.** The ability to deploy the system in any location.

- **Migration Transparency.** Allow minimum or no impact to the existing system when upgrading service implementations.

- **Persistence Transparency.** If the desired service has not been used, you can load it automatically. If it has been used you can reuse the code already resident in memory.

- **Relocation Transparency.** The system should allow you to move a service from machine A to machine B without impacting clients.

- **Replication Transparency.** The system should be able to provide the same service from different locations. This supports failure transparency, and it can also be used to increase performance via horizontal scalability.

- **Technology Transparency.** As long as you get the service to do what the service is meant to do, the client shouldn't care what technology was used to implement the service.

These transparency attributes facilitate legacy integration with new technologies. Since the implementation of the service is hidden from the service consumer, the service-oriented approach enables the integration of older legacy software with emergent software. Once older applications are properly encapsulated under the guise of services, it is also possible to gradually transition a system by re-implementing services one step at a time. This removes the necessity to incur a risky "big-bang" system migration. Also, these transparency attributes are what makes emerging technologies such as Cloud Computing possible. Without transparency there can be no cloud!

4. **Simplifies software development** by decoupling business processes, decisions, and data. The agility gained from SOA comes from the inherent simplification of the software design. It becomes easier to assign development of different modules to different groups and isolates the way the program accesses the data. More importantly, because SOA can mirror the business processes, you can create organizational structures in IT that truly, mirror the business structures.

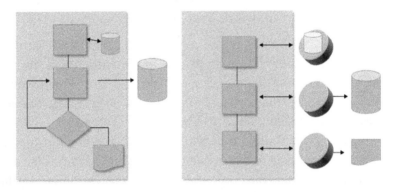

The diagram above shows this concept pictorially. It's far easier to decompose and assign each of the various business processes inside the box to the right, using external services, rather than having to adopt responsibility for the way data is accessed or manipulated.

Now that I have sung the praises of SOA, I want to bring you back down to earth just a bit. There are certainly many traps and difficulties in using SOA, and it makes sense to be aware of them so that you can use the well-travelled roads of successful past experiences as much as possible. This means that designing SOA is all about figuring out the concept of patterns and the way services fit into these patterns.

THE SOA DISTRIBUTED PROCESSING PATTERN

It's said that one of the keys to human intelligence is the ability for abstract thought and an instinctive reliance on patterns. By expediently matching new situations to a "library" of pre-existing patterns, normally referred to as "experience", humans have been able to react more quickly in the face of new challenges. The sky is covered with dark clouds? No matter the shape of the clouds, their darkness and conglomeration indicate a storm is on its way. A large animal growls and salivates as it menacingly stares at you? I doubt you will stop to investigate what this is all about. If you did, your chances at reproducing would be as low as those of an ascetic monk. There's no question that pattern recognition has been a key to our survival as a species.

Patterns have hierarchies, and the highest level pattern hierarchy deals with the overall system structure. I will discuss more about the use of patterns specific to SOA later. First I would like to discuss the broader Distributed Processing Pattern because the introduction of SOA has forced a rethink on how this pattern is defined. Just as a typical DMV office has the typical frowning employee at the window, the sullen clerk riffling and stamping papers in the back, and a file rack along the back wall, most traditional distributed systems models have converged to a pattern consisting of these three tiers:

1. A **Presentation** tier which displays the program's output and allows the user's input.

2. A **Business-Process** tier that deals with the "heart" of the application. The actual business rules and processes are performed here.

3. The **Data Tier**. Applications request user data via the presentation, process the request within the business-processing area, and interact with data as appropriate.

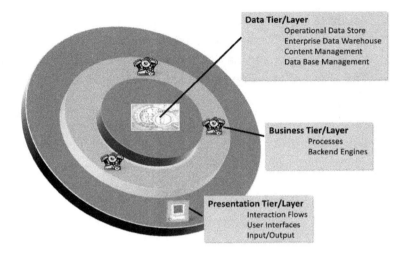

This three-component pattern has traditionally been referred to as 3-Tier Architecture. Furthermore, traditional proponents of distributed processing use this 3-Tier Architecture term to *physically* map each of the parts with distributed components. In this very literal interpretation of the model, the desktop devices perform presentation functions, and an intermediate server computer does some processing and then accesses data, usually via SQL or Store procedures. This fixed distributed model is typical of what was originally promoted by Data Base vendors as part of their preferred architectural model (e.g. Oracle Forms, using PL/SQL). The problem with this view of distributed processing is that it takes such a physical view of the distributed system that it soon becomes very static and inflexible, failing to accommodate new technology capabilities.

Because the PCs emerged outside the realm of the mainframe priesthood, the sad reality is that just as with a very intelligent blonde (not an oxymoron, all joking aside!) desperately trying to get a date, PCs had to sneak into the corporate world by pretending to be dumb terminals—a good fit within the static boundaries of a traditional presentation device. Also, while old intermediate systems were mostly used as communication switches or to act as specialized gateways, the physical view of the 3-Tier model tended to view today's servers merely as

125

database front-ends. Things have changed significantly. "Access" devices such as today's personal computers and wireless devices, such as your phone, have tremendous power. The traditional 3-Tier view can't accommodate their broader use.

Whereas the traditional distributed processing pattern separated processing into three *physical* tiers (presentation, business processing and data), in reality, data rarely resides in a single source, and business processes cannot always be executed from a single server. Also, in real life, computation can take place anywhere, and even though organizations tend to be hierarchical, the actual business flows look more like a network than a strict hierarchy.

If SOA is to mirror this meshed topology, then we must shift the paradigm somewhat. A proper SOA design should support true distributed environments; not just three tiers, but rather *an n-Tier meshed topology, with an intrinsic 3-Layer logical pattern.*

The fundamental distributed pattern with SOA is that there are three *layers; and multiple tiers*—something I describe as the n-Tier/3-Layer SOA Distributed Processing Pattern. The shift from Tiers to Layers has important implications: The layers in SOA are *logical* and are not meant to directly represent the underlying physical systems.

A typical SOA scenario is shown below:

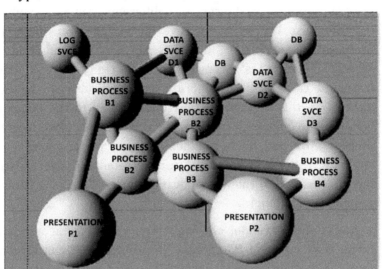

This n-Tier/3-Layer pattern exists independently of the actual number of computers or entities. For example, imagine that the service pattern above depicts airport Kiosks displaying flight information. The user inputs the desired airline via the touch-screen terminal **P1**. This entry originates a service request to business process **B1.** Business process B1 logs the request by calling an authentication and log service that front-ends the database **D1**. Once the request has been authenticated, B1 requests the assistance of business process **B2** (either one of the two B2's shown). Process B2 may call the assistance of **B3** for as many services as needed. It then extracts the flight information for the selected airline by calling service front-ending database **D2**. Finally, **B2** returns the information to B1 which then passes the result onto P1 to output the requested flight information.

When dealing with this level of system design, little is assumed about the physical nature of the environment. It might well be that, initially, all business processes depicted (**B1, B2, B3**) execute in the same machine in which databases **D1** and **D2** reside. A second instance could have **B2** running in a separate server, and so on.

The system can be scaled up by allowing the deployment of multiple service instances on different systems. Multiple instances also happen to improve the system robustness. The presentation services *P1* and *P2* may or may not reside in separate computers (remember the transparency tenets discussed earlier). Furthermore, assume because we have an increase in the number of transactions going to the computer handling the business processes, we now wish to move business processes *B2* and *B3* to another machine. No problem. A key attribute of the n-Tier/3-Layer service oriented pattern is that there is no need to change applications when deploying services in separate computers.

Say we find a vendor offering a cheaper and faster way to do things than our own *B3* service. No problem. *B3* can then run from the external vendor's system. As a final note, you may have noticed that not once have I mentioned whether these computers run on Microsoft or Linux software, or are a mainframe or PC. Why not? Because the technology transparency tenet is that all software should be able to run on any given platform.

The concept of Cloud Computing, based on computer infrastructure available as a virtualized computing service via Internet-like mechanisms, is emerging as one of IT's future directions. The idea is that the higher penetration of standards and the convergence of technologies is driving commoditization to the point where we no longer much care about the kind of technology providing the service we receive. Having an n-Timer/3-Layer pattern is a necessary (but not sufficient) condition to allow your solution to eventually garner the benefits of Cloud Computing in the future.

Having said this, while it's easy to appreciate the flexibility that this type of architecture provides, keep in mind that it does have its drawbacks! For starters, there could be overhead in computing processing and message delivery latencies. This type of architecture is designed not for performance but for flexibility. On the plus side, a smart service-oriented design can optimize the way services are called and how data is passed between components via judicious use of caching techniques. Secondly, n-Tier/3-Layer can be complex, especially when deployed in a distributed fashion. SOA demands an extra focus on management and control. Thirdly, you'll need to tighten your deployment guidelines or you might end up with a zoo of redundant services, similar to having a traffic cop signal traffic even though the semaphores are working just fine. Lastly, we began with patterns and end with a reaffirmation for their need.

A meshed system like the one shown has an exponential number of combinations, and it would not make sense to try and architect specific SOA arrangements over and over. Instead, the industry has now defined a series of SOA patterns that system architects can apply. Managing and taming the complexity of an SOA solution demands a disciplined use of patterns.

The story of how to make SOA work in the face of these challenges will be my next topic of discussion.

SECTION III
THE TECHNOLOGY SOLUTION

"Any sufficiently advanced technology is indistinguishable from magic."
Arthur C. Clarke

Trials

It's SOA. That's the magic trick. But how do we pull this rabbit out of the hat? And how do you get the rabbit in there in the first place? ◆ Talking about service oriented concepts is one thing, but actually implementing them is another ◆ SOA is flexible, but flexibility gives you and your team more opportunities to "screw-up" ◆ SOA is an n-Tier system. Managing it is like herding cats!

Techniques

Defining SOA architecture patterns ◆ Creating life-cycle processes that help manage new services to a library of services ◆ Understanding the overall SOA taxonomy, including the definition of services, framework, foundational aspects and techniques that make SOA work.

Tribulations

SOA has yet to attain the level of maturity of traditional mainframe systems ◆ Managing SOA is hard ◆ Defining support governance creates havoc, but traditional organizational structures won't do.

AN SOA TAXONOMY

It is one thing to say SOA is the most natural way to architect systems and another to figure out how SOA should be implemented. The way we define the SOA structure (its "taxonomy") is important because it has a direct impact on the best organizational governance needed for its successful use.

While there are many ways to split the SOA-cake, in my experience it makes sense to borrow from the world around us. After all, we've already established that there is nothing new under the sun when it comes to SOA. Humans have, after all, been using this service model quite naturally for thousands of years. Also, humanity has tested a variety of social structures that allegedly have improved over time. It's easy to be cynical when looking at the issues facing us today, but feudal structures are no longer considered appropriate (at least by most of us in western societies), and sacrificing prisoners to appease the gods is frowned upon these days. It makes sense to look at how we operate today as a possible model for defining a proper SOA taxonomy.

Let's start with the use of language, (human language, mind you; not the computer programming-kind). Think of sentences with their nouns and predicates, and the concept of service interface can emerge naturally from it. "**Give** me the lowest fare for a flight to New York in April," or "**Find** the address for Mr. John Jones," are service requests you could make equally well to your assistant or to a software program.

Just as a language's sentence has to follow specific grammatical rules, how we articulate the request follows an implied structure intended to guarantee the request is understood and that it is in fact actionable. Satisfaction of the service requires an agreement as to how the service request is going to be handled and an expectation of who is going to act on the service.

Acting upon language instructions would be impossible without a specialization framework. When you call for a taxi, you don't expect a hot-dog cart to show up, and if you need to summon emergency services, you dial 911 and not the pizza delivery service (you can tell I'm a bit hungry as I write this!)

In fact, much of the social fabric related to the various roles and institutions usually referred to as 'civilization' are nothing more than a broad framework for the services we deliver or receive.

The streets we traverse, the sewage and plumbing systems beneath it, and the way electricity is delivered via power grids, are infrastructure elements we all take for granted in support of the 'civilization' framework.

Finally, requesting services via the right language, using the means of civilization and the needed infrastructure would be all for naught if we were only capable of uttering nonsensical commands like, 'ride me to the moon on your bike', or even requests not followed by the magic words, 'here is my credit card'. There are protocols that must be followed to ensure the entire system works as expected and these represent the social and legal ecosystem from which everything else flows.

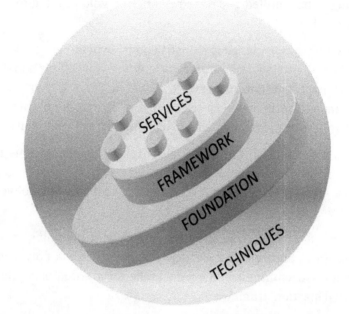

This is in essence the SOA taxonomy I will be discussing in more detail next. The elements encompassed by SOA are no different from the Language-Civilization-Infrastructure-Protocols pattern I've just discussed. For SOA, the equivalent pattern is Services-Framework-Foundation-Techniques:

I. **Services** as the language of SOA. It is not the same thing ordering a meal at McDonalds as it is at a five star restaurant (yes, I'm still hungry!). There are services and then there are services. A clear understanding of what constitutes a service is essential to the SOA approach.

II. The emerging SOA **Framework** as the civilization. Trying to approach SOA in the same mindset as a traditional design is not feasible. SOA demands the establishment of new actors and their roles. Here I'll discuss the proposed introduction of a common Enterprise Service Bus (ESB) as a potential common transport for all SOA interactions and the guidelines related to the access of data by services.

III.   The physical **Foundation**. SOA is a beautiful approach, but it still relies on actual wires and moving bits and bytes—a suitable infrastructure. Here I will cover the distributed model and the systemic approaches to scaling and managing SOA.

IV.   The **Techniques** needed to make SOA work. Imagine that you are given the opportunity to race against a professional NASCAR driver using a car superior to that of the professional. Or that you are to compete against Tiger Woods in a round of golf using better golf clubs. Odds are that, even with better equipment, you won't win. Ultimately, you can have the best equipment in the world, but it's how you use it that makes the difference in the outcome. Good equipment, like good infrastructure and services, can only be leveraged with appropriate techniques that only expert hands and minds can apply.

THE SERVICES

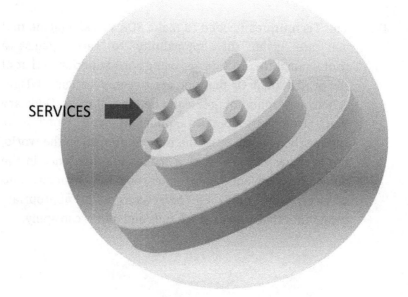

SERVICES

Because of SOA's roots as a reuse technique that evolved from the reuse of functions and libraries, it's not surprising that there is a degree of debate on what actually constitutes a service. There is a view out there that services are akin to "functions on steroids". The problem with this perspective is that functions are typically too fine-grained to truly stand alone or to be distributed efficiently. Dynamic libraries, functions and object classes are not actually services for the simple reason that these reuse-elements are not designed with the attribute of location transparency. Distributing them in a willy-nilly fashion would have severe performance implications and, thus, is not recommended practice.

In the SOA taxonomy there is a hierarchy of elements with specific purposes. There are the elements needed to allow code reuse, and then there are services and applications. The primary reuse-elements (libraries, functions, and objects) are ideal to allow the reuse of code within an application or a specific service implementation. With services, however, we are trying to reuse business processing elements; not necessarily code.

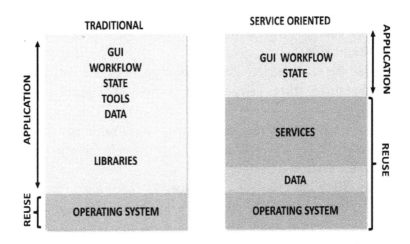

In the legacy view, an application is a monolithic piece of code that does everything for you: grabs the data, massages this data, performs calculations, determines the execution flows, presents the information, accepts and validates the user input and so on. With SOA, the application is simply the entity tasked with handling the business workflow, keeping all manners of state and acting as the orchestrators responsible for calling the appropriate services. The application drives the sequencing of service calls and interactions with the user for purposes of delivering a clear business function. An application is thus the brain of the solution. In SOA, however, the brunt work of implementing each specific business process or data manipulation aspect is expected to be performed by the underlying service fabric; not by the application.

The role of a service in this new paradigm is to provide a discrete function representing encapsulated logic with the following characteristics that must meet many of the transparency tenets discussed earlier:

- Designed and implemented independently from the specifics of the client or requester.
- Movable. The service can be executed anywhere "in the Cloud"
- Any service may be invoked by any qualified client, or by any other service, without having to change the implementation of the service.
- Can be encapsulated. While some services are entirely self-contained, others rely on other services for a portion of their logic.
- Replicable. A Service may be available from more than one server. It can't be assumed that it is the only allowed instance in the system.
- Interface-driven. The interface is decoupled from the implementation. The client sees only the interface and never has to worry about the details of the implementation. This formally defined service interface represents an unbreakable contract with the client.

In this context, it's easy to see why many other popular reusable objects or components such as Dynamic Libraries, Portlets and RMI-Callable Objects aren't really services because they are missing one or more of these characteristics.

The key point in describing a service is this:

> *For SOA purposes, a service represents a unit of work that even a non-technical person can recognize as providing a valuable stand-alone capability.*

Admittedly, this definition allows some wiggle room, but it hopefully helps to more crisply define what can and cannot be considered a service. Let me emphasize the "non-technical" bit: if you can't explain what the service does in non-technical terms then it is most likely not a service. "The service calculates the Mod10 checksum of the credit card number," will not mean much to most people. "The service checks that the credit card number is valid," sounds like a true service. This discussion is important, because maintaining a service life-cycle and properly managing and administering service repositories and deployment can be an extremely expensive and complex proposition.

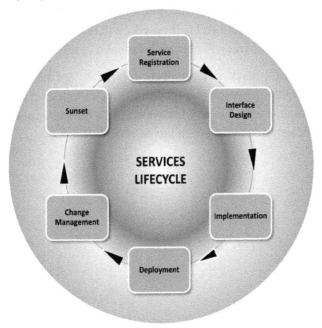

Creation and management of services follows a very similar lifecycle to the lifecycle of applications, but the types of governance, skills, controls and rules governing their workflow are different and must be handled by specialized technical staff. For this reason, identifying what does and does not constitute a service is not sufficient. There is also a need to understand the general role of the service.

There's an anonymous saying, "There are two types of people in this world: those who divide people into two types, and those who don't." I confess, I belong firmly to the former group. You can extrapolate that quote to: "There are two types of people in this world: those who classify services into several types and those who don't."

Knowing how to classify services according to classes, types and delivery patterns, as I will in the following sections, helps define the framework for their use, their limitations, and their ultimate scope. More importantly, if you plan to establish a well-constructed service portfolio to ensure that all services in the portfolio are created, deployed, maintained and sunset according to very strict life-cycle rules, then you will do well to identify the degree of control you will establish for each of these components.

Later on I'll discuss the aspects related to the governance of services, including organization and lifecycle, required to develop and maintain them. For now, however, let's delve deeper into the classes of services available in our SOA toolkit.

SERVICE CLASSES

The analogy that SOA Services mirror the way civilization is structured around individuals and institutions can help us to understand the value of classifying services by type. After all, if you think of a repair shop, for example, one can see that the services provided by the receptionist are not the same as the services provided by the repair technician in the backroom or the services provided by the cashier who will later process your payment. You would not normally consider putting the receptionist in the role of a mechanic or the repair technician in the role of cashier. Things work best when each individual performs the role for which they are optimally qualified. There is also the manner in which each individual renders his service. Some have a role as orchestrators of other people's work. The shop manager is someone who offers a coordination service that makes the business run coherently. Others perform a specific, specialized role. They do what they do without requiring the help of others (like the wife who orders you out of the kitchen!). Then there are those whose main role relies on accessing a data repository of sorts. They front end information resources. How much salary you confer and how much value and attention you place on each, ultimately depends on a combination of all these attributes.

Similarly, with SOA we can define three service classes: Access Services, Enterprise Services, and System Services.

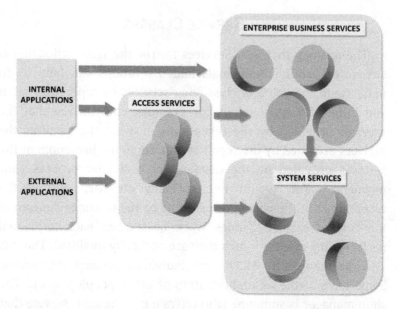

Access Services are often implemented as wrappers for legacy applications and encapsulate the internal business service logic while taking on a role as proxies to the clients. This role usually involves keeping and managing the state of a business flow on behalf of the external client. This is often needed in order to hide proprietary logic from external users. As a consequence, interfaces in this class of "services" will be extremely coarse and therefore somewhat verbose. In travel, for example, the Open Travel Alliance XML protocols tend to be extremely elaborate because of the very high level of service interface abstraction required for diverse companies to interoperate.

If you have control of the actual calling application, then you can implement the orchestration logic directly within them and, provided the application runs internally, inside your DMZ scope. They can bypass the Access Services by calling the backend Enterprise Business Services directly.

Access Services and **Enterprise Business Services** classes are best defined in terms of their business value—as something easy to explain in terms of the business services they provide. But just as there are business services, there are also system services.

System Services are the services that support the system and don't usually have a direct business mapping, even though they indirectly support the business. Still, remember that, as per our definition, you ought to be able to explain what these services offer to a layman, even if the services are not providing direct business functionality. Just because a service has a system focus, as opposed to a direct business focus, does not mean that the service should be so fine–grained that it simply serves some obscure function which could be better handled via a library or a subroutine.

All service classes should comply with the guidelines and standards established for service life-cycles. I do suggest, however, that the specific elements of the lifecycle will be different for each service class. Access Services will probably be public and should be normalized to industry standards as much as possible, while Enterprise Services should be governed by your internal architecture group. The company's operation team will be the likely user of the System Services.

THE SERVICE TYPES

Just as services can be divided into Access, Enterprise Business and System Services classes, they also need to be classified based upon their intrinsic roles and by the way they are internally structured so that you can assign their maintenance to the proper development organization.

Services that implement functionality requiring access to other services are known as **Composite Services**. Services of this type may at times keep a session state, but only for the duration of the execution (having services keep state across multiple service calls is generally not recommended, unless the service is an Access Service as discussed above). On the other hand, services that provide function without having to call upon other services are known as **Atomic Services**. These services provide coarse-grained functionality in a single-shot. A specific type of Atomic Services is **Data Access Services**. The latter supports one of the key principles in SOA: avoidance of data base visibility from functional services, whether Composite or Atomic, and the interfacing of all interactive data requests via service interfaces. The following diagram below gives an example of the kind of service classes and types you would see in a reservation system.

IT TRANSFORMATION

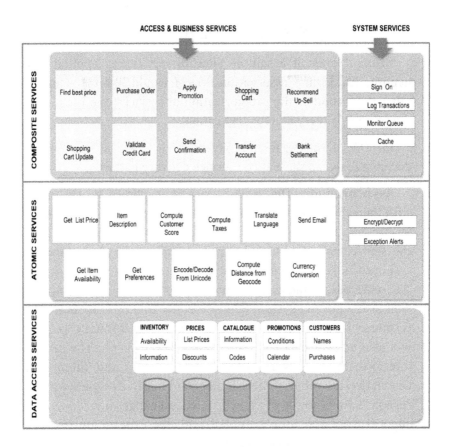

SERVICE DELIVERY PATTERNS

Before I present a sample view of services as applied to a hypothetical airline reservation flow, I would like to cover yet other dimension to the categorization of services: the manner of the service delivery and its disposition.

In SOA, as in life, for any given service request you will be deciding between these three service delivery patterns:

Asynchronous: The service request is posted by the client with the expectation that the action will take place at the server's leisure and that the client will not expect a related response from the service call. As the client is not waiting for an immediate response, he/she can continue to do whatever it is that clients do. The service is posted asynchronously and possibly queued up in a wait area until the system (the server) is able to process it. Any response resulting from processing the asynchronous request will also be sent back asynchronously to the client. The service interface designer is responsible for defining and filling-in a correlation identifier, if there is a need to match a request with its response. An example of asynchronous exchanges is a request for support from a vendor via email, with the expectation (but not certainty!) of a reply sometime later. Implicit in the way asynchronous services are handled is the idea that a queuing system of some sort must exist in the system infrastructure to properly handle the various aspects related to this pattern: How do we ensure delivery of the request? How do we prioritize the handling of the service? In the email example, the mail server takes care of all these details.

Query/Reply: This is the predominant service pattern for transactional systems. Here, a service request is made with the expectation that a response to the request will be given immediately. The fact that the client actually waits for a response gives this pattern very definite sensitivities as far as performance is concerned. If email exchanges are a representative example of asynchronous exchanges, you can think of chat or even telephone

146

exchanges as an example of Query/Reply. Instead of sending an email, you establish a two-way real-time dialogue between yourself and the service provider.

Event Driven. This pattern is also known as Pub/Sub because it relies on the Publish/Subscribe idea. In this pattern the service request is for an asynchronous response that will take place upon the satisfaction of the event criteria. This pattern is typically used in a manner similar to the synchronous pattern as the calling client need not wait for a response. However, on occasion, a design may call for the client issuing the subscription request to sit idly by until a response occurs.

With that covered, let me now display a sample generic service flow.

A SAMPLE VIEW OF SERVICES IN A SYSTEM

The diagram below shows a sample generic service flow, orchestrated from a putative airline reservation application with a client requesting, via a natural language interface, all available flights to a chosen destination. The example shows a number of service types interacting to construct the appropriate response.

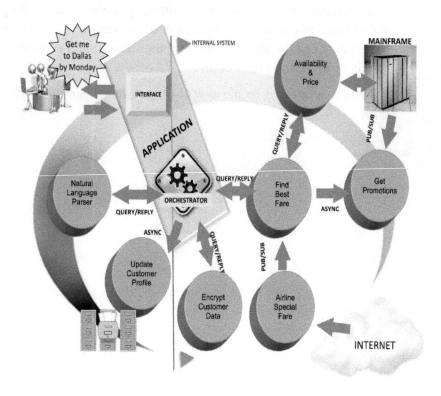

Hopefully most of the diagram is self-explanatory. The services shown to the left of the vertical line are meant to indicate those that can be accessed by the outside world and are thus considered to be Access Services. The Natural Language Parse, for example, could well be an external service provided by another company on a SaaS basis. The Update Customer profile could be available to external B2B partners to update the profile as per

148

commercial agreements. Clearly, the Find Best Fare service could also be made available externally if desired, but the example here depicts a Best Fare Service that is applying internal rules that we do not wish to expose to the world. The various services could be classified as follows:

CLASS/ PATTERN	QUERY/REPLY	ASYNC	PUB/SUB
Access	NATURAL LANGUAGE PARSER (Atomic)	UPDATE CUSTOMER PROFILE (Atomic)	
Business	FIND BEST FARE (Composite) AVAILABILITY & PRICE (Atomic)	GET PROMOTIONS (Atomic)	AIRLINE SPECIAL FARE (Atomic)
System	ENCRYPT CUSTOMER DATA (Atomic)		

Understanding the attributes of each service will enable you to apply predefined standards for their use. For example, Access services will be expected to provide public interfaces and will be hardened for public use. Access services are also cases where you may have to keep state across multiple service calls. Such state information may have to be kept in non-volatile storage (disk or replicated cache). Composite services will be allowed to keep some state, but only for the duration of the service call. Atomic services will have highly streamlined execution paths, including avoidance of state.

Ideally, everything will follow an asynchronous pattern, in the sense that not having to wait for a response is the most flexible way to optimize system resources and meet service level agreements. However, the reality is that you may need to adjust the overall solution against this ideal. Designing a system to do asynchronous messaging whenever possible may be seen as a desired goal, but fact of the matter is that you will need to use the Query/Reply patterns more often than not, particularly in transactional environments, to ensure prompt responses. Alas, I have witnessed actual designs that attempt to force asynchronous patterns in transactional systems (making everything flow through queues); resulting in very odd behaviors and unsatisfactory performance.

Finally, there is another category of "services" I have not yet defined. These are the services needed to facilitate or simplify the workings of SOA. I refer to these services as meta-services, and they are usually called upon to perform a specific SOA activity such as ensuring transaction integrity, branching the delivery of a service request, routing a service request to an alternate location and other tasks. In fact, there are various patterns identified for these types of services[39], but the most interesting aspect is that a portfolio of meta-services is being bundled. It comprises a large portion of what is rapidly evolving to be a separate SOA middleware enabling layer: the Enterprise Service Bus.

---

[39] ESB Technology Selection and Implementation Patterns by Victor Grundt and Chuck Rexroad provide an excellent coverage of these patterns. Published by IBM in December, 2007

ON SERVICE GRANULARITY

You're seated in a fancy restaurant ready to enjoy a nice gourmet meal. The waiter shows up with the menu, but instead of a list of entrees and appetizers, you are confronted with a catalogue of recipes. You order Tuna Tartare as an appetizer. The waiter stares at you with a bewildered expression. "Pardon?" he asks. "I'd like a Tuna Tartare," you insist. He doesn't understand, and it finally hits you, he's expecting you to guide him through each step of the recipe. "Heck," you think, this must be some kind of novelty gimmick (think Kramer's make-your-own-pizza idea in a classic Seinfeld episode), and so you begin the painstaking process of giving instructions to prepare the appetizer:

"Get 3 ¾ pounds of very fresh tuna. Dice the tuna into 1/4-inch cubes and place it in a large bowl." The waiter scribbles furiously. "Got this part, sir, I'll be right back!" he says as he dashes to the kitchen to begin preparing your order.

When he returns, you ask him to mix 1 ¼ cups of olive oil, 5 lime zests grated and 1 cup of freshly squeezed lime juice. He runs back to the kitchen before you get a chance to tell him to also add wasabi, soy sauce, hot red pepper sauce, salt, and pepper to the bowl. . .

You get the idea.

There are different ways to ask for services. Let's think of a more realistic computer design choice. Say you need to calculate the day of the week (What day does 10/2/2018 fall on?). If you were to define "Calculate-Day-of-the-Week" as a service, then you would be expected to allow this service to run in any computer, anywhere in the world (remember the transparency credo!), and to be reachable via a decoupled interface call. If you were to answer, "Okay! No problem", I would then have to ask you whether this is actually a sensible option. What would the potential performance impact be of having to reach out to a distant computer *every time* a day of the week calculation was needed?

Recalling the definition of services that I provided earlier, you insist that "Calculate-Day-of-the-Week" is definitely a service that provides a direct business value.

For SOA purposes, a service represents a unit of work that a non-technical person can understand as providing a valuable stand-alone capability.

You can argue that "Calculate-Day-of-the-Week" is in fact a unit of work that the salesperson, a non-technical person, can understand, and one that she will need to access via her Smartphone. In that case, I would then yield to the argument because you have shown that the calculation has business logic that is relevant to your company.

If, on the other hand, "Calculate-Day-of-the-Week" is needed only by programmers, and there is no requirement for it to be directly accessed by anyone from the business group, then this is something that should be handled as a programming function and not as a service.

If the reason "Calculate-Day-of-the-Week" is needed is because the calculation is part of a broader computation, say to find out whether a discount applies to a purchase ("10% off on Wednesdays!"), then the real service ought to be "Determine-Discount" and not a day of week calculation. As you can see, defining what constitutes a service can be somewhat subjective.

Your team should apply similar reasoning when determining services: Calculating the hash value of a field is a function; not a service. Obtaining passenger information from an airline reservation system is a service, but appending the prefix "Mr." or "Ms." to a name should not be considered a service.

Now, to be fair, there will always be those fuzzy cases that will demand your architecture team to make a call on a case-by-case basis. If obtaining a customer name is needed for a given business flow, then it can be considered a service. However, if obtaining the customer name is part of a business process that requires assembling of all a customer's information (address, phone number, etc.) you should really have a "Get-Customer-Information" service so as not to oblige the client to request each information field separately.

In general, when it comes to services, it is better to start with fewer, coarser services and then move on to less coarse services on a need by need basis. In other words, it's better to err on the side of being coarse than to immediately expose services that are too granular. It's ultimately all about using common sense. Remember the restaurant example. When you order food in a restaurant, it's preferable to simply look at the menu and order a dish by name.

Finally, even if a function is determined not to be a service, and therefore does not need to be managed with the more comprehensive life-cycle process used for services, there is no excuse for not following best-practices when implementing it. Just as with services, make certain the function is reusable, that it does not have unnecessary inter-dependencies and that it is well tested. You never know when you may need to elevate a function to become a service.

But most importantly, the secret sauce in this SOA recipe is the interface: Both services and functions must have well defined interfaces.

The Service Interfaces

Do you want to watch TV? Grab the remote control and press the ON button. To mute the sound, press Mute. Simple. The service interfaces represent a binding contract between the service provider and the client. Ideally, the contract will be as generic as possible so that it can be flexible, and you won't need to change it for trivial reasons. On the other hand, you have to ensure the interface is complete and sufficiently specific to ensure there are no ambiguities between the request and the response.

The contract should not assume any explicit knowledge between the client and the service provider. In other words, the more abstracted and decoupled the interfaces are between the client and the server, the better. Imagine if every time you drove to a fast-food window you are expected to order the meal differently depending on who is taking your order.

Web services have gained quick acceptance because they rely on high level interfaces like XML. SOAP (Service Oriented Architecture Protocol) improves the situation even more by enforcing an interface view based upon WSDL (Web Services Description Language) as opposed to a view based upon data structures. Other approaches such as REST (Representational State Transfer) utilize the Web stack to provide suitable abstracted interfaces. Regardless of the specific interface semantics, the point remains: A good interface should completely decouple HOW a service provider works from WHAT the service is offering. In the end, the client of the service doesn't care whether the TV channel is changed via electronic circuitry or via a little gnome living inside the television (an uncomfortable situation for gnomes these days thanks to the advent of flat screens!).

But returning to our restaurant metaphor. . . You have probably been in one of those fast-food places where you can enter your order via a touch-screen. The result is that, instead of an $8/hour employee taking your order, you have an $8/hour employer behind the Kiosk guiding you on how to input the order, and probably making you feel like an ignoramus. Unlike ordering your meal from a human being, ordering from a touch-screen exposes some of the intrinsic processes used by the restaurant, and forces you to follow a specific, usually awkward flow. This is one of the reasons touch-screens to order meals have failed to really take hold and, analogously, it's a reason that an older "SOA Protocol" like CORBA (Common Object Request Broker Architecture) failed to catch-on as well. As with the touch-screen example, CORBA forced the client to match the server interface in a way that was not sufficiently transparent. Similarly, we cannot rightly consider remote object invocation protocols such as RMI (Remote Method Invocation) or the analogous RPC/XML (Remote Procedure Call with XML) to provide true SOA interfaces. These protocols force the client to make assumptions about the object methods and data types, while failing to properly hide the implementation of the service, such as the way the called "service", represented by the object, is constructed or initiated, and the way various data types are handled.

The difference between a service and a function is subtle, but the way to disambiguate it is clear: If the "function" being called is potentially required to be placed in a separate environment or can be provided by a separate vendor, then it should be defined as a service. Yes, RMI/Java APIs are okay for "local services", but beware of this terminology. If you recall the transparency credo, you know that talking about "local" services is a mistake. If you intend to create a true service, then I suggest you expose it properly from its inception. As such, it should always be exposed as a decoupled service with a truly abstracted and portable interface.

Remote Object Invocation and other function-level interfaces fail to meet the implementation transparency credo required by SOA, making the resulting "service-less" SOA system as pointless as decaffeinated coffee or alcohol-free beer.

While some might argue about the "merits" of using RMI or RMI-like protocols to improve SOA performance, this performance improvement, if any, comes at the cost of flexibility. Why? The moment you have to grow the system and try to convert the "local" service into a real service, you are bound to face unnecessary decoupling work. This stage of the design process is not where we should be worrying about performance. Creating a function where a service is needed simply to avoid "the overhead" of XML or SOAP is not an appropriate way to design (in any case, said overhead can be minor when using coarse-grained services). Define the services you need first, and then you can focus on streamlining their performance.

Yes, there is a role and a place for RMI and Object Interfaces when you are certain you are creating a function and not a service. Functions are usually fine-grained and can certainly be used for specific intra-system calls to shared common objects. But the bottom-line is this: In case of doubt, use real SOA interfaces.

There is a beauty in respecting the transparency credo and enforcing the abstraction layer provided by properly laid-down service interfaces. It is that you will then be in a position to utilize the tremendous powers that the underlying service framework provides in rapidly leveraging service ecosystems for the quick delivery of solutions.

THE SOA FRAMEWORK

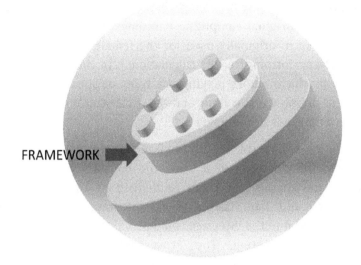

Early Ford Model Ts were the most successful automobile for a good portion of the twentieth century. If you had opened the hood of one of them, you would have found a very basic machine design consisting of an engine, a magneto (similar to an alternator) and perhaps a battery.

In contrast, when looking under the hood of a modern car, it's easy to be bewildered by its complexity. With their fuel-injection systems, anti-lock brakes, intelligent steering systems, safety mechanism and many other features, a modern car can be better described as a computerized mobility machine. About the only thing Model Ts have in common with modern cars is the fact that they both move.

Trying to explain the workings of a new a vehicle in terms of 1920's terminology is almost impossible. Such an explanation requires the use of a new language. The same is true for SOA. The traditional computing paradigm of centralized mainframe-based processing represents the Model T of computing. The designing and explaining of SOA, even if only to represent another computer environment, requires a new language.

This new language will have more in common with, say, the language used to describe a Broadway play or the workings of interacting organisms in biology than with the language used to describe the original computing paradigms (a "computer", after all, was a term originally used for the female staff in charge of manually performing census calculations). In this new language you would have actors playing the roles of specific services, a script to define the storyline, and the orchestrators to execute it. SOA is a play; not a monologue.

Still, regardless of the internal workings, a new car still requires the existence of a command console, an engine, and wheels and chassis. SOA can be defined by the Presentation, Processing and Data Layers. The Presentation occurs in the Access space, and the interface could be viewed as a "membrane" enclosing the system. The Processing layer provides the orchestration of services, and the Data represents the stuff that makes it all worthwhile.

Remember, the SOA meshed diagram I showed you earlier?

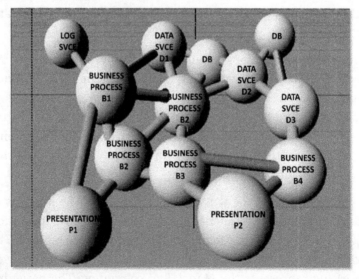

This diagram gives a somewhat chaotic and anarchic representation of the manner in which a truly distributed, service oriented environment operates. It behooves us to impose some order and structure so that the actual SOA system is something we can implement and operate appropriately. I refer to this structure as "The Framework"; the following are its elements:

- **The Access.** No matter the system, the objective is to ultimately interface with humans. I wrote early on about possible interface technologies in the future, from 3D Virtual Telepresence to technologies that can be implanted in our bodies to extend our senses in a seamless way. We are already living in a time when the access mechanism is becoming irrelevant to the engagement experience. You can check out your Facebook site from a PC, cell phone, iPod or game console.

- **The Membrane.** If we can envision a world in which we utilize a variety of access devices, we can also envision their touch points as a membrane. The advent of Cloud Computing already provides the cloud as a metaphor, but the cloud metaphor serves best in depicting the manner in which virtualized computer systems are integrated as a whole working unit. The membrane represents the interface to the information services.

- **The Orchestrator.** This is what I like to call "The Wizard of Oz Booth". The magic behind the curtain is represented by the process rules, information gathering decisions, and alternative workflows evaluated and chosen by the orchestrator.

- **The Fabric.** There is no civilization without infrastructure. Indeed, many could argue that civilization *is* infrastructure. And what exactly is infrastructure? It's anything we can bury beneath the ground, that is not dead, and that provides a service in as transparent a fashion as possible. However, I chose the term Fabric because this term better conveys the dynamic nature of the supporting infrastructure. Fabric has two connotations, one as an entity producing goods, and the other as the material substance that forms SOA.

- **The Data Keeper.** In a proper SOA environment, data should be abstracted to be accessed as a service. Similar to the role of your high school librarian, you will need a formalized Data Keeper. It will be responsible for abstracting the access and maintenance of data. This is to ensure no one has to worry about whether this data is being stored in old Phoenician tablets, Egyptian papyrus, Monastic scriptures, ferromagnetic storage or any of the modern or future ways data is stored.

In the future everything will be virtual, an abstraction. Enabling this capability is the role of the SOA Framework.

The Access Layer

Many of you who have been around long enough to remember the good old days of data processing may still long for the simplicity and maturity of centrally located mainframes. They could be easily accessed via a simple line protocol from basic screen devices and keyboards at each client location. Older "dumb-terminals", such as Teletypes, ICOT and 3270 devices, simply captured the keystrokes; which were then duly sent to the mainframe, either in character-by-character mode or in blocks. The mainframe would then centrally format the response. This response was then displayed by the access device in the same blind manner as Charlie Chaplin hammering widgets on the assembly line in the movie, "Modern Times".

For a period of time, with the advent of the PC back in the 80's, a debate ensued about the idea of moving all processing to client devices. For a while, the pendulum swung towards having PCs do the computations, earning them the "fat clients" moniker. After enjoying the exhilarating freedom of not having to depend on the DP priesthood behind the central mainframe glass house, local IT departments began to learn what we all were supposed to have learned during our teenage years: With freedom come responsibilities. As it turned out, trying to keep PC software current with the never-ending stream of versions updates and configuration changes, or trying to enforce corporate policies in this type of distributed environment, no matter how flimsy, soon became a Nightmare on IT Street.

Newton said it best: For every action there is a reaction. Soon voices from the "other-side-of-the-pendulum" began to be heard. Mainly as a strategy to counter Microsoft, which in the early nineties was still the eight-hundred pound gorilla that Google is today, the folks at Sun Microsystems began pushing for the "Network Computer" concept. This was in reality a cry for the dumb terminals of yore; only this time designating the Java Virtual Machine as the soul of the distributed machine. To be fair, given the maintenance burden presented by millions of PCs requiring continuous Windows upgrades, these network computers did make sense. After all, network computers were capable of executing applications autonomously from the central system and thus were not strictly the same as old-fashioned "dumb-terminals".

In the end, the pendulum did swing back towards Thin Clients. Enter the original Web Browser. This time the appeal of Web Browsers was, thanks to Tim Bernes-Lee, the inventor of the Web, the fact that they accelerated the convergence of technology platforms around a standardized access layer. Whereas in the past each company might have used proprietary access technologies or proprietary interfaces, web browsers became a de-facto standard. The disadvantage was that, well, we were once again dealing with a very limited set of client level capabilities. The narrow presentation options provided by HTML limited the interface usability. Java Applets solved this constraint somewhat but then ironically increased the "thickness" of the client as programmers placed more processing within the Applet. Thankfully we are now reaching the point where we can strike the proper balance between "thinness" and "thickness" via the use of Cascading Style Sheets and, more recently, Ajax and Dojo.

Now, a word about two of today's most popular client access solutions: Proprietary Multimedia extensions, such as Macromedia Flash and what I refer to as "Dumb Terminal" emulators, such as Citrix. Using Macromedia Flash is great if you are interested in displaying cool animations, enhanced graphics and such. It is fine to use languages such as Action Script for basic input field verification and simple interface manipulation (i.e. sorting fields for presentation, etc.), but writing any sort of business logic with these languages is an invitation to create code that will be very difficult to maintain. Business logic should always be contained in well-defined applications, ideally located in a server under proper operational management.

Technologies such as Citrix basically allow the execution of "Fat Client" applications under a "Thin Client" framework by "teleporting" the Windows-based input and output under the control of a remote browser. This approach makes sense only under niche needs such as during migrations, or when you need to make a rare Windows-based application available to remote locations that lack the ability to host the software. Citrix software has also been used successfully to enable rich interfaces for web-based meeting applications (GoToMeeting) when there is a need to display a user's desktop environment via a browser, or when users want to exercise remote control of their own desktops. Other than in these special cases, I recommend not basing the core of your client strategy around these types of technologies. Remember, when it comes to IT Transformation, you should favor open standards and the use of tools that are based on sound architecture principles rather than on specific vendor products.

I will close this discussion on Access technologies by noting that, just as we no longer debate the merits of one networking technology over another, network technologies have become commoditized. I suspect we will soon move the discussion of Access technologies to a higher level, rather than debate the specific enabling technology to be used. Access-level enabling technologies such as Ajax and others are becoming commodity standards that will support a variety of future access devices in a seamless fashion. So, pull out your mobile phone, your electronic book reader, and bring your Netbook or laptop, or access your old faithful PC, or turn on your videogame machine, if you don't want to fetch your HDTV remote control. It behooves you in this new world of IT Transformation to make everything work the same!

The Membrane as the Boundary Layer

Sooner or later it happens to most of us. We grow up and can no longer continue to live in the cocooned environment created by our parents—the comfort and coziness of our youth is gone (unless, as a result of the Grand Recession you are obliged to return to your parents home and are forced to experience the George Constanza-like awkwardness of adulthood, but I digress). Either way, we have to enter the real world, a world where people speak the language of credits and debits and where behaviors are no longer governed by Ms. Manner's etiquette or Mom's nagging but rather by a set of complex social rules that help us interface with the world. The way we engage with the world, the set of rules we follow, the processes and mechanisms we use to interact with others, the whole cultural context of how to say "please" or "keep the change", are equivalent to a boundary layer between us and the rest of humanity.

Having created a suitable SOA system (either homogenous or federated via Enterprise Application Integration tools), we need to enclose it in its own protective cocoon, lest the reckless world outside trample with its internal fabric. The trick is to prevent what is not wanted from getting in, while allowing what is wanted to access the system. Here, biology provides us with an ideal model in the workings of the living cell. Just as the membrane of a healthy cell acts as a barrier against harmful agents and judiciously allows the exchange of the enzymes needed to make the cell work in concert with the rest of the organism, we must maintain an SOA membrane that allows the necessary information exchange to take place while keeping the bad guys out of the system.

In IT terms, the membrane is known as the DMZ (Demilitarized Zone). Frankly, I never cared for this term. A DMZ is a buffer zone designed to keep warring factions apart—a zone void of hostilities. The term is deceiving because, in reality, the DMZ is the area where all access battles are fought. Also, the layer's role is not to keep warring factions apart but to allow the controlled exchange of participating partners. With the emergence of virtualization approaches such as Cloud Computing, we should take the perspective that the membrane is the region where safe trade occurs. In this area the presentation logic is placed alongside a number of public applications. This is the layer that deals with the Business-to-Consumer (B2C) and the Business-to-Business (B2B) interactions. In this layer you also must perform data transformations for data exchange with external entities.

In engineering terms the membrane consists of an arrangement of technologies carrying the interaction with the external world in each layer of the computing stack, from the security guard manning the entrance to the Data Center to the application displaying the sign-on screens. In the networking layer you have the protocol convertors, VPN gateways, IP routers and load balancers. Further up in the stack, the membrane includes firewalls with the appropriate system-level access passwords and permissions; including specific field-level encryption. Higher up, the membrane contains the needed data mapping and conversion services. Moving on to the application space, the membrane includes spam filters and user-level authentication mechanisms.

Rather than give a subliminal message, let me state it as loudly and plainly as a used car commercial before a Memorial-day sale: it's preferable to create the membrane with off-the-shelf technologies rather than to try to develop your own. The capabilities and features needed for this layer are usually standard to the industry, and thus it makes sense to use vendor solutions. In fact, a trend is to have many of the functions needed by the membrane handled by special-purpose hardware appliances.

Alternatively, if you plan to outsource operations, then let the hosting provider worry about the make-up of the membrane. Still, you have to define the required levels of service and make certain the monitoring tools and processes exist to ensure these levels.

Either way, the membrane is a component that's rapidly becoming commoditized. A good thing too, for this is not where you ought to seek competitive IT differentiation (that is, unless you are one of those hosting providers!).

To sum up, the membrane is not the area to invest in internal development. The challenge is to create and view the membrane as an integrated component that can be managed and monitored in a holistic manner even if it consists of an assemblage of products and technologies. If you are creating a membrane, you should focus on sound engineering work and vendor component integration; not software development.

Ultimately, a well-designed membrane should be trustworthy enough to allow some relaxation of the security levels inside the system. Also, a well-designed membrane should be flexible enough to allow support for a variety of access devices. Once you take care of your system's membrane you can then focus on what happens inside. This is where the real work takes place, with the Orchestrators.

The Orchestrators

Back in the XIX century (that's the 19th century for all you X-geners!), there was a composer who didn't know how to play the piano. Nor, in fact, did he know how to play the violin, the flute, the trombone or any other instrument for that matter. Yet, the man managed to compose symphonies that to this day are considered musical masterpieces. The composer's name was Louis Hector Berlioz, and he achieved this feat by directing the orchestra through each step of his arrangement and composition. His most recognized work is called "Symphonie Fantastique" and, according to Wikipedia: The symphony is scored for an orchestra consisting of 2 flutes(2nd doubling piccolo), 2 oboes (2nd doubling English horn), 2 clarinets (1st doubling E-flat clarinet), 4 bassoons, 4 horns, 2 trumpets, 2 cornets, 3 trombones, 2 ophicleides (what the heck is an ophecleide? A forerunner of the euphonium, I found out. What the heck is a euphonium? Well, check it out in Wiki!), 2 pairs of timpani, snare drum, cymbals, bass drum, bells in C and G, 2 harps and strings.

By now, you probably get the idea. Mr. Berlioz fully exemplifies the ultimate back-end composite services element: **The Orchestrator**. Berlioz composed some pretty cool stuff by knowing a) what he wanted to express, b) what specific set of instruments should be used at a particular point in time and c) how to communicate the notes of his composition to the orchestra.

Every SOA-based system needs a Berlioz.

There are several dimensions involved in defining the role of an orchestrator for SOA. First, as discussed earlier, most orchestrator roles will be provided within the context of an application; not as part of a service. That is, the orchestration is what defines an application and makes one application different from another. The orchestration is the brain of the application, and it is the entity that decides the SOA services calling flow.

In some instances, you might even be able to reuse orchestration patterns and apply them across multiple applications. Better still, you can build orchestration patterns by utilizing the emerging Business Process Modeling technologies (BPM). BPM simplifies the work of creating orchestration logic by providing a visual and modular way of assembling orchestration flows. A small commentary of mine is this: BPM is not SOA, but BPM requires SOA to work properly.

An apropos question is to ask how much orchestration should be automated in the SOA system as opposed to allowing the user to manually orchestrate his or her own interactions. To answer this question it is best to remember the complexity rule I stated earlier: *The simpler the user interaction, the more complex the system, and vice-versa.*

Then again, there are limits to the complexity of an orchestration. A full-fledged Artificial Intelligence system could become the ultimate orchestration engine but, unfortunately, such a machine remains in the realm of science fiction[40]. Cost-benefit compromises must be made.

Say we have a travel oriented system and need to find the coolest vacation spots during the month of September. Should we let the user manually orchestrate the various steps needed to reach a conclusion? Each step would indirectly generate the appropriate service calls for searching destinations, filtering unwanted responses, obtaining additional descriptions, getting prices, initiating the booking, and so forth. Or we could consider developing a sophisticated orchestration function that's able to take care of these details and do the hard work on behalf of the prospective traveler. But should we?

The answer lies in the size of "the market" for a particular need. Clearly, there is a need for a travel orchestration capability

---

[40] Some do disagree. At the end of the book, I discuss some speculations on the possible emergence of more capable AI systems.

that can take care of all the details mentioned. After all, isn't this why Travel Agencies emerged in the first place? If the orchestration is needed by only a few users, then it is best not to spend money and effort attempting to automate something that is too unique. On the other hand, if the request becomes common, then it is preferable to create an automated orchestration function that organizes and integrates the use of SOA services.

The orchestrators design should always accommodate the transparency tenets in order to allow horizontal scalability. In other words, if you provide the orchestration via servers located in the system membrane, you will need to design the solution in such a way that you can always add more front end servers to accommodate increased workloads; without disrupting the orchestration processes in existing servers. Because orchestration usually requires the server to maintain some form of state, at least for the duration of a transaction, you will need to incorporate some form of session-stickiness in the orchestration logic. Later on, I will write more about why I recommend that this is the one and only area where a "session state" between the user and the orchestration should exist, even as I still advise to keep backend services discrete and sessionless.

ESB and the SOA Fabric

A number of new needs have emerged with the advent of SOA. First of all, there was no standard way for an application to construct and deliver a service call. Secondly, there was no standard way to ensure the service would be delivered. Thirdly, it was not clear how this SOA environment could be managed and operated effectively. Fourthly . . . well, you get the idea . . . the list goes on and on.

SOA demands the existence of an enabling infrastructure layer known as middleware. Middleware provides all necessary services, independent of the underlying technical infrastructure. To satisfy this need, vendors began to define SOA architectures around a relatively abstract concept: the Enterprise Service Bus, or ESB. Now, there has never been disagreement about the need to have a foundational layer to support common SOA functions—an Enterprise Bus of sorts. The problem is that each vendor took it upon himself to define the specific capabilities and mechanisms of their proprietary ESB, oftentimes by repackaging preexisting products and rebranding them to better fit their sales strategies.

As a result, depending on the vendor, the concept of Enterprise Service Bus encompasses an amalgamation of integration and transformation technologies that enable the cooperative work of any number of environments: Service Location, Service Invocation, Service Routing, Security, Mapping, Asynchronous and Event Driven Messaging, Service Orchestration, Monitoring and Management, Testing Tools, Pattern Libraries, etc. Unfortunately, when viewed as an all-or-nothing proposition, ESB's broad and fuzzy scope tends to make vendor offerings somewhat complex and potentially expensive.

The term ESB is now so generic and undefined that you should be careful not to get entrapped by buying a cornucopia of vendor products that are not going to be needed for your specific SOA environment. ESBs resemble more a Swiss army knife, with its many tools, of which only a few will ever be used. Don't be deceived. Vendors will naturally try to sell you the entire superhighway, including its rest stops, gas stations and the paint for the road signs, when all you really need is a quaint country road. You can be choosy and build your base SOA foundation gradually. Because of this, I am willfully avoiding use of the term "Enterprise Service Bus", preferring instead to use the more neutral term, "SOA Fabric."

Of all the bells and whistles provided by ESB vendors (data transformation, dynamic service location, etc.), the one key function the SOA Fabric should deliver is the assurance *that the services and service delivery mechanisms are abstracted from the SOA clients.*

A salient feature that vendors say ESBs are good for is their ability to integrate heterogeneous environments. However, if you think about it, since you are going through the process of transforming the technology in your company (the topic of this book after all!), you should really strive to introduce a standard protocol and eliminate as many legacy protocols as possible.

Ironically, a holistic transformation program should have the goal of deploying the most homogeneous SOA environment possible; thus obviating the need for most of the much touted ESB's transformation and mapping functions. In a new system, SOA can be based upon canonical formats and common protocols; thus minimizing the need for data and service format conversion. This goal is most feasible when applied to the message flows occurring in you internal ecosystem.

Now, you may still need some of those conversion functions for several other reasons—migration and integration with external systems being the most obvious. If the migration will be gradual, and therefore require the interplay of new services with legacy services, go ahead and enable some of the protocol conversion features provided by ESBs. The question would then be how important this feature is to you, and whether you wouldn't be better off following a non-ESB integration mechanism in the interim. At least, with the awareness that you will be using this particular ESB function for migration purposes only, you can try to negotiate a more generous license with the vendor.

There are cases whereby, while striving for a homogeneous SOA environment, you may well conclude that your end state architecture must integrate a number of systems under a federate view. Your end state architecture in this case will be a mix of hybrid technologies servicing autonomous problem domains. Under this scenario, it would be best to reframe the definition of the problem at hand from that of creating an SOA environment to that of applying Enterprise Application Integration (EAI) mechanisms. If your end state revolves more around integration EAI, it would be better suited to performing boundary-level mapping and transformation work. In this case, go and shop for a great EAI solution; not for an ESB.

If the vendor gives you the option of acquiring specific subsets of their ESB offering (at a reduced price) then that's something worth considering. At the very least, you will need to provide support for service deployment, routing, monitoring and management, even if you won't require many of the other functions in the ESB package. Just remember to focus on deploying the fabric that properly matches your SOA objectives and not the one that matches your vendor's sales quota.

A quick word regarding Open Source ESBs: There are many to choose from. However, the same caveats I've used for vendor-based ESBs apply. Open Source ESBs are not yet as mature, and the quality of functions they provide varies significantly according to the component. Focus on using only those components that you can be certain will work in a reliable and stable manner or those that are not critical to the system. Remember you are putting in place components that will become part of the core fabric. Ask yourself, does it make sense, just to save a few dollars, to use a relatively unsupported ESB component for a critical role (Service Invocation or Messaging, come to mind) versus using a more stable vendor solution?

In the end, if you are planning to use the protocol conversion features packaged in a vendor-provided or open source ESB, I suggest you use them in a discrete, case-by-case basis, and not as an inherent component of your SOA fabric. This way, even though faced with having to solve integration problems associated with the lack of standards, at least you won't be forced into drinking the Kool-Aid associated with a particular vendor's view of ESB!

The Data Sentinel

Data is what we put into the system, and information is what we expect to get out of it (actually, there's an epistemological argument that what we really crave is knowledge. For now, however, I'll use the term 'information' to refer to the system output). Data is the dough; information the cake. When we seek information, we want it to be good; to be accurate, relevant, current, and understandable. Data is another matter. Data must be acquired and stored in whatever is best from a utilitarian perspective. Data can be anything. This explains why two digits were used to store the date years in the pre-millennium system, leading to the big Y2K brouhaha (more on this later). Also, data is not always flat and homogeneous. It can have a hierarchical structure and come from multiple sources. In fact, data is whatever we choose to call the source of our information.

Google has reputedly hundreds of thousands of servers with Petabytes of data (1 Petabyte = 1,024 Terabytes), which you and I can access in a manner of milliseconds by typing free context searches. For many, a response from Google represents information, but to others this output is data to be used in the cooking of new information. As a matter of fact, one of the most exciting areas of research today is the emergence of Collective Intelligence via the mining of free text information on the Web. Or consider the very promising WolframAlpha knowledge engine effort (www.wolframalpha.com) which very ambitiously taps a variety of databases to provide consolidated knowledge to users. There are also other mechanisms to provide information that relies on the human element as a source of data. Sites such as Mahalo.com or Chacha.com actually use carbon-based, intelligent life forms to respond to questions.

Data can be stored in people's neurons, spreadsheets, 3 x 5 index cards, papyrus scrolls, punched cards, magnetic media, optical disk, or futuristic quantum storage. The point is that the user doesn't care how the data is stored or how it is structured. In the end, Schemas, SQL, Rows, Columns, Indexes and Tables, are the ways we IT people store and manage data for our own convenience. But as long as the user can access data in a reliable, prompt and comprehensive fashion, she could care less whether the data comes from a super-sophisticated, object oriented data base or from a tattered, printed copy of the World Almanac.

How should data be accessed then? I don't recommend handling data in an explicit manner, the way RDBMs vendors tell you to handle it. Data is at the core of the enterprise, but it does not have to be a "visible" core. You don't visualize data with SQL. Instead, I suggest that you handle all access to data in an abstract way. You visualize data with services and this brings up the need via a Data Sentinel Layer. This layer should be, you guessed it, an SOA enabled component providing data access and maintenance services.

To put it simply, the Data Sentinel is the gatekeeper and abstraction layer for data. Nothing goes into the data storages without the Sentinel first passing it through; nothing gets out without the Sentinel allowing it. Furthermore, the Sentinel allows decoupling of how the data is ultimately stored from the way the data is perceived to be stored. Depending upon your needs, you may choose consolidated data storages or, alternatively, you may choose to follow a federated approach to heterogeneous data. It doesn't matter. The Data Sentinel is responsible for presenting a common SOA façade to the outside world.

Clearly, a key tenet should be to not allow willy-nilly access to data by bypassing the Sentinel. You should not allow applications or services (whether atomic or composite) to fire their own SQL statements against a data base. If you want to maintain the integrity of your SOA design, make sure to access data via the data abstraction services provided by the Sentinel services only.

Then again, this being a world of imperfections, there are three exceptions where you will have to allow SOA entities to bypass the abstraction layer provided by the Sentinel. Every castle has its secret passageways. I will cover the situations where exceptions may apply later: Security/Monitoring, Batch/Reporting, and the Data Joiner Pattern.

Obviously, data abstraction requires attention to performance, data persistence, and data integrity aspects. Thankfully, there are off-the-shelf tools to help facilitate this abstraction and the implementation of a Sentinel layer, such as object-relational mapping, automated data replication, and data caching products (e.g. Hibernate). Whether you choose an off-the-shelf tool or write your own, it will depend upon your needs. However, the use of these tools is not always sufficient to implement a proper Sentinel. Object-relational mapping or use of stored procedures, for example, are means to more easily map data access into SOA-like services, but you still need to ensure that the interfaces comply with the SOA interface criteria covered earlier. In the end, the use of a Data Sentinel Layer is a case of applying abstraction techniques to deal with the challenges of an SOA-based system, but one that also demands engineering work in order to deploy the Sentinel Services in front of the Data Bases/Sources. There are additional techniques and considerations that also apply, and these will be discussed later on.

SOA APPROACHES & TECHNIQUES

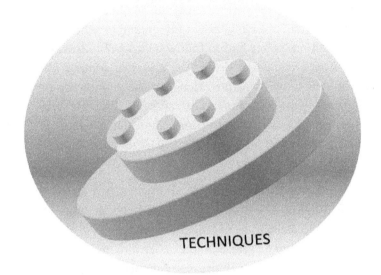

Remember when I wrote, "Architect for Flexibility; Engineer for Performance"? Well, this is where we begin to worry about engineering for performance. This section, together with the following SOA Foundation section, represents the **Level III** architecture phase. Here we endeavor to solve the practical challenges associated with SOA architectures via the application of pragmatic development and engineering principles.

TAMING THE SOA COMPLEXITIES

On the face of it, I wish SOA were as smooth as ice cream. However, I regret to inform you that it is anything but. In truth, SOA is not a panacea, and its use requires a fair dose of adult supervision. SOA is about flexibility, but flexibility also opens up the different ways one can screw up (remember when you were in college and no longer had to follow a curfew?). Best practices should be followed when designing a system around SOA, but there are also some principles that may be counter-intuitive to the "normal" way of doing architecture. So, let me wear the proverbial devil's advocate hat and give you a list from "*The Proverbial Almanac of SOA Grievances & Other Such Things Thusly Worrisome & Utterly Confounding*":

- **SOA is inherently complex.** Flexibility has its price. By their nature, distributed environments have more "moving" pieces; thereby increasing their overall complexity.
- **SOA can be very fragile.** SOA has more moving parts, leading to augmented component interdependencies. A loosely coupled system has potentially more points of failure.
- **It's intrinsically inefficient.** In SOA, computer optimization is not the goal. The goal is to more closely mirror actual business processes. The pursuit of this worthy objective comes at the price of SOA having to "squander" computational resources.

The way to deal with SOA's intrinsic fragility and inefficiency is by increasing its robustness. Unfortunately, increasing robustness entails inclusion of fault-tolerant designs that are inherently more complex. Why? Robustness implies deployment of redundant elements. All this runs counter to platonic design principles, and it runs counter to the way the Level I architecture is usually defined. There's a natural tension because high-level architectures tend to be highly optimized, generic and abstract, referencing only the minimum detail necessary to make the system operate. That is, high level architectures are usually highly idealized—nothing wrong with that. Striving for an imperfect high level architecture is something only Homer Simpson would do. But perfection is not a reasonable design goal when it comes to practical SOA implementations. In fact, perfection is not a reasonable design goal when it comes to *anything.*

Consider how Mother Nature operates. Evolution's undirected changes often result in non-optimal designs. Nature solves the problem by "favoring" a certain amount of redundancy to better respond to sudden changes and to better ensure the survival of the organism. "Perfect" designs are not very robust. A single layered roof, for example, will fail catastrophically if a single tile fails. A roof constructed with overlapping tiles can better withstand the failure of a single tile.

A second reason for why SOA is more complex is explained by the "complexity rule" I covered earlier: The more simplicity you want to expose, the more complex the underlying system has to be. Primitive technology solutions tend to be difficult to use, even if they are easier to implement. The inherent complexity of the problem they attempt to solve is more exposed to the user. If you don't believe me consider the following instructions from an old Model T User Manual from Ford:

"How are Spark and Throttle Levers Used? Answer: under the steering wheel are two small levers. The right- hand (throttle) lever controls the amount of mixture (gasoline and air) which goes into the engine. When the engine is in operation, the farther this lever is moved downward toward the driver (referred to as "opening the throttle") the faster the engine runs and the greater the power furnished. The left-hand lever controls the spark, which explodes the gas in the cylinders of the engine."

Well, you get the idea. SOA is all about simplifying system user interactions and about mirroring business processes. These goals impose greater complexity upon SOA. There is no way to get around this law.

There are myriad considerations to take into account when designing a services-oriented system. Based on my experience, I have come up with a list covering some of the specific key techniques I have found effective in taming the inherent SOA complexities. The techniques relate to the following areas that I will be covering next:

State-Keeping/State Avoidance. Deciding under what circumstances state should be kept has a direct relevance in determining the ultimate flexibility of the system.

Handling Transactional Services. Formalized transaction management imposes a number of requirements to ensure transactions have integrity and coherence. Matching a transaction-based environment to SOA is not obvious.

Direct Access Data Exceptions. As you may recall from my earlier discussion on the Data Sentinel, ideally all data would be brokered by an insulating services layer. In practice, there are cases where data must be accessed directly. The question is how to handle these exceptions.

Mapping & Transformation. Even if the ideal is to deploy as homogenous a system as possible, the reality is that we will eventually need to handle processes and data transformations in order to couple diverse systems. This brings up the question as to where best to perform such transformations.

Handling Bulk Data. SOA is ideal for exchanging discrete data elements. The question is how to handle situations requiring the access, processing and delivery of large amounts of data.

Caching. Yes, there's a potential for SOA to exhibit a slower performance than grandma driving her large 8-cylinder car on a Sunday afternoon. The answer to tame this particular demon is to apply caching extensively and judiciously.

All the above techniques relate to the actual operational effectiveness of SOA. Later on I will also cover the various considerations relating to how to manage the SOA operations.

State Keeping/State Avoidance

Managing SOA complexity brings up the question of session state. By 'state' I mean all the required information that must be maintained and stored across the series of interactions needed to complete a full business exchange. Maintaining the state of a service interaction implies remembering at what stage the conversing partners and the working data are in effect. It will often be at your discretion when designing services to either depend more or less on the use of state information. At other times the problem at hand will force a specific avenue. In either case, you should remember this simple formula: *State-Keeping = Complexity.*

Maintaining state might be inescapable in automated orchestration logic, but it comes with a cost. State-keeping constrains the options for maintaining high availability and indirectly may increase SOA's fragility by making it more difficult to add redundant components to the environment. With redundant components you must ensure that messages flowing throughout the system maintain their state, regardless of the server resources used. Relying on session states, while also allowing flexible   service flows, is hard to do. It's done, yes, but there's a price to pay in increased complexity and performance penalties related to the need to propagate the state of a particular interaction across several nodes. Therefore, a key SOA tenet is that you should use *sessionless flows* whenever possible. In other words, every request should ideally be atomic and serviceable regardless of the occurrence of previous requests.

Let's say you want to know the name of an employee with a given social security number? No problem. As a part of the request, enter the social security number and receive the name. If you next want the employee's address, you can enter either the social security number or the name as part of the request. While atomic, sessionless, requests such as these do require the client to maintain the state of the interaction and hold the information elements related to the employee, this approach does simplify the design of systems using server clusters.

Still, although the preferred tenet is to avoid session key, on occasion, it becomes impossible for the client to keep the state, forcing the server to assume this responsibility. In this case, the approach is to use a uniquely generated "session-id" whereby the server "remembers" the employee information (the state). You will have to ensure that the session key and associated state data is accessible to all servers in a loosely-coupled cluster, making your system design more complicated.

For an example of keeping a session-based state, consider an air booking process whereby the client is reserving a pair of seats. The server will temporarily decrease the inventory for the flight. For the duration of the transaction the server will give a unique "reservation id" to the client so that any ongoing requests from the client can be associated with the holding of these seats. Clearly, such a process will need to include timeout logic to eventually release the two seats in the event the final booking does not take place after a predetermined amount of time.

This discussion leads to another tenet: *Maintaining state, either in the client or in the server, along the lines mentioned is ultimately acceptable. Keeping the state inside the intermediate nodes? Not so much.* Why? An intermediate component should not have control in timing-out a resource that's being held in the server. If it did, it would be disrupting the server's ability to maintain integrity in its environment. Also, an intermediate component will not have full awareness of the business semantics of the service request/response. Relying on an intermediate component to preserve state is like expecting your mail carrier to remind you that your cable bill is due for payment on the 20th of each month. He might agree to do it, yes, but the moment you forget to tip him during the holidays, he might quite easily "forget"!

Ironically, many of today's vendors offer solutions that encourage the processing of business logic in their intermediate infrastructure products, encouraging you to maintain state in these middleware components. They do so because enabling middleware is an area that does not require them to be aware of your applications, and thus is the easiest area for them to offer you a "value-add service" in a productized, commoditized fashion. You should resist their melodious, siren song and refrain from using their tempting extras services. If not, you may find yourself stuck with an inflexible design and with a dependency on specific vendor architecture to boot.

My advice is to avoid these vendor-enabled approaches. There is much that can get complicated in the maintenance of state, especially when the business process requires transactional integrity, referential integrity and security (and most business processes do). The moment you give up this tenet and maintain session state inside the SOA middleware as opposed to the extreme end, represented by the Client and the Server, you will be ensuring years of added complexity in the evolution of your SOA system.

Handling Transactional Services

Related to the issue of Session-Keeping is how to ensure that complex business transactions meet the following so-called ACID properties:

- Be **A**tomic. The transaction is indivisible and it either happens or doesn't.
- Be **C**onsistent. When the transaction is completed, all data changes should be accountable. For example, if we are subtracting money from one bank account and transferring it to another account, the transaction should guarantee that the money added to the new account has been subtracted from the original account.
- **A**ct in Isolation. I like to call this the sausage-making rule. No one should be able to see what's going on during the execution of a transaction. No other transaction should be able to find the backend data in a half-done state. Isolation implies serialization of transactions.
- Be **D**urable. When the transaction is done, the changes are there, and they should not disappear. Having a transaction against a cache that fails to update the data base is an example of non-durability.

Since we are dealing with a distributed processing environment based on services, the main method used to ensure that ACID is met is a process known as **Two-Phase Commit**. Essentially, a Two-Phase Commit establishes a transaction bracket prior to executing changes, performs the changes and, after ascertaining that *all* needed changes have occurred, a commit finalizes the changes by closing the transaction bracket. If during the process, the system is unable to perform one or more of the necessary changes, a rollback process will occur to undo any prior partial transaction change. This is needed to ensure that, if unsuccessful, the transaction will, at the very least, return the system to its original state. This process is so common-sense that, in fact, all this business of transaction processing has been standardized. The OpenGroup[41] consortium defines transactional standards and, in particular, the so-called X/Open protocol and XA compliance standards.

However, transactional flows under SOA tend to be non-trivial. This is because a transaction flow requires the keeping of session states throughout the life of the transaction and, as earlier discussed, state-keeping is to SOA what Kryptonite is to Superman. Say you want to transfer money from one checking account to another. You access the service *Subtract X from Account*; then you create another service, *Add X to Account Y*. This simple example puts the burden of transactional integrity on the services client. The client should ensure that the *Add to Account* service has succeeded before subtracting the money from the original account. An approach like this breeds as much complexity as a cat untangling a ball of yarn, and it should be avoided at all costs. Far simpler is to create a service, *Transfer X from Account X to Account Y*, and then let the service implementation worry about ensuring the integrity of the operation. The question then is what type of implementation is most appropriate.

While SOA based transactional standards are in place[42], actual vendor-based implementations supporting these standards don't yet exist in the way mature Database XA compliant implementations exist. In general, you'd be better off leveraging the backend transaction facilities provided by RDBMS vendors or by off-the-shelf transaction monitors such as CICS, MTS or Tuxedo. All in all, it's probably best to encapsulate these off-the-shelf transaction services behind a very coarse meta-service whenever possible, rather than attempting to re-implement the ACID support via a Two-Phase Commit at the services layer.

---

[41] http://www.opengroup.org/

[42] http://www.oasis-open.org/committees/tc_home.php?wg_abbrev=ws-tx

It should be noted that what I am essentially recommending is an exception to the encapsulation of databases via a Data Sentinel when it comes to implementing transactional services. This is because integrating with off-the-shelf transactional services will likely require direct database access in order to leverage the XA capabilities of the database vendor.

As more actual off-the-shelf transactional service solutions for SOA appear in the future, we can then remove the exception.

The Data Visibility Exceptions

The Data Sentinel is not unlike the grumpy bureaucrat processing your driver's license application forms. After ensuring that you comply with what's sure to be a ridiculously complicated list of required documents, it isolates you from directly accessing the files in the back.

While you, the applicant, the supplicant, cannot go around the counter and check on the content of your files directly (not legally, anyway), the DMV supervisor in the back office is able to directly access all office files. After all, the supervisor is authorized to bypass the system processes intended to limit direct access to the data. Direct supervisory access to data is one of the exceptions to the data visibility constrains mentioned earlier.

Next is the case of ETLs (Extract Transform Loads) of large sets of data as well as its reporting. These cases require batch level access to data in order to process or convert millions of data records which wreck performance if carelessly implemented. Reporting jobs should ideally run against offline replicated databases; not the on-line production data bases. Better yet is to plan for a proper Data Warehousing strategy that allows you to run business intelligence processes independently of the main Operational Data Store (ODS). Nevertheless, on occasion, you will need to run summary reports or data-intensive, real-time processes against the production database. When the report tool is allowed to access the database directly, bypassing the service layer provided by the Data Sentinel, you will need to ensure this access behaves well, and that it runs as a low priority process and under restricted user privileges. The same control is required for the ETL processes. Operationally, you should also schedule batch-intensive processes for off-peak times such as nightly runs.

A third potential cause for exception to data visibility is implied by the use of off-the-shelf, transaction monitors requiring direct access to the databases in order to implement the ACID logic discussed earlier.

A fourth exception is demanded by the need to execute large data matching processes. If there is an interactive need to run a process against a large data base set with matching keys in a separate data base ("for all customers with sales greater than $X, apply a promotion flag equal to the percentage corresponding to the customer's geographic location in the promotion database"), then it makes no sense trying to implement each step via discrete services. Such an approach would be extremely contrived and inefficient. Instead, use of a Table-Joiner super-service will be required.

Data Matching and Integration Engines

Encapsulation of data via data services via Data Sentinel works well when the data is being accessed intermittently and discretely. However, there are cases where the data access pattern requires matching a large number of data records in one data base to large data volumes in another data base. An example could be a campaign management application which must combine the contents of a customer database with a promotion data base to define discount rates based on the customer's place of residence. Clearly, the idea to have this service call a data service for every customer record would be both unsound and impractical from a performance perspective. The alternative, to allow applications to perform direct data base joins with the various data bases is not ideal either. This latter approach would violate many of the objectives SOA tries to solve by forcing applications to be directly aware and dependant of specific data schemas and data base technologies.

Yet another case would be when implementing data extraction algorithms such as MapReduce that necessitate the orchestration of multiple backend data clusters. This type of complex orchestration against potentially large sets of data cannot be left to the service requester and is best provided by sophisticated front end servers.

Both examples reveal the need to make these bulk data matching processes part of the service fabric; available as coarse data services. The solution then is to incorporate an abstraction layer service for this type of bulk data join process. Applications can then trigger the process by calling this broadly-coarse service. In practical terms, this means that when implementing the SOA system you should consider the design and deployment of data matching and integration engines needed to efficiently and securely implement this kind of coarsely defined service. In fact, you are likely to find off-the-shelf products that, at heart, are instances of Data Matching Engines: Campaign Management

Engines, Business Intelligence systems, Reporting Engines servicing users by generating multi-view reports.

Now, using off-the-shelf solutions has tremendous benefits, but the use of external engines is likely to introduce varied data formats and protocols to the mix. Non-withstanding the ideal to have a canonical data format throughout, there will always be a need to perform data transformations.

Data Mapping & Transformation

A basic tenet should be to keep transformations to a minimum. However, it is not always feasible to create completely homogeneous systems. Even if one wishes to use standard communication means between systems, the reality is that there will always be a need to handle data and protocol mismatches. We frequently must interface the new system with legacy components or support a federated environment with differing protocols and presentations. More often than not, the system will need to interface with a third party component that does not use the standard format, semantics or protocols. The question that now emerges is how best to make these components talk to each other? In what components should we deploy the transformation logic?

There are various schools of thought about how to approach this thorny subject of transformation. We end up with the following alternatives:

- *Broker makes right*
- *Sender makes right*
- *Receiver makes right*
- *Sender and Receiver use a common ("canonical") format*

Broker-Makes-Right is akin to the United Nations whereby a diplomat delivers a speech in his native language, and the various translators must translate it for the listeners.

This may work well in the UN where the translators are actual human beings capable of human understanding. However, relying on automation, the best you can hope for is to have the intermediate perform straightforward X-to-Y transformations by following pre-defined mapping rules. Unlike UN translators, automated brokers lack the understanding to intelligently optimize the mapping based on cognition. Broker mediated transformations only make sense when mapping low-level formatting mismatches. Do you need to convert an integer to a string? No problem. Use an intermediate component. Want to append a null termination to strings coming from A and destined for B? Again, an intermediate component works fine.

Then there are cases where it is never advisable to let the broker perform automated conversions. For example, currency conversions from Euros to Dollars may require the knowledge of specific exchange discounts or the application of exchange fees, or anything else that can be dreamed up by government bureaucracies. These types of "business-based" conversions must be placed in the upper layers that are capable of handling business rules and not in an intermediate broker.

Sender-Makes-Right advocates argue that the sender of the message should know the capabilities of the recipient and adjust the format and characteristics of the delivery to match the recipient's capabilities. An analogy is that of a teacher communicating to a group of kindergarteners. The teacher will not use complex words and will make an effort to adjust her language so that the children will understand what she is trying to convey. Sender-Makes-Right assumes the sender knows-it-all and will be able to adapt a message to be understood by almost any recipient.

Receiver-Makes-Right proponents believe there is no way a sender will always know the capabilities and limitations of the receiver. Secondly, they argue that the sender is not necessarily the most powerful component of the system. Receiver-Makes-Right proponents argue that the recipient of a message should be able to extract what is needed and transform, as appropriate, the sender's format. Obviously, if the scope of information delivered by the sender exceeds what can be handled by the receiver, it is the receiver's prerogative to dispose of the excess. If the sender has less knowledge than the receiver, then it is easier for the receiver to map the sender's format and complement the needed information through other means. An example is the manner in which Google applies complex heuristics to infer user requests.

A final form is what I call the Esperanto approach, more commonly referred to as the **canonical** style. Here, both the sender and the receiver agree to use a common language, and both take responsibility for translating their respective formats into this common standard.

Which is the best approach? Clearly each method has unique issues and advantages.

My experience is that the transformation should take place as soon as possible. For starters, this means that broker-mediated transformations should be avoided, if at all possible. The entity doing the transformation must have an understanding of the business processes being mapped. Intermediate brokers usually lack this knowledge.

It is ideal to establish a canonical (i.e. standard) format, and then allow both the receiver and the sender to translate their respective formats into the chosen canonical form (performance considerations can be dealt with later). For example, in today's world, English is the common standard used by most people—A German businessman can generally communicate with a businessman in Japan by speaking in English. In SOA terms, this canonical form may well be a specific set of XML structures.

If a standard protocol is feasible, you will need to decide whether this format will be a subset (a lowest common denominator) of all formats, or whether you will allow the format to carry functions that exceed the capabilities of either one or both of the communicating entities. If the former, you will be forced to "dumb-down" the functionality; if the latter, you will need to restrict the information conveyed by the canonical format on a case-by-case basis. Still, it's preferable to make the standard format as comprehensive as possible. It's always easier to restrict usage of excess functionality than it is to introduce new features during implementation.

If no standard format is feasible, because you can't control the sender or receiver, then you should adopt either a Sender-

Makers-Right or a Receiver-Makes-Right approach. In general, the entity that has the better understanding of the business process should take ownership of the mapping. For example, if you are a tourist in a foreign country and use of a canonical language (aka "English) is not possible, then it behooves you to try to speak the local language (i.e. Sender-Makes-Right). After all, it's unrealistic to expect the local folk to understand your language. On the other hand, if you are visiting the tourism board in that foreign country, you can reasonably assume someone there might speak your language.

Typically, the sender has a better understanding of the meaning (i.e. "semantics") of a request. Consider the example where the requester searches for an employee record by name. The name is in a structured fashion: LastName, FirstName. The server, on the other hand, expects to get the request with a string that contains the "last_name+first_name" (this is a common scenario when the server is a legacy application). The scenario is obvious (I mentioned this was a trivial example!). The requestor (the sender) should create the necessary string. Building the string is much easier for the sender than it is for the receiver. The sender knows the true nature of the last name, while the server's logic could fail if it tried to derive the last name from regular expression parsing. (I can't tell you the number of times I have encountered systems that assume that DEL is my middle name!) Cleary the simple parser used by such software fails to take into account the fact that some last names include a space.

This recommendation still leaves open the question of where to do the mapping, everything else being equal. My personal view is that when everything is equal, you should put the mapping logic in the server of the request (i.e. Receiver-Makes-Right), simply because it gives you a centralized, single point of control for the mappings. Relying on a Sender-Makes-Right scenario places much of the burden on what could eventually become an unmanageable array of clients. Also, I suggest that if you decide for one or the other, that you don't ever mix the approach. That is, if you decide to do a Sender-Makes-Right, do so throughout the system, or vice versa. The hybrid case with mixing Receive-Making-Right with Sender-Making-Right can make the system far too complex and unmanageable.

The corollary to this discussion is that there is a hybrid approach that I believe provides the most flexibility and solves the great majority of transformation needs: *using a comprehensive canonical form, combined with a Receiver-Makes-Right, for cases where the super-set capability exceeds the receiver's ability.* The logic to this approach is that it is easier to down-scope features than it is to second-guess a more powerful capability.

Consider a typical search application scenario: A client sends a search request, and the server then prepares a response which includes the found elements; plus ranking scores related to each item returned. The sender converts the ranking weight factors from a relational database into a "standardized" ranking score system defined by the canonical form. Now, let's assume the client (the receiver of the response) is not prepared to get or use this extra information. The receiver simply discards the extra information. The down-scoped information loses some of its value, but the client will still be able to present the search results, although not in a ranked fashion. As long the key results are obtained, no major harm occurs. A future, more competent client will be able to use the ranking information. Note that this approach only works if the information being ignored is not essential to the response. If you need to ensure essential information is not discarded, you'll have to define this information as core to the canonical standards.

Yes, transformation work is sure to have an impact on performance. Next I will cover a technique used to remediate this problem: Caching.

Caching—SOA on Steroids

One of the most oft heard critiques against SOA is that the overhead of SOAP/XML formats make it intrinsically low performing. Yes, we all know that standards are often the result of consensus and aren't always optimized, but SOA's flexibility is needed to avoid recreating the monolithic "all-is done-here" view of the older development culture. There is no doubt that SOA architectures can be affected by message transmission delays. This is due to larger message sizes resulting from standardization and overheads associated with modular designs.

So, how to solve this conundrum?

A common mistake is designing with the idea of avoiding these performance problems "from the start". The outcome is that you have designs that are too monolithic and that introduce inflexible interfaces with tightly coupled inter-process calls "in the interest of performance". Talk about throwing out the baby with the bathwater! A better approach is to design for flexibility, as the SOA gods intended, but to introduce the safety valve of caching throughout the system. Caching is the technique used to preserve recently used information as close as possible to the user so that it can be accessed more rapidly by a subsequent caller. Think of caching as a series of release valves to ensure the flow of services occurs as pressure-free as possible from beginning to end.

The idea is to design a system that allows as many caching points as possible. This does not mean you will actually utilize all the caching points. Ironically, there is a performance penalty to caching, and you should, therefore, make certain to follow these tenets when it comes to its use:

- Ensure that the caching logic operates asynchronously from the main execution path in order to avoid performance penalties due to the management of the cache.
- Ensure you use the appropriate caching strategy. There are several different strategies that apply to specific data dynamics.

Should you clear the cache based on least-used, oldest or most recently added criteria? Will you implement automatic caching space recollection techniques (i.e. have a daemon periodically releasing cached elements in the background), or will you do so only when certain thresholds are crossed?

- The rules for caching should be flexible and controllable from a centralized management console. It is imperative to always have real-time visibility of the various cache dynamics and to be able to react appropriately to correct any anomalies. Use the recommended cache flag field in the message headers to give you more controlled granularity of these dynamics.
- Allow pre-loading of caching, or sufficient cache warm-up, prior to opening the applications to the full force of requests.
- Always remember that blindly caching items is not a magic bullet. The success of caching depends significantly on the items you cache. If the items change frequently, you will have to update the cache frequently as well, and this overhead could upset any caching advantages.

Even though there are vendor products that provide single-image views of distributed systems caching, I recommend using them only for well-defined server clusters and not broadly for the entire system. You will be better off designing custom-made caching strategies for each particular service call and data element in your solution. There are several caching expiration strategies, such as time-based expiration, size-based expiration (expiring the oldest x% of cache entries when a certain cache threshold is reached) and change-triggered cache updates using a publish/subscribe mode.

Selecting the right expiration and refresh strategy is essential in ensuring the freshness of your data, high hit cache ratios (low cache ratios can make overall system performance suffer because of the overhead incurred in searching for a non-existing item in the cache), and avoidance of performance penalties due to cache management. Also, if you can preserve the cache in a non-volatile medium, in order to permit rapid cache restore during a system start-up, do so.

Clearly, choosing what data to cache is essential. Data that changes rapidly, or when precision is critical, should not be cached (e.g. available product inventory should only be cached if the amount of product in the inventory is larger than the amount of the largest possible order). You'll need to assess how fresh data must be for any given situation. The optimum strategy must be determined carefully via trial-and-error. You can also apply analytical methods such as simulation (see later) to better estimate the impact of any potential change to either the characteristics of the data being cached or the preferred caching approach.

Finally, I can't emphasize enough the need for accurate caching monitoring via use of real-time dashboards. These dashboards are a core component of the infrastructure needed to properly manage a complex SOA system.

Managing SOA

The Control Layer

You should maintain control of your SOA environment by ensuring that all SOA messages in your system comply with a service framework that incorporates a standardized service stub, containing necessary control elements for each message. Whether using a federated ESB or your own canonical approach, you must ensure that every SOA message contains the following elements:

- *Versioning*. This will enable you to gracefully introduce new versions of services and interfaces. The service routing fabric (often part of the ESB) will be able to use this information to help decide to which implementation of the service the service request should be sent. Clearly, service versioning should be used sparingly and judiciously as it could become a de-facto means of creating new families of services and thus make future control of service implementations more difficult.

- *Prioritization*. The SOA middleware may be in the position to deliver services under pre-defined level agreements.

- *Sequencing/Time-stamping*. It's always a good idea to introduce an ordinal counter for each service request. Ideally, if the response to the service is atomic and can be associated with a request, the response should also incorporate the ordinal number of the request. This type of information can be used for debugging purposes, or even to give the client the ability to associate a response to a request without having to keep state. Time-stamping all services is a good way to ensure the potential tracking of performance metrics and the ability to debug message routes.

- **_Logging level_**. In principle, all service calls should be "log-able". Once a system has been stabilized, you will probably want to log only a few key service calls. However, given the need, you may want to increase the detail of logging on demand. Setting up a log-level in each service message will enable the middleware to decide whether or not the threshold for logging requires the message to be logged.

- **_Caching Ability_**. This setting works in two ways. From a requester's perspective, the flag may indicate to a caching entity that under no circumstance should there be a cached response to the request. From a responder's perspective, the flag might indicate to the caching entity whether or not the response should be cached.

I recommend that you task your architecture group to define the specifics of an Enterprise Service Framework (ESF) to ensure all your applications generate services with the _standard_ headers you've defined. The ESF should be instantiated as a common repository of dynamically linked libraries that will be a part of your programmers toolkit; one that will have the appropriate headers transparently appended during the service call.

In the end, the establishment of standard headers under an ESF is a foundational practice necessary to support system-wide dashboard monitoring, preventative systems management and proactive performance planning.

Best Performance Practices

As mentioned earlier, using "thin" services that require multiple trips to the server to obtain a complete response is one of the most common performance mistakes made with SOA. Most other SOA performance problems occur due to basic engineering errors such as miss-configurations (low memory pools, bad routings, etc.) which can be fixed with relative ease once identified. Performance problems caused by inappropriate initial design are much harder to correct:

- **Inefficient implementation.** The advent of high level and object oriented languages does not excuse the need to tighten algorithms. Many performance problems are the result of badly written algorithms or incorrect assumptions about the way high-level languages handle memory and other resources.

- **Inappropriate resource locks and serialization.** Just as it is not a good idea to design a four-lane highway that suddenly becomes a one lane bridge, best practice design avoids synchronous resource-locking as much as possible. Its' best to implement service queues whenever possible to take advantage of the multitasking and load balancing capabilities provided by modern operating systems. Still, avoid using asynchronous modes for Query/Reply exchanges.

- **Unbalanced workloads.** This is a scenario more likely to occur when services must run from a particular server due to the need to keep state, or because the services are not configured correctly. The more you can avoid relying on state, the more capable you will be in avoiding unbalanced workloads.

- Placing the **logic in inappropriate places.** Don't let grandma drive that Lamborghini. Emerging web site implementations were developed with an organic view that placed business logic in the front-end portals. So-called Content Management Systems were developed to provide flexible frameworks for these web portals. Unfortunately, this architecture pattern leads to monolithic, non-scalable designs. Despite the assumed performance overheads implied by modular designs, it is best to put the business logic in back-end engines that can be accessed via services through front-end portals.

Designers, aware of SOA's inherent inefficiencies, tend to architect the system in a traditionally monolithic manner. However, it is a mistake to shy away from the use of services during the design phase just to "preemptively" alleviate performance concerns. You risk reducing flexibility in the design; thus defeating one of the main reasons for the use of SOA.

There are many other, better ways to remedy the performance concerns of SOA:

- Applying best practices in service design. Watch for service granularity, service flows and the use of superfluous execution paths. For example, avoid "in-band" logging of messages (control messages mixed with the application data-carrying messages). That is, quickly copy the messages to be logged and handle them asynchronously to the main execution path. Make the logging process a lower priority than application work (alerts must be the highest priority!).

- In SOA, caching is essential. Caching is to SOA what oil is to a car's engine. Without caching, there is no real opportunity to make SOA efficient and thereby effective. However, provided that the necessary enablers are in place (i.e. ability to use caching heavily), performance is an optimization issue to be resolved during system implementation (remember the dictum: Architecture is about flexibility; engineering about performance.)

- Finally, with SOA there is a need to proactively measure and project the capacity of the system and the projected workloads. Modeling and simulation must be a part of the SOA performance management toolkit.

Performance Planning with Modeling & Simulation

SOA environments are characterized by an eclectic mix of components, service flows, processes and infrastructure systems (servers, local area networks, routers, gateways, etc.). This complexity makes it difficult to predict the capacity of the needed infrastructure. In addition, trying to evaluate the impact of changes in how services are routed or used is more an exercise in the art of divination than in the scientific method. Understanding the dynamics of an SOA system usually takes place over a period of time. Having to wait months to optimize a system is not usually a good option.

An alternative approach is to create a model of the system in order to simulate its current and future performance. Depending upon the complexity of the model, you will be able to simulate the actual system latency and the predicted response times of a variety of service flows.

Simulation can help identify potential bottlenecks and streamline processing times by pinpointing areas where resources can be best optimized. Imagine knowing the answers to these questions in more concrete terms:

- *What are the transaction response times?*
- *How many servers, data bases, or links do I actually need?*

Without the ability to simulate, system designers and administrators are left with the choice of deploying what they believe to be the best system, praying, and then taking a reactive approach based on the on-going measurement of actual performance data via monitoring tools. By then, it might be too late or too expensive to fix the system.

In general, simulations fall within one of the following levels of detail:

Rapid Model (also known as "NapkinSim"). You've probably been simulating in this manner for quite some time. If a clerk takes 10 minutes to serve a customer, and on average two customers arrive every 20 minutes, what is the average wait time? "Simple," you might say, "the answer is zero." The answer, however, is not simple and it is not zero. The answer depends upon the sequence in the way customers arrive. If two customers arrive at the same time, one of them will have to wait at least 10 minutes. When running a simulation tool you will soon come to realize the importance that inter-arrival distributions have on simulation results.

Aside from the simplest SOA problems, you cannot predict the desired resource-requester relationship by resorting to simple pen and napkin arithmetic.

Mathematical Analysis. Significant work has been done to analyze the so called M/M/1 problem (single queue with exponential arrivals and services). However, most mathematical approaches cannot satisfactorily cope with dynamic or transient effects and quickly become too complex for multi-server environments. In real life most queuing problems cannot be solved easily by resorting to linear equations. Indeed, the norm is for complexity to quickly drive the problem area to behave like a non-linear system. This in turn requires the use of complex mathematics. What then is the alternative?

Queuing Simulation. Regardless of the level of abstraction chosen for the system under simulation, you will want to have the most precise and reliable information for its expected behavior. In this case, simulation known as Queuing Simulation can be very helpful.

Queuing simulation is particularly suited to SOA because you can simulate almost any process in which a "client" requests a service and where a "resource" provides that service. No doubt about it, queuing simulation is the most viable and obvious way to model and predict how an SOA system will behave.

To be clear, the simulation approach is not a panacea. First of all, you have to learn about the simulation tools. Secondly, detailed modeling can be time consuming. Modeling should not be viewed as a way to get quick answers to questions. You should also keep in mind that simulations yield only approximate answers which, in many cases, are difficult to validate. In the end, simulation is merely a more precise way to venture a guess. You should not accept simulation results as gospel. It's all too easy to forget that the simulation is an abstraction of reality; not reality itself. A thorough validation of the results must be made, especially prior to publication of the results. Simulations should be supported by careful experiment design, an understanding of the assumptions, and reliability of the input data used in the model. Despite these caveats, you will find that simulation can be an invaluable tool for your day to day business activities.

While you could develop a simulation by writing a program yourself, you could also use one of the many simulation tools on the market. Today's simulation tools are not as expensive as in the past, but they do demand the discipline to capture and create the base model and to keep the simulation model current for future simulation runs. A modern simulation for SOA should provide a visual, interactive modeling and simulation tool for queuing systems that have the following attributes:

General purpose. You can simulate almost anything that involves a request, a queue, and a service, whether this includes a complex computer network or the service times at a fast food counter. This capability will give you the option of simulating the SOA system at various levels of granularity, from the underlying packet-level communications layers to the upper service flows.

Real-time. Unlike other costlier programs, you can view how the resources in your system behave as the simulation progresses.

Interactive. You can dynamically modify some essential parameters to adjust the behavior of the simulated components even as the simulation runs!

Visual Oriented. Allows you to enter the necessary information via a simple and intuitive user interface; while removing the need to know a computer language. In addition to running the simulation, it also provides you with important information to help you fine tune it.

Discrete oriented. Discrete-event systems change at discrete points in time, as opposed to continuous systems which change over time.

Flexible. You can see the dynamic effects of the simulated system or the accumulated averages representing the overall mean behavior of the system.

Prophesy is available for free

I am making Prophesy available for free. Prophesy is a simulation product that I developed and marketed back in the roaring 90's (when in retrospect I should have been putting my efforts into developing something for the exploding World Wide Web—but that's another story). Prophesy meets the requirements listed above, but unfortunately, the product is aged. It's no longer supported, and it will run under Windows 7 only via the Windows Virtual PC feature (using a Windows/XP Virtual Machine), This feature is available from Microsoft for free if you have a Windows Professional license.

Visit **http://www.abstraction.com/prophesy** to download it for free and to hopefully use it as a learning tool, but be reminded the tool is no longer supported.

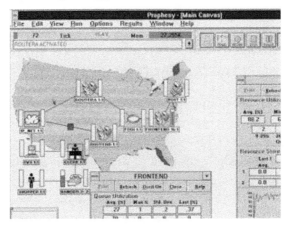

ENGINEERING WITH SOA: THE FOUNDATION

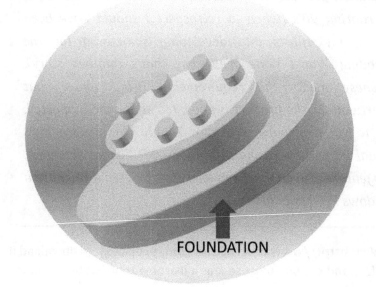

FOUNDATION

THE ROLE OF ENGINEERING

Let's face it, developing a new system can be such a "sexy" undertaking that it's only natural to want to place most of the focus on the cool stuff, such as leading-edge technologies (wireless, social media), design and development of algorithms, flashy user interfaces and the implementation of complex system features. This type of focus often results in the neglect of the more "pedestrian" aspects of the actual implementation. It's not much fun dealing with nuanced matters such as ensuring that back-up processes are in place, that the system actually includes fallback and recoverability capabilities, or that the system is truly secured and stable.

It's true that most of the actual engineering processes tend to come from pre-defined, out of the box vendor products (clustering, default configurations, etc.), but the target operational metrics should come from the enterprise needs and not from the vendor defaults. From the outset your very own engineering planning should focus on ensuring these targets are met as early as possible.

From a governance perspective you will need to ensure you have a dedicated engineering team, able to tackle all detailed implementation and operational questions and also able to interact with the architecture team in a continuous and equal basis. The engineering team should be able to push-back on some architecture elements in order to validate that the solutions are sufficiently practical and implementable. In this sense, the engineer is not unlike the building contractor who interprets the architect's blueprints and guides the building construction via the selection of actual materials, enforcement of building codes, and performance of the necessary detailed adjustments to the design. Architecture may be an art, but engineering is a science.

Still, in the same veneer as development, engineering needs to be an iterative process. Engineering must initially deal with high level designs and approaches. However as additional "construction" data is gathered, the engineering process should also adapt to the various fine-tuning variables: capacity metrics, configuration parameters, availability, performance strategies and others.

In the end, the final acceptance test must include testing of engineering aspects as well as software development. That is, the final testing should take a holistic approach to coverage of the system operation as well as to its functionality. Having a system that provides nice applications that do not scale cannot be considered a successful outcome. That's why the engineering objectives are paramount. These healthy engineering key objectives are known in a tongue-in-cheek fashion as the "ities" of the system: Availability, Security, Serviceability, Reliability, etc. I will next cover three of the key engineering areas targeting these "ities":

- System Availability and Reliability
- Security & Continuance
- Systems Management.

SYSTEM AVAILABILITY & RELIABILITY

Achieving the ability to provide services from any number of loosely coupled servers is essential in facilitating the deployment of redundant systems. Redundancy is the key to continued availability. Traditional mainframe environments were designed to be monolithic and had fewer components. Following the precept that, if you put all your eggs in one basket, you better make sure that it's a good basket, mainframe systems were designed to be extremely reliable and were embedded with high-availability features. On the other hand, SOA systems tend to include more moving parts. More moving parts means a higher possibility of failure. Also, these moving parts may be components that have not been engineered or manufactured with the same high level of quality control applied to the more expensive mainframe. No use debating it: Out of the box, most mainframe systems deliver far higher availability levels.

SOA must overcome these inherent availability issues. The method used to achieve redundancy in SOA is by introducing redundant elements; usually via clustering. This is true of whether you use virtual environments or not. To enable full utilization of the clustering capabilities provided by application server vendors, you should reduce state-dependent services. This reduction will facilitate the logical decoupling that allows you to design a very resilient system that consists of active-active components in each layer of the stack, from dual communication links, to redundant routers and switches, to clustered servers and redundant databases.

In the following diagram, a sample mainframe system has, for the sake of discussion, a 90% availability (mainframe systems usually have much higher availability ratings. I am using this number to simplify the following calculations).

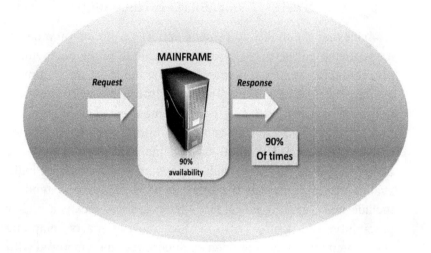

Now, let's say that you deploy a two-component SOA environment; with each component giving 90% availability...

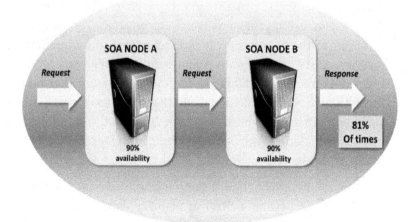

In this latter SOA system, you should expect the overall system availability to be no greater than 0.90 * 0.90 = 0.81! That is, by virtue of having added another component to the flow, you've gone from 90% availability to 81%. The reason for this is that both components are in a series, and both have to be functional for the system to operate. In SOA you must adjust by adding additional fallback components:

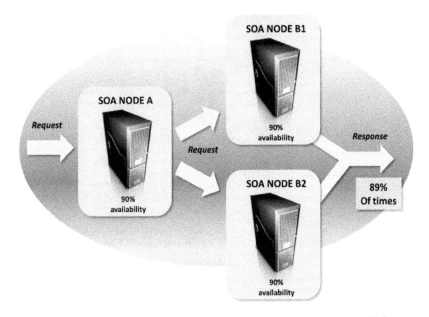

The overall availability of two systems working in parallel, such as in Cluster B above, is calculated by this formula:

$$B = 1 - ((1-B1) * (1 - B2))$$

In other words, Cluster B has an availability of **1- (0.10 * 0.10) = 0.99 or 99%**

The total system availability thus obtained is now:

0.90 * 0.99 = 0.89

Not quite the 90% received from the mainframe solution, but very close. By increasing the number of Node B systems even more, the availability will increase somewhat. However, the overall system availability can never exceed the availability of the weakest link: the lowest available cluster in the chain. In this case, we could increase the availability further by adding a second "A" component.

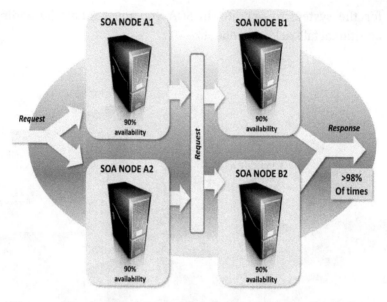

The combined availability of the Node A Cluster is now 0.99, and thus the combined system availability is now 0.99*0.99 > 98%. This resulting system availability is higher than the availability capability of any single one of its components! This is when the concepts of decoupling services via interfaces, avoiding state and encapsulating business services and data, so that services can be deployed to allow horizontal scalability and availability, makes the SOA approach truly shine.

Remember that the system will only be as resilient as its weakest point. This means that the fall-back philosophy outlined here must be replicated for each level of the operational stack. It serves no purpose to put dual servers in an environment that, for instance, relies on a single communications link or on a single router.

Secondly, you should never forget the importance of controlling the introduction of new software, configuration changes and data to the system. Take Google as an example. Google is reputed to have a supremely parallelized environment consisting of not one, not two, but actually hundreds of thousands of CPUs. In theory, such an environment ought to be almost infallible. Yet, on January 31, 2009, as a result of a trivial mistake during a configuration change, the entire Google system failed. For nearly one hour, millions of search requests received results with the same warning message: "This site may harm your computer"[43]. It turns out that someone accidentally added the generic tool URL of '/' to Google's list of potentially malicious addresses, resulting in the flagging of all URLs on the Internet! In this case, computers did not fail, the network did not fail, but thanks to perennial human frailty, the "super-available" Google system failed.

---

[43] "Google Glitch Briefly Disrupts World's Search" The New York Times. http://thelede.blogs.nytimes.com/2009/01/31/google-glitch-briefly-disrupts-worlds-search/?partner=rss&emc=rss

SECURITY & CONTINUANCE

Security and Continuance aspects should be dealt with simultaneously. They represent the two faces of the same coin. As discussed earlier, the continuance cause is advanced by the design of fault tolerant systems. If you don't believe me, consider this example: Soon after the People's Republic of China opened its economy and began the process of establishing a Chinese Stock Exchange, a group of advisors from a leading US computer company were asked to check out the country's new electronic trading system, developed to support that exchange. Upon inspection they found that the entire system was based on a single server computer with no fallbacks and no backups. When they were told by a very proud systems engineer that the system was able to process upwards of 300 transactions per second, the American team was flabbergasted. How were they able to process such throughput in what was, after all, no more than a single mid-size server? "Well everything is being kept in memory," was the response. "But . . . doesn't that mean that if someone hacks the system or the system goes down for whatever reason, you are bound to lose all the stock exchange transactions held in the memory?" the baffled Americans asked[44]. The Chinese programmer, who clearly at the time was not yet well versed in the principles of Capitalism, thought it over for a moment and then replied, "Well . . . Stock Market . . . very risky business!"

The fault tolerance issues of the trading system could be resolved by using redundant servers and by handling the transactions according to ACID rules, but then the system security should also become an intrinsic element of this design. But how much security is appropriate? Instinctively, most security managers would love to encase the system in layer-upon-layer of

---

[44] If you remember discussion on ACID attributes for transaction systems, this would be an example of a transaction environment lacking in inherent durability.

firewalls and encryption—something I like to call the "Fort Knox in a Box" approach. If you were to carry out the most rigorous of these security recommendations, you would end up with a system that's not only very expensive but also so heavy and burdensome that no one would be able to use it.

There is always the tradeoff between security, business continuance, cost and performance. What's the right level? Therein lays the conundrum.

This might be considered controversial but, in my view, as long as the relaxed position does not compromise the core business similarly to the stock market application mentioned in the preceding anecdote, the right level can only be found by calibrating the amount of security or continuance coming from the more relaxed position. In other words: start simple. Simpler security guidelines are more likely to be followed than complicated ones (in my experience, stricter parents always wind up with the most rebellions kids!). However, this approach only works well when you have designed the system to be flexible, so that it can quickly accommodate new security layers, and when you can act proactively to preempt any security exposure.

The stock market solution mentioned in my story was too flimsy from the get-go, but at least there's still a chance to harden the system. In my experience, trying to loosen-up a system that has been initially over-engineered often results in a structurally weakened system.

When it comes to security and business continuance, one should apply reasonable criteria that can be measured against the actual likelihood and impact of exposure. Paranoia is a good attribute to have when it comes to designing security systems, but hysteria is not. I knew a security manager who wanted to encrypt all the messages flowing in the central serve complex; no matter that this complex was decoupled from the outside world by virtue of a DMZ. The argument was that disgruntled employees would still be able to snoop at the unencrypted messages. Assuming, of course, that those disgruntled employees had access to the central complex (not all employees did). The proposed security "solution" was one that would have cost the company many more millions of dollars in extra hardware to protect it against a possibility that was strictly speculative.

I know of at least one large web project that initially had contemplated the placement of encryption on every web page; causing the overall system to perform at snail's pace. An effort was made to improve performance, but the system had been designed with such an inherently complex structure that it could not be improved upon. The entire effort had to be scrapped, and a less burdensome and more efficient system had to be created from scratch.

The degree of security should be commensurate with the consequences of a breach. If we are to protect a nuclear silo, massive security layers make sense. Trying to apply that level of security to protect your web server might be overkill. Adopting a strategy to not encrypt all the internal traffic was deemed to be an acceptable risk, given the circumstances.

For instance, consider the need for compliance and certification of industry standards, such as the Payment Card Industry (PCI) security standard, requiring encryption of all critical credit card information. Even if a literal reading of the standard might allow the transfer of plain credit card information in an internal, controlled environment, one can make the decision to encrypt this information anyway. However, an acceptable compromise implies that only those fields related to the PCI certification need to be encrypted; not all the messages flowing in the core system.

A security strategy that safe-guards assets on a case-by-case basis according to criticality is more appropriate than trying to encase the entire system in accordance with its most critical element.

SOA Systems Management

On February 1, 2003, the Columbia space shuttle disintegrated over Texas upon re-entry. The cause of the tragedy was the damage sustained to the wing during liftoff. This had been a two-week space mission, mind you, and many at NASA had been aware for days of the potential problem after seeing videos of debris hitting the leading edge of the shuttle's wing during liftoff. In fact, after receiving a request from the Debris Assessment Team (DAT) to have spy satellites take pictures of the shuttle as it circled the Earth, the NASA's Columbia Mission Management Team leader answered with a "... this is not worth pursuing, for even if we see some damage to the shuttle, we can't do anything about it".

Just as with Apollo XIII, when NASA ingenuity and genius saved, against all odds, a mission in great peril, it is now believed that, had they been given the opportunity, NASA engineers could have come up with at least two strategies that would have saved the Columbia crew, if not the shuttle itself.

It's only human nature to close one's eyes when we believe we are powerless to rectify a problem. I've been there. There were times, after deployment of a complex system, when I wished I could simply close my eyes in order to avoid "finding" any problems. I suppose we never outgrow our instinct to "peek-a-boo" with reality, but alas, part of adulthood is the realization that reality often finds a way to bite us on the behind. Despite the unspoken desire to avoid looking at brewing problems, hoping they will go away (or at least pretending they don't exist), it's better to recognize that operating an SOA environment is, in fact, a more complex proposition than operating and managing a traditional mainframe-based environment. SOA demands our full attention, and it necessitates the deployment of system and network management components to enable proactive identification and resolution of issues before it is too late to handle them with grace. Successful control of this environment requires that these concepts and tools be in place:

- Management and Monitoring at each level of the system stack
- Deployment of a centralized Logging Server
- Real-time operational dashboards.

It also must be said that none of the above would be useful without adequate planning of remediation strategies to deal with failure. These strategies must be part of the overall system organizational governance and will be covered later on when I discuss the administrative and management aspects related to managing the IT transformation.

The Systems Management Stack

Managing an SOA environment requires a unified view of all levels of the system components. As mentioned before, the way to ensure a unified management view across all layers is to create a Management Dashboard, Centralized Logging Repository and Single Sign-On Capability. These components ultimately rely on the introduction of probes to monitor all resources and to track the flow of services across the SOA system.

Unfortunately, the software utility industry has yet to catch-up with the overall SOA management demands. After all, it took decades for the systems management suite to evolve around the mainframe model, and the integrated management view required by modern SOA systems is still evolving. This does not mean that you should take the, see no evil, hear no evil view of the NASA administrator who ignored the request to check out the Shuttle. It simply means that you should endeavor to create the needed probes and components that will give you a minimum of capability in this area.

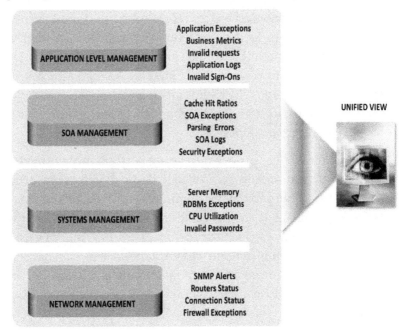

Notice from the diagram the suggestion that you manage security at each layer of the management stack. Security is not a layer, but rather an attribute of each layer.

In so far as the entirety of the management cycle is concerned, you should have capabilities for:

- Continuously monitoring the overall health of your system, with the ability to be notified on a trigger basis of events demanding immediate attention.
- Providing the ability to direct specific diagnostic checks on any component or layer in your system on an on-demand basis.
- Maintaining a comprehensive logging repository for all events and traffic taking place in your system. Clearly, this repository could grow to prohibitive levels, but you should at least have the ability to keep a solid log of all messages and events in your system for a period of time, with appropriate summary analytics for the log events that might have to be discarded.

Ideally there should be a unified view where alerts from one layer can be correlated to alerts from another. For this to occur, you will need a canonical way to represent all alerts and events of the various system layers. Unfortunately, chances are that you will have to deal with the formats and interfaces provided by the vendor of choice for each specific layer. If you can afford it, you could add an additional integration component that normalizes the various formats and events around a canonical form that can be used for future analytics.

As for the system probes measuring performance within each component, you should ensure that these monitors never add more than a few percentage points of overhead to the system (<5% is as high as it should be, in my opinion). Ideally, you will have the option of heightening or lowering the degree of monitoring, depending upon circumstances. You can have low level monitoring for steady-state operations and more intrusive monitoring for those cases where more detailed diagnosis is needed.

Finally, make sure to exercise appropriate change management controls in configuring the monitoring and tracing levels. I can't count the number of times I have witnessed failures caused by someone "forgetting" to remove diagnostic tools from a production system.

Dashboards and Centralized Logging

"Doctor," the patient says, "When I press on my calf with my finger, it hurts..."

"I see," the doctor replies.

"And then when I press my finger on my thighs, it hurts too!"

"Really?" the doctor mutters skeptically.

"I tell you doctor, I must have something serious because it also hurts whenever I poke my arms, my chest and my neck! It hurts all over!"

"Have you considered," the doctor asks, "that it might be that your finger is broken?"

Establishment of a control layer will give you access to the needed sync points from which to control the parameters affecting the dynamics of the system. The SOA Fabric (which includes the human element!) will have to react to the conditions you've set in these message headers. In the end, while the management infrastructure is there to provide you with real time snapshots of the system, it will be up to you and your staff to properly diagnose the problems that do arise.

Having an SOA Fabric, a Control Layer, and a Centralized Logger gives you the opportunity to view and manage the SOA system in the same grandiose manner as Captain Kirk on the bridge of the Starship Enterprise. The point being that part of the early transformation plans should include the design and development of a centralized dashboard capability for management of the SOA system. Attempting to run an SOA system without a dashboard that offers you a 360 degree on-demand view of all the elements of your system is not unlike Slade—the blind man in "Scent of a Woman"—driving a Ferrari at high speed on the streets of the city. The Dashboards would not be possible without a Central Logging Server and the placement of event triggers that can drive the dashboard displays. This server must be part of your initial system design, and you should treat it the same as you would any other database used for business analytic purposes. To the extent that you capture logged data over time and obtain detailed analysis of your system dynamics (resource utilization versus performance/failures), you will also develop the capability to pro-actively plan the future evolution of your system and to better understand the thresholds that might trigger failures under stress conditions.

Needless to say, logging and monitoring should minimize interference with the actual operation of the system as much as possible. Logging should always be conducted on an off-band basis. This means that all logging events should be sent to the Central Logging Server on an asynchronous basis. Do you want to log an entire message? Copy it and log the copy, but do not make the production messages flow through the logging logic. In other words, you should duplicate the message containing the logging information and send it to the log server without increasing the latency of the main message flow.

You should be able to run reports against the various logs in the database to proactively identify deficiencies and trends requiring attention. Ideally, you will extract and backup the appropriate summaries and all the logs that you are mandated to preserve for business or legal compliances reasons.

I for one don't believe you need to make this Central Logging Server a fault-tolerant element in the system, but you should certainly make sure it receives the appropriate amount of attention to ensure its high reliability.

Clearly, the entire area of system management for SOA is very complex, and I have just scratched the surface. The key message to keep in mind is that managing SOA is not the same as managing traditional legacy environments. You will need new tools, new methodologies, new processes, and prayers to new gods to make it all work!

SECTION IV
EXECUTION: GETTING IT DONE

'Vision without execution is hallucination.' - Thomas Edison

Trials

Aligning the IT organization to the emerging blueprint ◆ . Defining the organizational structure needed and duration of transformation ◆ The organizational structure needed for execution is not necessarily the same structure to establish once the transformation has been completed ◆ Ensuring support of ongoing operations ◆ Remember, ultimately it is the business that drives the pace of execution. ◆ How to get it done.

Techniques

How to ensure there is a system level competency in the organization ◆ Planning resources, identifying gaps, recruiting right skills, training, socializing and motivating the team ◆ Executing according to a well-paced crawl-walk-run plan ◆ Focusing on obtaining early successes ◆ How to strengthen QA and deployment processes.

Tribulations

In the end, success won't happen without aligning the will of the organization and, more fundamentally, people around the objective. You'll need to know how to handle office politics!

GETTING IT DONE: MANAGING THE TRANSFORMATION

There are all kinds of books dealing with IT management techniques and the many methodologies that have evolved since the start of modern day computing. However, at its core, IT management is still an art; not a science. In fact, while the use of structured methodologies can be helpful in the context of specific project tracking, it should not be relied upon as the panacea that ensures the success of the project. Fact is that, oftentimes, processes and methods are applied only to satisfy the control instincts of bureaucracies and, applied dogmatically, can do more harm than good by getting in the way of the actual project execution.

But if strictly following "management" methodologies (mythologies would be a more proper name!) is not particularly useful, then what is? Well, it's not that techniques should not be applied. It's that the techniques that should be applied are those that result from intuitive management assessments; adjusted to the specific conditions of a given project. That is, IT projects tend to have so many variables that effective management of the project should be tailored specifically to that project. There's a reason why project management is not done by robots. You can't run projects, especially major projects, with fixed "how-to" type instructions in a book written by a management consultant guru that's intended for the masses and expect success. The name of the game is intuitive flexibility and best practices. It's about guidelines; not law. It's about common sense[45]; not blindly following administrative dictums.

---

[45] "Common sense is not a single thing. Instead, it is an immense society of hard-earned, practical ideas—of multitudes of life-learned

Project success is also about focus. A common belief is that Magellan was the first explorer to circumnavigate the world. Fact is that, while Ferdinand Magellan was indeed the captain of the expedition launched to go around the world in 1519, he never made it. Instead of keeping his focus on the goal of reaching the Moluccan Islands (Indonesia) by going west and then returning via the east, he got distracted and became embroiled in local native politics. Ultimately, he met his death in a battle between Philippine tribes. Leaderless, only 18 severely ill and famished men, out of the 237 men who set sail in five ships to circumnavigate the globe, made it back alive to Spain.

The typical transformation project usually takes more than 24 months to complete (a shorter project time span would suggest you are not actually undertaking a transformation but rather a renovation; a quick-fix). Now, the average stay time for a CIO is 24 months. Do the math. No matter in what space-time continuum you happen to live, the expected project length vis-à-vis the average CIO tenure presents an inescapable conundrum. Typically, the management team completing the project (if the project is completed at all!) will be different from the one that began it.

Indeed, the single most important reason for a project's failure is that the sponsorship team is no longer around when it finally gets going. Once the new team is handed over the reins, they often feel obliged to pooh-pooh the work done by their predecessors. Anything that occurred prior to their arrival has to be wrong. Otherwise, why were they hired if not to fix the mess?

It doesn't matter. You could spend the time of your tenure as an IT executive either twiddling your thumbs or planning some sensible deliverables. Choose the latter. In the end, even if you don't complete the project yourself, having a successor complete

---

rules and exceptions, dispositions and tendencies, balances and checks."—Marvin Minsky

the project successfully is something you can proudly note in your résumé. Similarly, if you are part of the new team, it is still in your best interest to leverage all prior "rights" and to "right" all prior "wrongs".

Next I'll cover the management approaches that are pragmatically helpful, whether you are starting a transformation project or are in the process of fixing "other people's" messes.

And so, we will now shift away from the technical aspects of IT Transformation and move into the equally complex management issues of transformation.

GOVERNANCE AND ORGANIZATION

Moving to a transformative environment, SOA requires the establishment of governance and competencies adapted to handling the specific features of this emerging technology framework. Gone are the days of purely hierarchical structures with their military style command lines. SOA requires a comprehensive, holistic management approach. Indeed, transformation management requires the understanding that there are a variety of ways to view and control a project.

LOGICAL VIEW

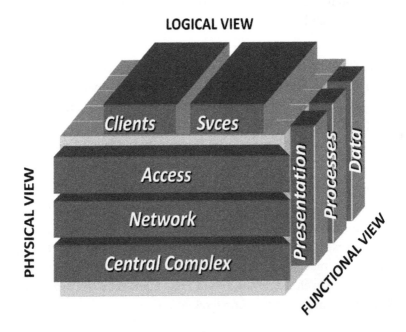

Just as with the proverbial elephant being felt by a group of blind individuals (some touch the legs and "feel" a tree trunk, others the ears and sense a flag, and so on) the system will appear different to the various constituencies. The engineering teams will focus on the physical elements of the solution: access technologies, networking and the central computers. The business partners will be more concerned with the views of Clients and Services, including the manner in which information is presented, processed, and consumed. Software developers will want specific service implementations along a 3-tier Model View Controller (MVC) paradigm. Meanwhile, enterprise architects and project managers will want to maintain the "whole image"; becoming the guardians of the holistic view of the system.

It is important to note that there is a time dimension as well. The optimum structure for execution is not necessarily the ideal way to structure the ongoing support of the deployed system. Ideally, the structure to execute the transformation should be one that gradually morphs into an organization that is capable of maintaining and supporting the new system on a steady-state basis.

The challenge is made more complex by the fact that business-as-usual operations must be maintained, even as the transformation is being executed. This means you will need to accept the existence of a dual organization structure for the required transitional period: the organization needed to support the legacy environment and the one executing the transformation.

The question is how to gradually sunset the skills, while ramping-up the new organization needed to support the future end-state. Most important is how to do so with regard to the issues presented by human considerations. People are not replaceable machines, and the transition from legacy to new requires a carefully crafted, staffing plan that encompasses retraining, reorganization, and evaluation areas.

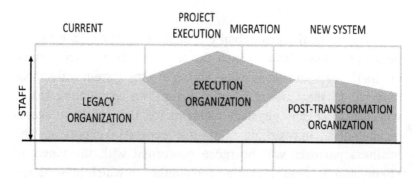

It's always disconcerting to mix the "old" with the "new". The feeling is similar to one I had this morning when I accidentally substituted toothpaste for shaving cream. I blame the shape of those new toothpaste containers, although I have to admit the mint in the toothpaste gave me a curiously refreshing shave (completely unlike the nasty feeling I received when I confused hemorrhoid cream for toothpaste!).

There is no escaping the reality that for a period of time, you will need to handle a mixture of "old" and "new": old processes running in parallel with new processes, long tenured people not yet fully trained in dealing with younger staff who are not yet knowledgeable about the existing processes, senior staff versant in the "old ways" working with newer staff unacquainted with the cultural traditions, and so on. This is not an easy task. We all know that dual organizations are usually a recipe for conflict and duplication. You should therefore make certain that the specific governances and responsibilities during this messy period of transition are clear and agreed to by all concerned.

If there is a new tactical requirement, should you give it to the legacy team to "patch" the legacy system, even if in the long run the solution might be a throw-away? Or should you try to develop a hybrid solution that can be expanded to fit the strategic standards?

In the end, as leader of the effort, you will need to broker the assignments of emergent work so that new work takes place in the right sphere. In general, the easiest way to scope responsibilities is to task the legacy team with maintaining daily operations and service levels and have the transformation team fix its sights on the new deliverables. Problems occur when new, urgent requirements demand a shifting of focus from the end state delivery. New requirements must be handled only when truly urgent and necessary and must be the domain of the legacy group only on an exception basis. At the start of the transformation you will need to agree with the line of business as to how to jointly handle tactical requirements. You will also have to agree on the thresholds that must be crossed in order to trigger urgent and necessary changes to the legacy environment.

IT Transformation efforts require the involvement of not only the technology group but other groups as well. This means that the business, finance, legal and general operations teams all need to be involved at some point. However, there are three specific groups whose roles you need to make certain are in place from the very start: Product Management, Architecture, and the SOA Team.

The Product Management Team

The control center for the transformation project is driven by a Product Management Team or PMT (a "product" in this context, need not be something your company will necessarily sell to the outside world. A product can be any specific project deliverable). The PMT should be the official technology touch point for business requests and should have the ability to refine those requests via use of business analysis processes, estimate the cost of the effort, and prioritize the potential work versus other commitments. Obviously, the product management team needs to work in line with the architecture and development teams in order to articulate the appropriate response to the requirements.

Having product management to also help with administering the project plans will provide this team with the needed visibility to assess urgent tactical requests. Items to consider in tactical requests are:

1. Is the request simple enough for the tactical group to handle? In other words, the request should not divert resources from the transformation project.
2. If the request is somewhat complex, and the tactical group will institute a stop-gap solution, how will the transformation team ensure that the requested feature or functionality will be present in the strategic deliverable?
3. If the request is fairly complex and delivering under the legacy scheme is not cost-effective, how should the request be handled vis-à-vis the transformation activity? In this case, negotiations with the business group should prioritize the request against other expected transformation deliverables as well as assessing the impact on the transformation plan.

Notice that I have resisted using the more traditional term "Project Management Office" (PMO) when referring to this group. I believe this term and governance have emerged from a belief that project management can be performed by anyone "smart enough", regardless of specific subject matter expertise. Take for instance the popular "Apprentice" TV Show in which Donald Trump assigns the contestants to "project manage" an activity challenge and then fires the person who, in his opinion, has performed the assignment least effectively. Perhaps this concept works for TV but, in the real world of software and systems development, the manager responsible for the project had better be someone who understands the technology and has an understanding of the team skills involved in the project. The manager of an IT transformation project cannot have only an administrative function.

I recommend that the actual management of a deliverable be assigned to the appropriate technology manager and not to a generic "project manager". Instead, the Product Management Team should be seen as the facilitator and enabler for the actual project work that will be conducted by a solution delivery manager. The PMT can have a direct role in specific project related activities: Business Analysis, Project Justification and Initiation, Project Planning, Project Tracking, Vendor Relationship Management, Quality Assurance, Implementation and Migration Planning, etc. and should act as a coordinating umbrella for a Project Management Steering Board that includes representation from all other constituencies as well: Development, Business, Finance, and Operations.

Speaking in practical terms, a key area of friction to look out for in this team is when delineating a clear line of responsibility for the person who will ultimately be accountable for a project deliverable. The reasons I advise against using the term "Project Management" for this role are: "Project Management" naturally implies this entity is responsible for managing the project and thus ultimately empowered to make project-level decisions. If in fact, this group is managing the project, there is no issue, but what often occurs is that the actual project execution is driven by the Development Manager. The term "Project Management" obscures the line of responsibility and causes confusion and tension. Secondly "Project Management" does not properly encompass other areas of responsibility that this function should include: business requirement gathering, lifecycle administration, project communications and tracking, assisting in defining the overall product delivery strategy, and ultimately enabling the project delivery.

From an organizational viewpoint, the project coordinator attached to a specific project should have a dual reporting line to both the delivery manager and the product manager director. The interaction with the former should be both daily and intense since it relates to the minute-by-minute project activities, while the later should only be on a periodic basis for overall status reporting and to receive overall direction regarding project tracking standards and processes. Yes, the reporting of the status may "blow the whistle" on project issues that require the product manager to validate the actual health of the project with the delivery manager. This should occur in the spirit of "check-and-balances" and should not be seen as empowering the product manager with actual supervisory or executive authority over the development team. In any case, proper procedures should be followed that allow any conflict between the product manager and the delivery manager to be escalated to their respective managers for resolution.

No one ever said life wasn't complicated!

The Architecture Team

The architecture group is responsible for ensuring that no work is duplicated, that the company aligns with the standards, and that the best technology practices are followed.

Think of the architecture team as the "special forces" team made up of senior technical advisors who maintain a holistic picture of the entire technical environment, both present and future.

When empowering the architecture team, it is wise to keep an eye out for those headstrong individuals who, in their quest for architecture purity, or because of ego, tend to push their own point of view or technical religion, rather than addressing customer needs. A good architect should be an expert and, by definition, an expert is someone who can solve any given problem in multiple ways. If you encounter an architect continuously hammering home the same solution to every problem; all the while blindly refusing to consider any other alternative, then it's time for you to provide some serious direction.

While the architecture team should enforce the standards, it should also demonstrate flexibility in adjusting and enhancing these standards on an on-going basis. The way to do so is by staying in tune with the business requirements and with the system analysts, engineers, and developers who are responsible for delivering the solution.

This is what often happens. You form a small group of bright, technical people with the objective of having them develop the framework, tenets and standards needed by the organization. However, if this group is not given the responsibility to actually deliver specific components, it becomes all too easy for them to move to the realm of platonic, impractical beauty. In this realm, all architecture constructs are conceptually beautiful and theoretically comprehensive, but essentially non-workable and non-functional (the original Open System Interconnection developed in the eighties comes to mind). Should the situation be allowed to fester, you will soon hear your programmers mocking those "fools on the hill" whose only ability is to produce extremely abstract architecture papers that will never be followed through. Meanwhile, the very talented architecture team will grow increasingly frustrated as they watch the fruit of their work ignored by those "spaghetti-code hackers". I don't have to tell you that this is not a healthy and productive state of affairs.

Giving architects a degree of development responsibility sends them the message that they will not be able to get by simply through publishing a series of holistically irrefutable, enterprise architecture bibles. Instead, the architecture group should be tasked with delivering something, i.e. actually coding stuff! This approach is to prevent the emergence of what author Joel Spolsky calls, "Architecture Astronauts"[46], or what they were called in my day, "Blue Sky Architects".

Accordingly, while the architecture group should have clear governance in defining and directing the standards, they should also be tasked with delivering code. To keep this team well grounded, a good assignment would be to give them responsibility for the development of system framework services, libraries, and toolkits.

Alternatively, line development functions should have a seat at the table in the development of technology standards. The architecture team has the overall responsibility for organizing and running technology forums that ensure that the technical team has a say in the process. These forums should allow everyone in the development community to speak their mind and state their personal viewpoints regarding standards and tenets.

Still, at times, some line developers will need to be reigned in, simply because it is not feasible to pursue the whims and wishes of those whose motivation might be to pursue "cool-hacks" rather than to ensure the long-lasting services of his or her deliverable.

---

[46] "Joel on Software" by Joel Spolsky, 2004 Apress.

In the end, however, instead of acting in a "dictatorial" manner, it is always more advantageous to bring these discussions to the forefront and to address them openly.

I have found that when the architecture group does their work correctly, and involve the entire development team, they will emerge as the natural leaders. The best case is when line programmers actually seek the advice and help from the architecture group. When you see this happening, you'll know you are on the right track.

The SOA Group

In addition to having a strong, effective architecture group, you must create a group dedicated to SOA. Since the data governance has historically been well defined for the roles of Data Base Administration, Data Analysis and Data Architecture, there is a tendency to also organize SOA in a manner similar to DBMS governances. Don't. Services are not data. While it is true there may be some similarity to the work of DBAs and SOA Service Analysts (e.g. Data Base Schemas vs. WSDL Interfaces), SOA is different enough to make it wise to establish the SOA governance separate from the data team.

Make this SOA governance responsible for the following service life-cycle areas: service interface validation, testing, service repository management, service deployment, versioning and services sun-setting. Note that since the actual service development is performed by the actual development organization, the role of the SOA Group is one of coordination and control. This function usually consists of a small group (two to four individuals) whose role is similar to that of a Data Base Administrator, but with a special focus on all things "services".

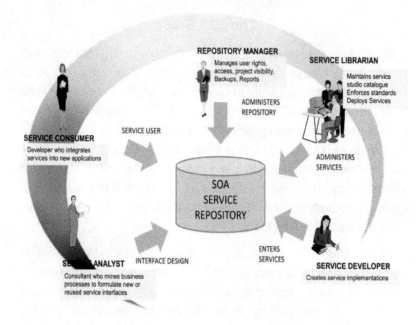

In the diagram above, the SOA Group covers the roles of Service Analyst(s), Repository Manager, and Service Librarian(s). Of these three, only the Service Analyst is required to have a programming background (the stronger, the better!). The Repository Manager will have a background related to operations (someone with experience managing LDAP servers comes to mind). The Services Librarian may well come from a data organization.

It is essential that the team be formed of very competent staffers. Now, before you say, "Duh, that's obvious!" let me remind you that we often fail to elect our politicians based purely on their competency. We vote for them because, "He's the type of guy I could have a beer with," or simply because we like the image he projects. As managers, we often incur the same biases and tend to empower those on our staff who better match our ideal image of competency. It often happens that, when forming a new team, it will be filled with "volunteers' whose primary motivation is to escape current roles rather to eagerly contribute to the new group. Don't make the SOA group the Gulag of IT.

Competency does matter, but it is not always easy to define "competency". Recently there has been a trend to evaluate employee competencies around the concept of "certifications". For example project managers are expected to show PMI (Project Management Institute) certifications, testers have their own certifications, DBAs get their certifications (usually from DB vendors), and so on.

Entire industries have spawned from the certification business. Now, I am not suggesting that certification is a bad thing in and of itself, but I have met many who have specialized in collecting all kinds of certifications and yet are not particularly competent. I suppose I could give them a certification for their ability to obtain certifications, but that's about it! My point is this: Be suspicious of anyone flashing a long list of certifications. Either this individual has had too much time on his or her hands and has not focused on actual work experience, or this person's certification portfolio proves he's a genius; making you wonder why the need for all those certifications in the first place. Forget the diplomas. Ultimately, competency is something that an employee either does or doesn't have. You'll know if he has it by seeing at what he delivers.

Transitioning the Team

Aside from start-ups or other new ventures, when it comes to employee resources, you're going to have to deal with a varied mixture of "legacy" skills and attitudes. It should go without saying that any serious transformation effort is going to face a certain amount of resistance and push-back—especially from those who, rightly or not, feel threatened by the change represented by the transformation. Building a team supportive of a transformation will require a great amount of patience, good communication, and a dosage of well-focused leadership.

A famous sculptor once remarked that creating the statue of a horse from a block of granite was all about removing the "non-horse" parts from the block. No matter the organization, there is always an existing team that can be crafted, via training and reassignment, to support the transformation goals. As with the proverbial sculptor, you will need to remove the "non-team" parts, represented by what might be an ossified and unmotivated staff (pardon me for sounding so Zen-like!).

Traditional team dynamics demonstrate that the greatest resistance to change is usually generated by only a few. Since it is not realistic to assume you will be able to build, completely from scratch, a new technology team, your mission then is to weed-out the unredeemable trouble-makers from the worker-bees, who though perhaps afraid of change, are nevertheless professionals who will gladly follow through once given clear direction. As an added bonus, with the benefit of fresh eyes and renewed objectives, you will also be able to identify the diamonds-in-the-rough, those underappreciated team members who have been waiting patiently for a chance to shine (and believe me they exist in nearly every organization) but have never been given a proper role to play. When given a chance and a fresh challenge, these individuals can become natural stars when allowed to spread their wings.

Add to this dimension the need to make a frank assessment of the skills of those in the group, vis-à-vis the skill-sets needed for transformation, the time and funding available to repurpose these skills, and the realization that you will need to fill the natural skill gaps presented by the introduction of new technologies. Consider too the fact that, yes, you are dealing with human beings, not machines, and you can see why this area of the transformation process is usually the most sensitive and difficult. It doesn't matter if you have the most wonderful architecture in place, or that you are using the most amazing technology, or that your project plan is a paragon of beauty, if you can't deal with the human dimension, the project is not going to succeed.

Dealing with this type of challenge requires a clear understanding of team inter-relationships. Most importantly, it involves applying a wise combination of informed intuition, fairness, and decisiveness in order to resolve or remove the elements that might impede the effort. In the end, once you have defused those who are interested in obstructing the project, you will be able to follow the kind of staffing plan that allows you to make delicious lemonade from the mix.

In the end, staffing the new system with existing resources, requires a case-by-case assessment of individual competencies and attitudes. This will involve working closely with your Human Resources team. When defining a more appropriate taxonomy of the various skills in your existing area, you will find that certain workers can be retrained to handle new technologies.

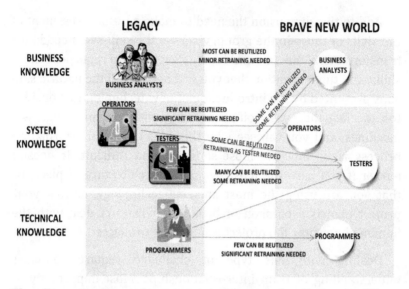

The diagram above shows a generic, sample roadmap of how different resource types can be utilized for the new system. Business analysts, for instance, will usually make the easiest transition; simply because the business processes supported by the new system are, for the most part, the same as those of the legacy environment. A few motivated legacy operators may be able to continue operating the new system after significant retraining, but many might be better off assigned to performing Q/A functions in the new system—after all, who better to spot inconsistencies or trouble in a new system than someone already acquainted with the operation of the old?

After reviewing the HR files for the current staff, you will be able to place each member within a general category that will hopefully give you a sense of the type of resource you have available. Alas, you will also find that a certain percentage of existing workers will never be able to make the switch over to the new system under any capacity.

The following classification is done somewhat in jest, and I admit it's not exactly scientific but, well, it is the result of my own professional observations. Enter here some worker profiles that you are likely to encounter in a legacy team:

The Curmudgeons. I use this as a term of endearment—think of the two elderly men seated in the balcony at the start of the Muppets show. The dictionary defines curmudgeon as a crusty, ill-tempered man, usually old in years. Key word: *usually.* Though not necessarily elderly, they are individuals who have done things one way for so long that they simply find it inconceivable to do them any other way. My experience is that, in this group, you will find some of your best potential assets: those ready and willing to contribute their tremendous experience in helping you succeed with the new system. At the same time, you will find some of the worst: those who are the most apathetic and disenchanted to the idea of change. No middle-of-the-road folks here. Your challenge is to identify who is who!

The Natives. Recall the history of the Spaniards landing in Mexico. Don Hernando Cortez found the Aztecs, who by all accounts were, prior to his arrival, quite content with their role as regional super-power, enjoying their life-style and religious customs that included the not-so-generous practice of human sacrifice. They exemplify those individuals who have been in the legacy system for so long that, when faced with something new, suffer a great deal of angst. Some will be able to switch, simply because they have retained a genetic ability to change when confronted with change, but others will have a hard time adapting to the new world. It is among these employees that "retraining" efforts often fail.

To put it in very direct terms: It is almost suicidal to depend on someone who has just recently been trained in a new technology to deliver a key element for the new system. Take, John Doe, who has been proficiently coding in COBOL for the last twenty years. He is not a curmudgeon, and comes forward saying that he's concerned about his job "once the new system is delivered," and that he wants to be trained in Java. I know there are always exceptions to the rule, but the typical John Doe who has been retrained to learn Java and is then given a Java application to code will, in most cases, deliver a very well written COBOL program that just happens to use Java syntax. What's the difference? Coding in Java entails coding in object oriented paradigms and the application of specific best practices that apply to modern development environments (calling the right external classes, using methods the right way, etc.) Multiply the John Doe effect by the number of individuals you hope to retain, and you can see what a royal mess your system will be in.

Truth be told, someone who has been working for decades with procedural languages such as COBOL will not have an easy time moving to modern object oriented technologies. Object orientation is more than learning the syntax of a new language. It's also about dealing with the conceptual shift represented by object oriented concepts and development methodologies. Some of the most serious coding disasters I've witnessed involved programmers who had to develop mission-critical applications using programming languages they were unfamiliar with.

I realize that what I am saying may not sound politically-correct, but the reality is that only a handful of procedure-oriented developers will ultimately be able to manage the transition to utilizing new technologies. You would do better to hire a recent college graduate with baseline training in modern systems; apprenticing him to those on your current staff.

Does this mean that John's only route is retirement? Not necessarily. My suggestion is to look at John's true value. This lies in his understanding of the core business processes he has been coding for the last several years. He may also know a great deal about how to interpret the business requirements of the business team and also have years of experience in how elements of the system needs to be tested. In other words, aside from his intrinsic inability to become an experienced Java developer, John Doe can be a very effective help to the new project and, in this context, his job should be protected. Yes, he should still learn Java, because learning it will at least give him the ability to communicate with the trove of expert Java developers (likely to be more junior) and to understand the specific constraints and capabilities the new system offers vis-à-vis the requirements.

The Juniors. These are the recent company hires. They are usually young, just out of university, and have not yet specialized strongly in any legacy segment. They are the ones who can be most easily retrained to focus on the new system. Even then, the actual success or retraining will be based more on their individual capabilities. You need especially to keep an eye out for those who, while stand outs when working with the outdated system, may not be all that competent when working with the new system.

The mark of a good leader is not in his or her ability to wipe a slate clean, but rather in his or her ability to identify the various hidden strengths inside the organization and to get everyone to contribute to the maximum of his capability. Bottom line is this: A proper analysis of the skill-sets in your organization can be well-timed to use each employee's skills in a way that is consistent with his abilities. This can only occur, however, when one is completely honest about how unrealistic it is to try to make change happen without ruffling some feathers. This, after all, is the nature of change.

Filling the Skill Gaps: Contracting, Outsourcing and Off Shoring

Let's say you're going to need to augment your work force with external resources. Think of the augmentation strategy in terms of layers. At the core, you have your trusted employees as your resident resource. The core team is the base and lever of the project. In the next layer we have in-house contractors. They are resources brought in by third party companies. They will work as part of your organization and will be paid on an hourly basis. The strategy is to implement an option-to-hire policy so that, as you bring in the much needed expertise, you can also exercise the option to hire those contractors who prove worthy of becoming part of the inner core.

In yet another outer layer, you have the augmentation resources provided by external companies working on a statement-of-work basis. While this model means you won't have to deal with the day-to-day management of these third parties, and you will not have visibility of each individual resource contributing to the effort, you should nevertheless be prepared to exercise appropriate ongoing oversight to ensure deliverables are met and that you are not surprised by missed deliverables.

Some like the idea of using outside contracting services on a per hour basis. I don't recommend this approach. The only exception would be for trusted former employees who for personal reasons have left the company but still wish to continue working, albeit remotely. Otherwise, external per-hour contractors should only be used temporarily as subject matter experts to fill specific gaps. Should you face this need, it is best to secure these outside resources on a retainer mode rather than on a per hour basis (how is it possible to oversee the number of hours clocked by someone working remotely, anyway?). Examples of resources best used in this manner are: DBAs, architects, security advisors, and performance engineers.

Finally, some companies prefer to use off-shore resources, either via statement-of-work or on a retainer basis. I personally feel that most companies are ill-prepared to deal directly with off-shore resources (cultural and geographic concerns apply). My recommendation is that, if off-shore resources are to be used, that they be managed by a local third party contractor who will take responsibility for the day to day interactions with them. It is also common and preferable these days for the off-shoring company to keep a touch point local presence. Still, off-shore services should only be relied upon for very specific, non-mission critical components that can be developed with a minimum of explicit functional descriptions and should never ever be used for core, mission-critical deliverables. Valid assignments for off-shore work are: reports, data mappings (ETL), general tools development (diagnosis, test tools, etc.)

You should also adjust the way you augment resources vis-à-vis skill sets and specializations. A development project that has a well qualified team of developers and a few good project managers will perform better than a team composed of many good project managers but very few qualified developers. The prized quality of a good project manager is his/her ability to enable the work of the developers and then keep out of their way as much as possible. I have seen enough horrors stories of management trying to fix a project in trouble by adding more and more project managers! As if a sinking ship needs more captains when what it really needs is buoyancy! The best project management work I have seen come from project managers who were hired as outside resources. They tend to focus more on the delivery of the project since they don't have to worry about internal governance disputes.

Likewise, many prefer to engage the services of external consulting firms to design the high level architecture plan. Needless to say, these high end services are usually very expensive. In any case, it's ideal when the architecture is developed by an internal team. Nevertheless, I can see the involvement of external consulting powerhouses in helping to refine specific, specialized niches in the architecture. External consulting firms are also often used to "audit" a given architecture or project implementation. However, my feeling on this is that they are usually used in this function when a project is already in trouble or, frankly, when executive management feels the need for external validation of the project. In all fairness, this validation may not be indicative of a lack of trust towards you or your team, but simply a necessary "cover-thy-derriere" to better defend the project to the board or to regulatory entities.

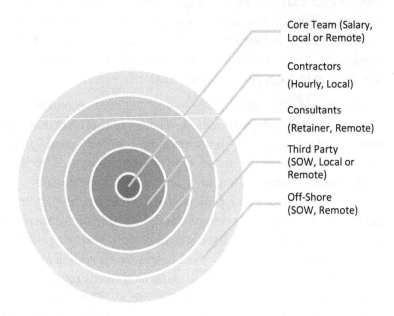

Core Team (Salary, Local or Remote)

Contractors (Hourly, Local)

Consultants (Retainer, Remote)

Third Party (SOW, Local or Remote)

Off-Shore (SOW, Remote)

In any case, the architecture team should definitely be part of your core team; not augmented with external resources. You still need to have a dedicated architecture team to lead the technology side of the project since the expensive, high level consultants will probably be long gone once the project begins to get intense. The architecture team should be in place to develop the common framework modules; perform R&D on new components and, in general, serve as an enabler to the programming community at large. They should establish the desired architecture by example, and they should also be able to establish governance, whereby line programming staff have the opportunity to voice their views and preferences in influencing the architecture direction. As discussed earlier, the architecture team will have a number of roles, from defining architecture to enforcing it. Keep in mind the key dictum that the architecture team should also do programming. If you create an architecture team whose only responsibility is to create architecture, they are bound to become like the gods of Mount Olympus, handing down un-implementable architecture specifications to the mere mortals involved in programming.

Finally, nothing will better ensure the success of your project than a strong group of developers, even if this means you will have to sacrifice the size of the team in order to achieve a higher degree of quality. Measuring the performance of a group of experienced programmers has shown that the difference between the best and the worst performance averaged a factor of 10 to 1. Think about it: A good programmer is on average ten times more productive than a lousy one![47]

Getting great programmers is, of course, never easy. If you identify great development resources to augment your team, try to bring them onboard in any capacity you can. Beware of the prima-donnas (the best programmers are often the ones that brag the least). They can be contractors or consultants and, if possible, should be hired. You should be prepared to pay better than market salaries and entice them to join your effort in light of its exciting challenges. Good programmers go for the thrill of the challenge even more than for the salary.

There are some who say that IT departments in your average Fortune-500 company can't aspire to the recruitment of top development talent. The allegation is that good developers prefer the smart, entrepreneur, technology-led start-ups over those big

---

[47] The Mythical man-Month—Frederick P. Brooks, Jr.

boring corporations. I'm not sure that I subscribe to this view. Granted, many of the brightest want to make their fortune quickly and so head for the cool and sexy frontiers of new development. However, cool and sexy can also be an attribute of a transformation technology project, and I do believe that a well-formed and *well-led* technology transformation project will appeal to many a talented programmer.

On Leadership

The Leadership Style

If you are lucky enough to have responsibility for a large portion or even the totality, of a transformation project, you will be called upon to make a number of decisions on an as-you-go basis. Mike Shanahan, former coach of the Denver Broncos, is reputed to have arrived at each game armed with a pre-scripted number of plays. But even he needed to make adustments when unforeseen circumstances, such as interceptions, fumbles or holding penalties, altered his original plan. Likewise, a strong planning stage and clear definition of the architecture, tenets and standards can facilitate the decision-making for a transformation project. However, in the end you are bound to encounter situations that demand impromptu judgment calls.

Being a good leader is often about making the correct decisions (emphasis on "correct"). On the other hand, due to the complexities involved, it is not reasonable to expect a 100% success ratio in all transformation involved decisions. What are the performance expectations? Unlike in baseball, for example, where a 40% batting success ratio would ensure you riches and your name in the Baseball Hall of Fame, in the business world a success ratio of 40% would get you only into the Hall of Shame. If you achieve a Pareto-like 80% success ratio in any of the myriad of low to middle impact decisions you'll make, you'll be doing fine. But when it comes to major decisions, you'll have to consider yourself lucky if you're able to survive one major blunder, let alone two.

Admittedly, this analysis may be slightly facetious since the truth of the matter is that often the criteria for success is not a binary right/wrong and tends to come with a high degree of fuzziness (that's why the art of "spin" has evolved to the point where it is now). The point remains: A necessary (but not sufficient) attribute of good leadership is making correct decisions. Many projects get derailed because those in leadership make decisions that are either too conservative, or too aggressive (depending upon the circumstances); too political, or too vague or plainly just wrong.

Don't believe those who say that leaders don't need to be knowledgeable in the problem domain. "As long as he surrounds himself with knowledgeable individuals, he'll do just fine," the saying goes. This might be true for managers but not for leaders. The truth is, making the correct decision is not possible if you lack the knowledge to determine right from wrong. It helps if, as a leader, you have experienced a transformation project while working as a foot-soldier. In this way you will have gained a broader frame of reference to help you make the right calls. Moreover, it also helps to be humble in accepting the fact that, no matter how knowledgeable or experienced you may be, it is impossible to know everything. You should have a clear view of your limitations and be sure to surround yourself with a trusted team of collaborators who can expand upon the knowledge you have. A second key attribute of good leadership is listening to both your team and others.

In his book "Infotopia" author, Cass R. Sunstein, writes about the Jury Theorem. This theorem states that the probability of receiving a correct answer, when applying the rule of majority opinion, increases towards 100% as the voting group increases. The only caveat is that, for this to work, each member of the voting group must be more likely to be right than wrong. A group of experts voting on an answer will tend to be correct more often than will a lone expert, for example.

The theorem also shows the opposite: If the individual members of the group are more likely to be wrong than right, the resulting probability outcome for correct decisions will trend towards zero. In other words, you should seek answers from your team, provided your team's experience makes them more likely to be right than wrong. The opposite is also true. Don't ask people to give you advice about things they know little about.

I once attended a "decision-making" meeting where my boss at the time, trying to appear inclusive, invited opinions and votes on a particular technical approach. This was a subtle and complex technical question, mind you. Problem was that in the room they were only two actual technology people. The rest were non-technical: the HR guy, an accountant, the boss' assistant and a couple of administrators! Only one of the non-technical individuals had the courage to answer, "I don't know. That's not my area." Regardless, the decision was made on a straight up and down vote. Needless to say, the decision adopted that day was the wrong one.

Now, I am not saying that decisions cannot be made by multi-disciplinary teams. It's just that the teams that make the decision should have the appropriate, relevant, domain-level expertise. When you do this, it's best to approach the art of decision making with the objective to reach consensus based decisions (but consensus does not imply unanimity!). When faced with a problem, it makes sense to gather your trusted advisors together and proceed to methodically evaluate each approach. Keep an open mind and consider all proposed solutions as part of the brainstorming exercise. Basic pruning principles are the Occam Razor principle (also known as the KISS principle for "Keep It Simple, Stupid"), stating that given two alternative choices, you should lean toward the simpler one, as common sense solutions are to be preferred. In the end, leaders should not assume that this process of consensus making is the basis for abdicating responsibility in making a decision. At times, project leaders mistakenly hold back on a decision far longer than advisable because they seek consensus at all costs. Ultimately, there should be the realization that not making a decision is no different from making a decision to do nothing. If you are comfortable with the impact of doing nothing, then fine. However, you should realize that, sometimes, consensus will not be possible, and you will need to make a call based on your own gut feeling[48]. On occasion you might even cash in on your prerogative as "the decider" to overrule a recommended decision from your staff. Beware of exercising this right too often, however, as this position should only occur when you feel very strongly about your decision and have objective elements (i.e. "knowledge") to defend it. Either way, you should allocate the time and effort to ensure that the staff and all appropriate stakeholders are made aware of the final decision, including the reasoning behind it.

Finally, leadership is not about managing. Managing is not difficult if you follow the methods laid down through the generations. Good management is a science, but leadership is an art. The third attribute of good leadership is treating your team with respect, motivation, and inspiration. Management is something you can draw up on an organization chart, but leadership is something that gets engraved in the trust of your collaborators. Leadership is about making certain your team knows they are building the proverbial cathedral as opposed to a church wall, and that they are encouraged to take ownership for the success of the project. Leadership helps ensure everyone on the team feels comfortable with the viability of the objectives, and that appropriate recognition will be shared with all involved upon the success of a project.

Because leadership is all about success, it's only natural that, although workers must follow managers, they want to follow leaders. Having said this, "No leader will succeed without a strong supporting team."

---

[48] Making decisions based on "gut feelings" is not necessary that bad IF and only IF you have experience in the field related to the decision, and is not based on blind faith. In fact, author Malcolm Gladwell shows in his best-seller book "Blink" that experts develop the ability to make appropriate decisions in their field of expertise almost sub-consciously.

The Leadership Team

Let's be realistic. Your resume notwithstanding, you are not Superman (Batman, perhaps, but not Superman!). It's one thing to have a pulse on the status of the transformation and be aware of the skill sets of your team, and another thing entirely to have more than twenty-four hours in a day to manage the minutiae involved. If there is a single element that can ensure success, it's to surround yourself with a great leadership team—a group of direct reports, fully attuned to your objectives and capable of working cooperatively amongst themselves and with other corporate constituencies.

Mad Magazine once published a cartoon showing the Lone Ranger with his Indian sidekick, Tonto, surrounded by attacking Indian warriors. The Lone Ranger turns to Tonto and asks, "What do we do now?" Tonto replies, "What do you mean by "we" Kemosabe?"

This story highlights the importance of having a team that shares your challenges. It also works the other way around. Your direct reports should feel comfortable when coming to you with a problem to be resolved, knowing they have your trust. Still, a former US President used to say "Trust, but Verify." From time to time you should reach out to the base levels in your organization in order to assess the morale and effectiveness of the entire team. If you are the type of manager who "walks-the-floor" (and you should be), you will be able to do spot-checks to directly determine whether your organization is running like a well-oiled machine or an episode of a bad reality show.

Beyond trust and alignment of purpose, you should also try to establish the right mix of skills in your leadership team. Multidisciplinary teams will ensure you receive a variety of perspectives rather than the same, repetitive advice. Singularity of purpose does not entail singularity of opinion. Within this multidisciplinary framework it would be ideal to have a balanced combination of management and technology skills.

Be prepared to mentor your direct reports to ensure that, in the end, you have a team that is congruent with the values you wish to imprint. Intrinsic elements, such as excellence, satisfaction, work attitude, commitment and integrity, need to be defined and enforced in practice and not merely on laminated sheets or through mug-imprinted company mottos. They should be established through example and should be measured (sensed, more than measured) on a day-to-day basis.

When it comes to organizing your direct reports and setting governance, make sure to assign roles to match skill sets with the teams they will be overseeing. If you have a highly technical, self-motivated team, don't let them be managed by someone whose style is to micro-manage activities. In this case, it would be better to have a manager who's not highly technical and has a hands-off style. Highly motivated, technical teams need a manager who will serve only as a facilitator; someone who will remove obstacles and then get out of the way, and not someone who will try to direct on a day-to-day basis.

Alternatively, some teams may benefit from a more technical-style rather than administrative manager. If you have the kind of team whose genetic makeup requires them to be more closely directed (traditionally, teams involved in the day-to-day operations tend to fit this profile), you will want to choose a manager whose style is more hands-on and more procedurally oriented. Teams formed by junior programmers, who are competent and yet inexperienced (these teams are usually put in charge of maintenance, but should not be), can benefit significantly from a manager who provides technology direction and mentoring.

Think of building your team in terms similar to that of a sports team coach focused on bringing in the right players and using them in the proper context. In the end, most successful working teams, like most successful sport teams, become so primarily by becoming unified under a shared culture.

Culture, Style & Pushback

No, this is not a section best covered by one of those lifestyle magazines, but rather an area that is often neglected in books on IT management. Your leadership is all about imprinting a specific culture onto your team. Whether your team works with a spirit of openness or secrecy, confrontation or collaboration, urgency or relaxation, depends upon the behaviors you promote as a leader. In IT, more than in any other profession, a well-motivated team is likely to deliver better results than a team that is discombobulated and demoralized.

Once you have set up the team structure and staffed it with the best resources you can garner, you should strive to be the best manager you can be. Remember that driving a team is not unlike driving a car. You need to know the proper gear to use, whether turning, reversing or going straight ahead. Managers with a one-dimensional style fail to realize that a project is a living thing. Projects should be driven with precision and in line with circumstances. This does not mean that you should relax the speed of delivery. "If you have everything under control, you are not going fast enough," are the words of Mario Andretti. Not only should you expect to operate to the very limits of your control, but you should also accept that, if you have staffed your team with the right balance of skills and styles needed to achieve success, you will have to deal with the negative consequences of personality issues, tensions and frustrations.

And speaking of frustrations. . . Assuming that your transformation effort attempts to establish a corporate wide architecture, you are likely to find significant push-backs—especially in the area of architecture (tenets and standards, remember?)

For your comfort and delight, following are the top ten, favorite push-backs I've come across:

1. We have a time to market issue. We need to deliver this in two weeks. When the architecture is in place, we will migrate to it.
2. I know you expect us to follow the new architecture standards, but I can't afford to train people for it just now.
3. I know you have some of the architecture running, but it has never been tested. We certainly don't want to be the first ones to use it!
4. I know you have the architecture running, and it has been tested, but we'd feel more comfortable using our better-tested Excel macros.
5. We are 80% architecture compliant anyway, so what's wrong with the use of a different programming language?
6. We like your architecture but it doesn't really apply to our project.
7. I not aware of this new technology; so it mustn't be ready for prime time yet.
8. I recently read in PC Week that protocol XYZ is better!
9. You mean you really want to deploy this stuff? I thought it was only meant as PR to impress our customers!
10. We really want to be compliant, we really do, but we think that sticking with Cobol right now is safer.

How do you handle these types of remarks? Well, we have tenets and standards to provide an overall framework to help align the enterprise as much as possible. But you do have to be flexible, particularly when the business drivers are such that, if you are not, you could become road-kill. It's best to accept that architecture exceptions are going to take place and codify an appropriate exception-process (even then, there will be exceptions to the exception-process, rest assured!). Bottom line, evaluate the argument against the exception criteria, which will hopefully include minimal remediation to ensure the architecture process can be brought back on track. Is there a need to sometimes develop a cheap-and-dirty tactical solution to solve an immediate business need? Okay, no problem! Just make sure to fund the on-going work and make certain that this tactical solution is eventually re-factored into architecture compliance; plus take into account the migration from tactical to compliance. I've discovered that sponsors of tactical solutions rarely deny this very reasonable request. Other arguments may be easier to dispense with, but you should never, ever, close your mind to them. Perhaps protocol XYZ is better and cheaper than the one you have been considering! Give everyone a fair shake, and allow them to justify their rationale. If the argument was "religiously" motivated, dogmatic, or driven by some other precious self-interest, justifying it will be difficult. Still, if there is a reason for considering an alternative, then please do so.

In the end, I circle back to the point of culture. As long as the team is committed to the success of the project, and the reasons for the negative issues are frank disagreements based upon well-meaning differences of opinion, you should be able to manage the situation to your advantage. Think about it for a moment. We all know that pressure creates diamonds, and friction polishes them. In my experience many successes are brought to fruition under the heat of deadlines and in response to initial failures. If from the onset, you've made sure to create a great team, you will get the results you want in the end. Just be sure to have plenty of coffee and donuts on hand to support the effort!

The Office Politics

IT transformation does not take place in a vacuum. You will surely encounter the wonderful world of office politics. Make no mistake about it, in today's corporate world, office politics is intrinsic to the business and is an unavoidable result of that little trait we refer to as "human nature".

Beyond the politics caused by individual personalities, it helps to understand the motivations and behaviors you're likely to encounter within the office (I've already covered some of the personality types you're likely to encounter within your team). The attributes covered below are more descriptive of individual behaviors rather than ingrained personality traits. After all, a colleague who supports a particular project may well be an enabler for that project, but if that colleague is not keen about your endeavor, he or she may become a barrier to your success. People, I should highlight, are much more complex than any single trait, but it sometimes helps to define the types of workers you may encounter in order to better deal with them.

As you move your efforts forward from conception to execution and then on to results, you may well encounter the following behavioral traits:

The Proceduralists

These are the individuals who expect you to fill form after form, get approval, document steps, and generally follow whatever process has been established without regard to reality. They simply expect you to align with the process, no exceptions, because "it's company policy". Many are well-meaning and will only espouse sensible needs (yes, you have to fill-in that expense account and process that invoice the correct way!), but many milk the system, exploiting the detritus represented by generations of legacy business processes that no longer serve any purpose, and driven by a need to feel important or pursuant to their own self-interest in a desperate attempt to avoid becoming superfluous.

The Concerned

Typically, this group is afraid of change, and your transformation activities place them outside their comfort zone. There is a subcategory of "the concerned"—those who seize your project as an opportunity to advance their future status in the company. They will show up at your meetings or fire up memos with items "they are concerned about", without ever recommending solutions. I can only conclude that they do so for the following reason: If the area of concern turns out to be a true problem, they will be able to brag about having called you on it. If on the other hand, a problem never results, they can always insinuate that the problem did not occur because they had forewarned you about it. They are usually a difficult group to confront because, when questioned about their motivation, they have a ready answer, "I'm only expressing my concern because I really want to see this project succeed."

Most of the time, the concerned are nothing more than a minor annoyance to your project but, occasionally, they can have the negative effect of casting doubt on it and jeopardizing the support needed for ongoing funding or adjustments. They can also create fear and obfuscation that can have a detrimental impact on your team, sidetracking them into constantly having to respond to concerns being raised.

Of course, there will be times when the concerns raised are legitimate. I suggest that, as a means of distinguishing true articles of concern from those that are politically motivated, you query the individual on suggestions as to how to remediate the issue. Better yet, assign him the task of solving the concern in question. This simple request is usually enough to silence all but the most sincere. Typically, the issue will not be brought up again.

The Sunshiners

These are the individuals who argue that because everything is fine, change is not needed. Hopefully, by the time you get your project going, you will have this group on board.

The Mavericks

In this group there are those who believe that they, better than anyone else, know how the project should be done. These people are often those who've attempted something similar in the past (a variation of the Sunshiners). They tend to be what I define as "The Mavericks." These are the younger "know-it-alls" who think that if they cobble together an open source tool they found on Google with that "cool-parser" they just learned about and then add a function created in their garage, that they're going to come up with a great "solution" that will do what you're trying to do for a gazillion dollars less (if not free) and in no time at all. The point being that putting together a mission critical enterprise system is serious business that requires mature planning and design and should never be approached as a tactical endeavor.

Now, if you just can manage to reduce the ego of the Maverick, what they do have on their side is the fact that they usually mean well (to be fair, to them you are probably just an old fogie who's not up to snuff on the ways of the modern world!). To be fair, on occasion the Maverick may be right; plus they often bring a fresh perspective to a project. They should be listened to, but take their advice with a grain of salt.

The Rolers

No, they are not the one's urging, "Let's Roll!" (they would then be called "The Rollers" and would be enjoyable to be around!). No, they are the ones who feel the transformation is stepping on their toes. "It is our role," they say, "to define the requirements; not that guy from that other department." How you handle the Rolers depends on their motivation. If the case is one in which they want to be part of the process, then I suggest you include them as much as possible. After all, you can actually increase the chances of success for your transformation project by including supporters in a productive manner. On the other hand, if the motivation of the Rolers is to sabotage your work and create barriers (usually in a passive-aggressive way), then be careful in how you handle them.

Depending on your actual corporate organization, you should be able to solve this problem via negotiations and delineation of roles. However, if in fact you encounter problems with them after the project has been initiated, you probably haven't been doing your homework. Reality is, part of a project's conception and justification is to ensure that all possible constituencies are identified from the get go, unless you or your executive sponsors are deliberately pushing a transformation with the knowledge that it is going to overlap people's real or perceived roles (and yes, that usually happens). If the appearance of "Rolers" comes as a surprise to you, it means you're going to have to a do a great deal of mending and adjustments to try and save the effort.

The Academicians

In every technology organization, you are bound to find one or two individuals holding PhD degrees; who are frustrated about the way development is being handled without proper "discipline" and who try to introduce novel "ontologies", or "well-formed algorithms," or who insist that all testing should be mathematically provable. I say this in jest. I do think there is a place for this type of resource if they are put in an R&D position; provided they can communicate with others on the team without coming across as demeaning or superior.

THE RELATIONSHIPS

Relationship between Technology and the Line of Business

Perhaps you've noted that I have repeatedly suggested the importance of having a good and respectful relationship with your business group, and that their involvement and support is essential to the success of a technology transformation program.

Without question, you should expect the business team to be heavily involved during the early phases of the project. In the early stages you need to work with the business partners to get the project approved (without their sponsorship, it simply won't), to define the detailed requirements, and to establish delivery commitments. Business should also be closely involved during the later stages for purposes of project acceptance and delivery. Their role at this point will, by necessity, be slightly adversarial. After all, they are one of the key players in determining the quality and success of the deliverable.

The role of business during the execution phase is not quite so clear. Their involvement during this phase will depend upon a number of factors, ranging from the cultural style of your organization to the idiosyncrasies of the individuals on the business team. Another variable is the type of project, the specific deliverable within the project, and how well or how badly the project is coming along. You may have a business team, perfectly happy to assume a "laissez-faire" attitude regarding IT as a form of "vendor", and taking the position that they are your customer to whom you will deliver the committed product or service. At the other extreme are those business groups that firmly believe the IT organization to be their butler; tasked to do their bidding. Then, of course there are a variety of attitudes in between these two extremes.

There are problems with both extreme views. Yes, if you are in a company that views technology as a commodity enabler, the perspective that technology is a "service" function might well apply. However, if you are in this type of company, you probably shouldn't be involved in a transformation technology project to begin with. Let's face it, a technology transformation project cannot truly succeed when there is a view of IT as simply a "vendor" or a "service-center" for the company." The days when the business could strike IT for being late with "the monthly report," or could set arbitrary deadlines for those "immediate changes to the way the discounts are computed", and then have the IT folk limp away Quasimodo-like with a submissive, "Yes, master!" are over (I know, many business friends of mine would easily argue that those days never occurred!). There is only one way for the business and technology teams to interact with each other when confronted with a major project like a transformative project: as partners . . . equal partners.

Establishing an equal partnership view between technology and business tends to be more controversial than it should. Oftentimes this view is opposed implicitly, or even overtly, by certain lines of business. You often hear, "The business is paying for this, and so it's our prerogative to decide things." Reality is that the business group is not the one paying for the project. The company is the one paying for it, through the business. Everyone has fiduciary responsibility for the well-being of the company; not just the line of business.

The fact is, having the technology team act as an "order-taker" is only feasible under certain scenarios, such as when delivering a stream of tactical initiatives, or when delivering basic support services to the business. The partnership- as-equals relationship is a better way to establish a decision making framework that will hopefully serve both respective governances. This type of relationship also demands shared responsibility and the ability of the technology team to understand business needs. For a trusting partnership to exist between business and technology, the technologists need to become acquainted with the business imperatives, while applying the knowledge and imagination needed to effectively leverage the emerging technology to provide a clear competitive business advantage. Technology should endeavor to proactively identify business enabling approaches, and to socialize and communicate to business the universe of what is possible. By doing so the business leadership can enjoy a wider menu of options and be better armed in the priority-setting exercises that are sure to follow. Let's not forget that, ultimately, to be deemed successful, technology must deliver a business benefit.

So, where is the line drawn in the decision making? First of all, I have yet to experience even the most "hands-on" business team attempt to make detailed technology decisions when it comes to infrastructure choices. The types of router, firewall, hardware or system management tools to use, for example, are decisions best left to the technology team. Alternatively, it is not a good idea for the technical team to debate with the business team as to the aesthetic, branding or usability aspects of a user interface. Render to Caesar the things which are Caesar's, and to technology the things which are technology's. Seriously, you can have your technical staff express their preference, but there are certain decisions that should be made by the business team, as long as they don't have a true direct or indirect impact on the complexity of the solution. For example, if the business team demands to use Flash for the interface, you can oblige, but don't let them force development of business logic within the Flash scripts if it violates established architecture tenets.

A partnership relation between the technology and business teams entails a balance in the sphere of decision-making, mutual respect (at the very least, the team making the decision should listen to the other team), and ideally should achieve some degree of consensus in the overlapping areas of decision making. This is easier said than done when the impact of a decision spans both the technology and business areas. An example would be the choice of a solutions vendor or even the decision on whether to develop a certain capability internally or to purchase it externally.

Even if you have defined a tenet stating that you will only develop solutions that match your core competencies, there may still exist gray areas open for debate. For example, say you are selecting a campaign management vendor. Campaign management is an area that will typically have very high visibility for the marketing and sales business group, and rightfully so. The business will likely have a strong opinion regarding the tools to be used, based upon the analysis of functionality and the perceived friendliness of the interfaces. Technology, on the other hand, will want to evaluate the underlying architecture and standards used by the vendor, including the schemas used for customer data bases and the integration capabilities offered by the tool. Who decides in this case? The short answer is not "the one that screams the loudest." Rather, this is a situation that calls for reasoned discussion and consensus building. You should always maintain the business arguments in the sphere of functionality. If your technical team is arguing for a different vendor or solution, you will need to validate if, in fact, the solution favored by the technical team meets the core business requirements (emphasis on "core"). In the end, this type of debate might have to be escalated in order to obtain resolution. However, even if it is determined that the business preferred option is the one to be followed, you should ensure that the minimum integration objectives can be met. In the case where the business is pushing for an external solution (e.g. a Microsoft based solution when your entire platform is Linux based, or a solution that relies on the vendor's proprietary architecture, etc), you will be required to explain the reason why you and your team find this type of solution unacceptable. If you are over-ruled, you should make sure to document the reasons behind your team's position and the expected impact the decision may have. In the end, this latter outcome rarely occurs. I believe that ninety percent of the time, a viable compromise can be reached.

The key aspect to remember is to engage the business as an equal partner; not as an order-taking entity, and to include them in the project as much as necessary; while clearly delineating who is responsible for what decisions. It's not always easy to engage the business this way, I'll admit, but the alternative of enduring a dysfunctional relation would place the success of the project in jeopardy.

Engaging vendors

Yes, vendors can be engaging and nice—especially when they invite you to dinner or to an all-expenses-paid conference. However, this topic is about how to engage with vendors—a topic that's often neglected in IT management books and forums. The more you rely on external products, especially in the context of IT transformation, where large budgets are at play, the more likely you are to have a long line of vendors knocking at your door. This is particularly true when vendors are desperately trying to meet their quarterly sales quotas. Don't feel pressured. It's up to you to manage the pace and mode of engagement with them. After all, the vendor decisions you are mulling over are likely to have a significant strategic impact, and ill-advised decisions could put you in a specific vendor prison for years to come. If you recall, in the section on tenets I suggested that any technology transformation strategy be architecture-led rather than vendor-led. You should always be in a position to choose or replace a vendor on the basis of your own needs and strict best-of-breed and cost considerations.

Still, it's not painless to switch vendors. Nothing completely removes the migration burden imposed when switching vendors or changing the reliance on a specific technology suite. This is why it's so important to identify early on which choices in vendor selection are strategic in nature, which are commodity led and which have a chance of becoming too 'sticky' or addictive. For example, the choice of a data base vendor for your core data is likely to be strategic. What about performance profilers? Not so strategic; especially if your tenets have you selecting best-of-breed components.

It goes without saying that the selection of a strategic vendor should be based more along the lines of choosing a strategic partner. It's more like a marriage than a one-night stand. You are not simply selecting the product but the partner as well. As a part of your vendor selection you are also selecting their vision, their culture and, most importantly, a business relationship between your respective companies. I am not going to sugar-coat it: If you decide to go with a strategic vendor for technology transformation, it's highly unlikely that you will go for a garage-operation outfit (the only exception being when you see an extraordinary value proposition or a potential acquisition play). Chances are that you will be engaging one of the "big-guys": IBM, HP, Oracle, Microsoft, etc. No need to apologize for this. You should, however, be wary of completely buying into their "integrated" value propositions. You should be able to maintain some degree of decoupling and freedom when choosing a particular vendor as a base. Yes, chances are that in the end you will most likely purchase more products from the strategic vendor, but you will be doing so because it makes sense (the add-on product integrates better, it is part of a bundle deal, etc.) and not because you have to.

In the case when you need to select a particular point solution suite (not necessarily a strategic vendor), you will likely pursue the Request for Proposal approach. Coming from someone who has been on the vendor side as well as on the RFP issuer side, I would recommend the following tenets regarding RFPs:

- Focus the RFP around your needs. Avoid over-elaborating the RFP with too much background about your company or other details not pertinent to the request at hand.

- Select only those vendors that you truly plan to consider for the selection process. Too often I've seen vendors invited to an RFP purely out of political considerations or to meet an imaginary goal of "minimum number of vendors to consider". Remember that vendors usually have to spend significant effort and money responding to an RFP, and it's not fair to have them go through the exercise if there is no chance in hell you're going to choose them.

- Analogously, don't have an RFP asking for the vendor's color of underwear. Be wary of assigning an RFP to someone who is overly technical or to an external consultant without supervision. These people are likely to request extreme details that, in the end, might not even be relevant to the assessment. Clearly, the details requested by the RFP should be commensurate with the value of the business opportunity. Even then, discussions about details should occur during follow-up meetings rather than via a response the size of "War and Peace".

- Make sure the RFP explains all the key requirements, constraints, and criteria you plan to consider in the selection. Don't make the RFP so general that vendors can simply answer with a very high level response (Goldie Locks' rule applies: "not too detailed; not to generic").

- Define the RFP selection process precisely and follow-through on it. Avoid sending the RFP out on Friday expecting a vendor response by Monday. You may believe this approach gives you a good evaluation element by determining which vendors respond quickly, but I surmise that a vendor's quick response is not an ideal indication of how well his product will meet your needs. The purpose of the RFP is to obtain a set of responses that you can compare against your requirements.

- Let's be honest, if you already have a product in mind and merely want to validate your choice, don't do an RFP. Don't waste the vendors' time. In this case, I suggest that you are forthright with the alternate vendor. Call them up, explain the context of your query, and give them a chance to explain why their product is better than the product you are planning to use.

Treat vendors well and give them the time they need. Their alliance and partnership will be essential to the success of your project.

Given that you are involved with a presumably large IT transformation, chances are that you will also be approached by a myriad of intermediate and smaller size vendors offering a variety of niche solutions. Now, I'm aware, when you're involved in your day to day activities, busy as hell, battered by the tremendous workload imposed by the running of a major project, these sometimes persistent calls from vendors with requests to meet, can become a major burden. As a busy executive, there is the tendency to ignore their requests and, frankly, to not treat them with the respect they deserve. I advise against doing this. I'm not saying you should meet with every single one, and risk death by PowerPoint, but I am saying that you should at least give a cursory glance to a vendor's proposition (or at least have someone on your staff do so) by quickly checking his/her email or web site. My experience is that 99% of the time you will be able to quickly determine whether or not the vendor's product has an immediate potential for application in your environment. If not, you should politely tell the vendor to check back with you at a later date. Most vendors appreciate this type of response and will gracefully go away—at least for the time being. Still, there will be those vendors who continue to persist and persist and persist. With pesky vendors you do have moral ground to be a bit harsher in your refusal to engage them.

There will, however, be those cases where you are intrigued by a vendor's proposition. Perhaps they claim to have a better way of managing services, or perhaps they have a way to improve your systems performance that is patented and exclusive? Some of these potential benefits might not be applicable to your project today, but may be needed in the future. You can ask this particular vendor to call back within a specific timeframe, consistent with your project plan, and give them a chance to reengage. There will also be those times when you are sufficiently intrigued to schedule an immediate presentation from a vendor in order to learn more.

It is difficult to provide a general recipe of how to deal with vendors since, as in all human interactions, there will be those who are excellent representatives and those who are in the wrong business and should be selling used cars instead of software and hardware products. Just keep an open mind and take an objective view of their sales style and value propositions. Vendors whose sales tactics are suspect (e.g. badmouthing the competition, giving deceitful datelines, etc.) should be avoided.

Finally, once you have determined that a vendor may be suitable to your needs, and you have established the requisite inter-personal trust and relationships with them, and have agreed with the overall terms of their proposal and engagement model, it's time to delegate the handling of the detailed negotiations and engagement to your vendor management team. If you are to preserve a degree of ongoing goodwill with the selected vendor as the project proceeds, other than for key decision selections you may be called upon to resolve, it's best to avoid direct negotiations with the vendor yourself.

In the end, the best vendors are those who become as emotionally attached and excited as you are about the success of the project. Remember, a good vendor can be your best ally.

THE EXECUTION & IMPLEMENTATION STEPS

Milestone Based Project Management

"The world is at a loss to find a thoroughly satisfactory reason for the persistence of the German in forcing the fighting about Verdun. To the world the German had been defeated in the battle long ago. Two months have passed since a German gain of any importance has been chronicled. In that time there have been many heavy attacks, prepared by artillery fire and delivered by infantry in their final stage, but all have shattered themselves against the wall of the French defense. The German losses have continued to be heavy, indisputably heavier than those of the French, yet the attacks continue. It is no wonder that the neutral world looks on in amazement and asks why."[49]

The battle of Verdun in 1916, during World War I, lasted nearly nine months and resulted in the deaths of about a quarter million soldiers and the wounding of another one million. As tragic as this battle was, another battle, the battle of Somme, designed as a means to draw German forces away from Verdun, resulted in even more casualties than the battle of Verdun (speak of "remediation"!). In the end the Battle of Somme resulted in 1.5 million casualties (around 400,000 killed). In the entire battle that took place from July to September of 1916, the British and French managed to perform an "impressive" drive of 8 Km (5 miles) from the original battle position.

While these battles remain the paragon of human stupidity, many large IT projects face their own version of the Verdun battle (proportions kept!). One can imagine the Verdun battle being run with one of those Task-Oriented project management tools: "Delivery of supplies? Check!" "Trench digging? Check!" Transfer another division of 5,000 men to the front to serve as cannon fodder? Check!"

---

[49] NY Times. May 14, 1916, Sunday

From a task-oriented, project management perspective Verdun was on track. Imagine if instead there had been quantifiable milestones, "By week five we should have advanced two miles". Perhaps that approach would have served the Generals better in understanding that their project was headed for failure.

What happened in Verdun is typical of many failing projects: a component fails and the management team expends resources and time in an effort to save it. When it keeps failing, more and more resources are applied, until eventually the entire project begins to be measured by the particular failure. This type of behavior has been well studied under the guise of the Gambler's Paradox, (the more one loses, the more one continues to gamble in the hope of recouping losses, resulting in even greater losses).

If the project is managed by appropriately partitioning it into discrete modules and deliverables, and with quantifiable milestone targets, then things need not be so dire. Also, it's important to understand that a transformation project is typically so complex that it is unrealistic to expect all of its components to immediately work as expected. Good project management entails tracking down and detecting when a sub-project is being derailed and acting upon this issue with a clear understanding of the problem. This means approaching the management of the project via well-defined milestones. Some of the milestones may be there to serve as a kind of "canary in the mine"—something like the delivery of a simple demo to test nothing is rotten in the "Kingdom of Projectmark". The key is to understand whether the component in trouble is critical to the overall success of the project or whether an appropriate do-over is in order.

Needless to say, the key to tracking and assessing the status and impacts of the project dynamics is the Project Management function. If the methodologies and lifecycles of project management in the context of IT projects are not clearly defined, this area quickly tends to become a hotspot of friction. Why? Because of a mistaken idea that anyone with working knowledge of MS/Project can become an IT project manager. A major transformation project is not the place to copy the style of shows, such as "The Apprentice", where contestants (usually celebrities) are given project management roles as a part of their challenge. In this show it does not seem to matter that a contestant must "project manage" a challenge outside his or her area of expertise.

In the world of IT, delivery managers with a systems and software background have traditionally been more successful in the project management role. The role of *generalist* project managers in IT projects is better left for peripheral or support functions (managing a training track, for instance). Moreover, IT development artifacts can be extremely detailed and, if micromanaged (something very easily done with task-oriented project management), can cause situations where you are not able to see the forest for the trees. Traditional Gantt-chart management with day-to-day tracking assessment of projects via red-yellow-green color codes may look good on status reports, but do little in ascertaining the true status of a project.

Secondly, there are projects and there are projects. . . Smaller projects need to be handled in a way that assures the necessary ingredients for success are available to the team leader with a minimum of red tape. Smaller programs can benefit greatly from rapid application development methodologies[50] and from early prototyping. What defines a small project? Well, I'd say one where you have no more than five people working on a deliverable for a maximum of four months is as good a metric as any. We're also talking about something that should not cost over one million dollars including labor, hardware, and software capital costs.

---

[50] Use of Agile methodologies should apply to the actual software development process; not to the architecture and design-making processes. Using pseudo-Agile approaches under the mantra of "code now, design later" often results in failure.

Then there are the medium size projects. These are projects that can take up to a year, or even a bit longer if the executives in your organization are prepared to take Prozac and give you more leeway. The core development teams for this type of project should never exceed the magic number of ten. These projects tend to fall in the ball-park figure of around three million dollars. A medium size project needs to be managed with a savvy combination of high-level project management controls and the appropriate placement of deliverable milestones.

Larger projects should basically not even exist. Why not? Well, a large project should be suitably broken into as many small and medium sized projects as possible. Ultimately, a large project should only exist in the talking points of the individuals responsible for your company's public relations and in the radar of the very small team responsible for integrating all the various moving parts.

So what is Milestone Based project management all about? Basically, it's the definition and tracking of measurable, well defined milestones. The difference between a milestone and a traditional project management event is the fact that the milestone should stand on its own as a deliverable. Completing a piece of code is not a milestone. Completing a prototype or being able to demonstrate a complete sub-component of the deliverable, are examples of milestones. If the event is something that can be shown to anyone outside the development group, and is considered to be at least a partial success, then it qualifies as a milestone.

Tracking milestones has a number of benefits:

- Missing a milestone is a clear signal that the project is not on track

- A successful milestone motivates the team by providing a clear partial result

- Milestone deliverables can provide some benefits sooner

282

- A successful milestone can motivate the project sponsors to continue their support of the project, even when faced with budgetary constraints

More importantly, there is no way to sugar-coat a missed milestone. While missing one milestone should not spell gloom-and-doom, a project with two or more missed milestones is a project that needs to be seriously reviewed.

In fact, you should always allow room in a large project to anticipate the failure of a specific component and to adjust for the overall delivery because of this failure. The solution to the quandary might range from starting again from scratch (assuming the initial implementation was proven wrong), to completely eliminating the subsystem and remediating by providing a suitable minimum set of capabilities from other subsystems.

Milestone driven project management is superior to task-oriented project management in large projects because it focuses on what's important while simplifying the view from the top.

On Tools & Methodologies

In one of Pablo Picasso's most famous quotes he states that it took him four years to paint like Raphael but a lifetime to learn how to paint like a child. Indeed, a sign of expertise is mastering one's field to the extent that there's no longer a need to abide by "traditional" rules. Great songwriters like Jon Mitchell, Bridget St John and Nick Drake (of "Pink Moon" fame) tuned their guitars in an unorthodox manner; inventing new chords which helped them create uniquely melodious sounds.

Once during a job interview, I was asked if I preferred project management tool X over tool Y. I could not refrain from answering, "The tool is irrelevant! What matters are the people who use it!" Perhaps my answer did not endear me to the interviewer since I didn't land the job, but the point remains: A better tennis racquet won't make someone a better player (I proved this pseudo-scientifically by purchasing an expensive state-of-the-art beauty made of graphite that didn't save me from losing game after game). Expensive tools don't necessarily ensure a project's success. In fact, blindly applying processes or fixed methodologies can easily be more of a hindrance than an assist.

Make no mistake, tools and methodologies are needed, but as a colleague once wisely said, "Only beginners need to follow every step and use every tool. Experienced people have gained the necessary knowledge to know when to bypass steps." Along the same lines, author, Phil G. Armour, makes this great point in his First Law of Software Process[51], "A process only allows us to do things we already know how to do". The corollary to his law is that you cannot have a process for something you do not know how to do or have never done. This scenario is especially relevant in the world of SOA as well as with other emerging technologies, where tools and processes are still immature and evolving.

---

[51] "The Laws of Software Process."—Philip G. Armour

It follows that a large IT transformation project will require the use of repeatable processes in those areas that have been tried before. However, in an IT Transformation, the biggest challenge is about creating something new. Processes in this context are not things that you must follow, but instead are things that you will have to create. Indeed, a key element of your IT transformation deliverables is to define and document the required processes to ensure repeatable success and continued operation of the new system.

How do you know which processes are needed and which aren't? The answer is to assess you own experience, along with the experience of your team, and figure out whether there is a need for a process—any process at all. If there is no need for one, then don't have one! You do not need to apologize for this. After all, experience is all about knowing how to separate the essential from the superfluous. Do you still read your car's user manual before driving your car? (Did you even read the manual at all?)

If you are dealing with a senior development team, you can only enforce so many processes. If, however, you are managing a team formed of very junior developers, they will actually benefit from the strong direction and clarity the following processes can provide. Now, let's not confuse processes with standards. You should definitely have a well-defined set of standards, and your developers will probably want to have them as well. Do, however, keep in mind an oh-so-true observation Mr. Armour makes in his book: "What all software developers really want is a rigorous, iron-clad, hide-bound, concrete, universal, absolute total, definite, and complete set of process rules that they can break".

You will have to assess how flexible you should be about these rules on a case-by-case basis. Ultimately, the range of tools and methodologies you will need to consider for a complex transformation initiative is rather large. At a minimum you should concentrate on standardizing the use of the following:

- Project Management Tools
- Documentation
- Collaboration
- Libraries and repositories, such as Service Registries and source code controls

There is some disagreement about whether to enforce standards of tools that are considered individual productivity enhancers. The line here is not always clear. Is a software development environment (otherwise known as IDE) something you should insist upon standardizing across your entire development group? I can assure you, programmers are typically compliant with much of the BS (Big Standards) they have to put up with (filling out those much-hated time reports, going through ridiculously convoluted change management processes, facing draconian purchase order approvals, having to change passwords every nanosecond, and so on.) but I have learned that trying to force them to abandon their preferred IDE tool is likely to set off a revolution of Bolshevik proportions. If you can identify two or three IDEs that everyone can use, then settle for those. You should be prepared, however, to accept that a year down the road, those IDEs will no longer be "the best", and there's sure to be a new kid on the block everyone's dying to use.

Conceding a bit on tools driven by personal preferences does not mean that you should give up on enforcing truly important enterprise rules. How you do version control, for example, should be standardized and not left to a single programmer's decision. Version control is a shared function after all. Focus on putting your foot down in the use of tools that have an enterprise scope and have to be shared by several people, as well as on tools that support repeatable processes. But make sure you identify these preferred tools as quickly as possible during the tenet-definition exercise. Failure to do so could lead to the adoption and rampant propagation of ad-hoc tools, making more difficult the alignment of your enterprise efforts. Still, there's nothing wrong with keeping the pulse on advances in technology so that, should a new valuable tool emerge, you can evaluate it in an objective manner and, should you choose, adopt it in a disciplined manner.

On Documentation

One of my biggest professional upsets occurred when, as a young programmer, I lost weeks' worth of documentation I had diligently created for a bank settlement system I had just completed coding. I had entered the documentation via a vanilla text editor (those were the days before modern word processors!) and, sadly, I had neglected to follow proper backup procedures. I had no versioning or backups since I always saved my file under the same name (I was young, remember!). A fateful evening, as I prepared to leave work, I pressed the Return key to save my nearly finished document back to disk. Literally, at the precise moment that the disk's red light began to blink, indicating the save to disk was taking place, the office experienced a brief electrical brownout. It was an outage that left me with a corrupt file, my extensive documentation gone, and fits of crying and cursing.

Other work priorities and accelerating deadlines prevented me from redoing the document with the gusto and detail I had invested in it originally. Upon delivery of the system, I arrived with a quick cheat-sheet that summarized the workings of the system. I then verbally explained to the users the key features and manner of use of my application. In the end, the customer was so satisfied than it dawned on me that the lost documentation wasn't even needed!

Still, internally I was disappointed. I had a sense of missing the complete deliverable. To this day, I imagine how cool and grandiose my eighty page documentation manual would have looked sitting next to the eight and a half inch floppies containing my code. In time, though, I became grateful for this twist of fate. As I proceeded to improve upon and change the system, I realized that the original documentation would have been extremely cumbersome to maintain and that, with each successive new release, would have become promptly outdated. In the end, the system worked so well and lasted so long that it never did require those eighty missing pages of documentation.

Keep in mind that my experience preceded those Apple Mac commercials from the mid-eighties bragging about how skimpy their manual was compared to the PC's. I was an accidental pioneer in the school of thought that believes, "when it comes to documentation, less is more". This view on documentation is now common. Nowadays, receiving software with documentation is as rare as receiving more than one bag of peanuts on a commercial flight.

The trend towards less documentation is only viable as long as you define and design the system with usability in mind. Creating a complex and cumbersome system, and then trying to deliver it with no documentation, is a sure ticket to perennial support hell. Fact is that some documentation will always be needed but, even in cases where documentation is required, you can now avoid paper manuals. That era is long gone. Focus instead on creating electronic files using modern collaboration systems. The best systems are self-documenting in each of its layers. When it comes to source code, for example, ensure that programmers follow best coding practices and the automated documentation facilities provided by the programming language you've chosen. The wealth of material created during the analysis of requirements phase, as well as in day to day communications (emails, file transfers, etc.), regarding definition of features and functionality can also be seen as living documentation. Make sure this information never becomes lost in disorganized team mailboxes, but is instead properly indexed, catalogued, kept and propagated via Wikis, so that it is always available via a web portal to the appropriate users.

Ultimately, the online help screens, demos, and training materials; along with the various PowerPoint presentations to executives and the team will constitute the core documentation of your system. Systems which are easy to use, capable of self-diagnosis and auto-recovery from exceptions, and which provide comprehensive and understandable status information, need not rely on bulky external technical documentation. This is particularly true in the realm of SOA where systems should naturally mirror the business processes they implement.

Beware of project plans with a standalone task for "System Documentation". Documentation should be an organic element in the design and development process; not a separate task. If anything, the company's business process documentation should serve as a suitable reference. Ultimately, the best documentation is an intrinsic part of the deliverable; not a thick manual collecting dust in some cabinet.

The Art of SOA Testing

Testing an SOA system is more of an art than a science. It's closer to trying to untangle the many strands in a bowl of spaghetti that checking for faulty auto parts on a production line. It follows that, if you have a system that's designed with circular interdependencies and referential loopbacks (as most sufficiently sophisticated SOA system are), classical testing methodologies that evaluate simple cause-effect relationships will simply not work.

What's needed is a completely new approach; one that will take into consideration the dynamics of a complex SOA system. This approach should encompass comprehensive testing in each of these testing dimensions:

- *Functional Testing.* The validation of functionality as perceived by the end-user.

- *Sanity Testing.* Ensuring that the system will behave as expected when faced with corrupt data or out-of-bound conditions.

- *Performance Testing.* The system is tested under various degrees of traffic loads; stressing it beyond its point of rupture to determine how the system will behave.

- *Availability/Recovery Testing.* What happens if you unplug that cable or turn off that server? How well does the system recover from each scenario?

So, you may ask, "How is this different from traditional quality assurance?" SOA testing does not remove the need to do testing along the traditional testing stages (Unit, Component, Integration and System Testing), but it does change the emphasis placed on each. When testing traditional systems, each component is unit tested to ensure that it does what it is meant to do. However, there is the assumption that, during the integration testing phase, any missed functionality or bug in that component will ultimately be revealed. This is natural, because in non-SOA systems there is no real way to know if each component is truly performing according to specifications prior to the integration. In non-SOA systems individual components can't be seen as fully-functioning standalone units of work, and holistic performance and robustness testing of individual subroutines or libraries is not really feasible.

Things are different with SOA. In SOA, unit testing becomes much more important. After all, if SOA excels at anything it is with the ease in which you are able to validate the sanity of any given service. With SOA, you can actually plan to test each service as if it were a complete deliverable on its own. That is, each service can be tested for performance, recoverability, and sanity.

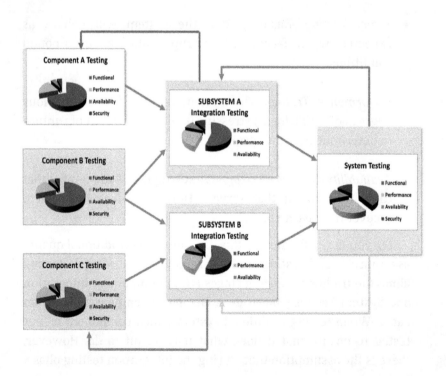

With SOA, performing a sanity-check of the system, without first ensuring that each service is in compliance with all traditional testing benchmarks, would be an exercise in futility. If the integrity of the parts is not proved, you can't expect to ensure the integrity of the whole. Each service should be completely tested for its ability to deliver the functionality it provides, its behavior when exposed to spurious requests, whether the request is garbled or contains request variables exceeding the valid data boundaries, and the efficiency of the service under varied conditions.

Ideally, component testing should be performed by an independent testing authority—the Service QA team—in order to validate that the programmer has actually delivered the component. This means that, in addition to the "unit testing" typically performed by the developer of the service, the Service QA team assumes responsibility for performing a "service test" that follows the same standards as that of a complete deliverable. That is, a service should not become part of the system unless it has first been certified by the QA team to be a part of the standard service development life-cycle.

Initially, the focus is to test the agreed service interfaces. However, as testing process progresses, you will also need to do performance and recovering testing on a per-component basis. Having this level of testing granularity also has the additional side effect of allowing you to keep track of a programmer's performance.

Knowledge that the services have been well tested, prior to moving to system level testing, will greatly simplify the integration testing. In SOA testing, integration and system testing ought to be more about testing core, service inter-dependencies, validating the overall system performance and dynamics, and testing the system capacity and scalability metrics.

If you see a thread here, it's that you should apply all testing cycles beginning with the service level. Think of testing as a fractal methodology, whereby the various testing harnesses that are ultimately applied to the entire system are first tried on each granular service and then applied to broader and broader service conglomerates. Testing with SOA is a true bottom-up exercise in that your key testing focus shifts from functional validity (at the service level) to a comprehensive system-level validation as you move up into coarser integration testing. Still, you should allow for the reality that testing at any given level will reveal defects and the need to correct them. SOA testing is not only a fractal process but an iterative one as well (see diagram). This testing approach aligns very well with rapid application development methodologies.

The concept of fractal testing demands the development of test scripts and test simulators that will enable the successive testing of services, components (represented by interoperating services), sub-systems (represented by an aggregation of services delivering well-defined business functionality) and, finally, system-level testing.

Testing thus becomes a recursive exercise that validates the viability of the system in a step-by-step basis. The functional testing, which includes the validation of the end-user functionality, including usability testing, can take place in parallel to the fractal testing exercise, but it is one that also requires a different focus. Since you will need to develop a comprehensive functional testing plan, you would do well to define the overall test patterns that you will apply to each gradient. It is essential that you define all known use-cases and give special attention to the more obscure cases. Programmers tend to test the most typical scenarios, and for the most part you'll rarely find bugs in these cases. The issues tend to appear when trying rarer use-case situations or unusual user interactions. In fact, you should make it a point to first test the rare examples and then work your way up from the rarer to more typical situations.

SOA testing enforces the introduction of suitable testing and system monitoring components that are not available for traditional non-SOA systems. The loosely-coupled nature of SOA systems requires that they exercise all available tools for network monitoring, service logging, and so forth. In the end, SOA testing is basically an exercise in system testing, even when simply checking the individual services. Because you can't expect to have all cooperating services available at once, you will need to allocate some project time to the development of service scaffolds to support earlier testing.

Remember, SOA testing is like dealing with Medusa—the mythical female Greek entity with serpent hair. Your job is to be the hero, Perseus, and confront this very frightening challenger, not by cutting off her head, but by giving her a great new hairdo.

Notes on Training

Ongoing training of all levels of your transformation team is critical both to the success of the project and the company. Ironically, training is often viewed as the ugly duckling in the budget cycle and as the line item that can serve as a "reserve cushion" when the inevitable need to make budget cuts occurs (you know the drill, around September, Finance begins to panic and all budgets must be reduced, "non-essential" travel curtailed, all hiring suspended). Training becomes a "use it or lose" it proposition, but who cares? Who wants to spend time on training during the last three months of the year when there are pressing issues to take care of, and the holidays are fast approaching?

Some companies have a training department, formally tasked to deal with training requirements for the organization. In my experience, these departments tend to focus on aspects related to the organization as a whole: company processes and values, inter-personal relations, and training in personal improvement areas commonly found in the catalogues offered by third parties. Depending on the company governance, you might have to work with the training department but, when it comes to IT Transformation, it's important that you take the lead in this area and do the transformation training yourself.

When it comes to transformation, training should be given much more respect. As with testing, training should be an inherent task in the overall transformation planning and not merely an after-thought. For starters, since you are dealing with the introduction of new technologies, make vendor training a part of any software or hardware acquisition. Everyone involved with the new technology should be trained in it. However, focus on train-the-trainer for those skills you wish to definitely preserve in house. In fact, vendor training arrangements ought to be primarily focused on train-the-trainer levels as opposed to basic 101 courses.

The same 101 training avoidance should apply in all cases. Invest in training that covers intermediate or advanced levels only. Don't waste time and money sending your people to introductory courses. Whenever possible, let them purchase and expense books and web-training programs dealing with introductory topics (the "Just-for-Dummies" series comes to mind). Permitting your team to read these books during company time is a much more efficient use of their time, and the company's money, than having them attend 101 courses. If this doesn't suffice, establish an internal training and mentoring program to enable transfer of knowledge from experienced staff to junior staff.

Also, don't forget the challenge of retraining those who will need to learn new skills due to the elimination of job positions caused by the transformation. Still, the same training principles should apply when retraining staff: don't allow introductory courses, focus on applied mentoring, etc. However, given that you are dealing with sensitive human resource aspects and morale issues created by the transformation, be aware that those individuals may approach training warily. They will certainly (and probably rightfully so) feel that their professional future is at stake, and that everything depends on their ability to become properly trained. In this case they deserve a more structured training and knowledge acquisition program. You must also work very closely with your HR department, as you may have to face the fact that a number of the staff will simply not be trainable. Tough calls will then have to be made about career progressions (transfer to another area, if appropriate, or departure from the company, if no other alternative exists).

An additional observation is that, if you check the training statistics for any given timeframe, you will notice that, typically, eighty percent of the training is utilized by twenty percent of the people ("Pareto's Principle" at work again!). Some employees shun all forms of training ("I don't need it!"). Others, however, become professional training participants; particularly those who like to make a career of collecting all types of certifications. You'll need to become more pro-active when developing training schedules for the team. It's best to circulate a training questionnaire and have everyone list their own training preferences (subjects, levels and available times), in order to gain a sense of how best to balance training efforts and to plan accordingly.

Attending conferences and conventions may or may not be considered valid training efforts. Depending on the specifics, attendance may be more of a boondoggle than a true training event. You will need to make sure the training budget is truly applied to efforts that will give expanded knowledge to the team.

Also, when speaking of training, it's best to think holistically about all affected constituencies. Don't forget the need to also train the users of the new solution, from the business stakeholders to the front end employee. Negotiate with the appropriate line managers so that you can tap their respective training budgets for this effort.

Finally, it should go without saying that it's often difficult to differentiate the training needed for the transition period from the training needed once the system has reached a steady state. Training for the transition period should be part of the migration plan and should be structured as a one-off basis. Planning for ongoing training will require further study and the appropriate development of recurring training tools, including web-based training, internal company training curriculum establishment, and even partnering with external training companies. Training programs and materials for steady-state are, in fact, part of the transformation deliverable.

Migration

Prototypical Migration Goals

The primary purpose of a migration plan is to successfully introduce the new system as seamlessly as possible. Simple migrations can easily accomplish this, but IT Transformation migrations require a more structured approach that must accommodate the inherent complexity and extended timelines involved. Migration is sure to drive transformation tasks and deliverables that need to be planned from the start; so defining the migration process once you're well into the transformation execution is a little too late. A transformation initiative should be planned with migration in mind as early as feasible. Depending upon the nature of your transformation initiative (is it an evolutionary change or a revolutionary scrap-and-replace effort?), you will need to approach migration with a clear set of goals. Typically, the migration goals you'll need to weigh represent a cost and focus compromise between the following objectives:

o *Value Acceleration.* The migration should provide benefit early on. One of the main reasons for the failure of a transformation project is extended delivery timeframes. This can cause the loss of support by new executive teams or financial pressures that lower its priority. When building a cruise ship, one doesn't attempt to have it set sail before it's completed. This is unlike IT Transformation. IT Transformation is more like a public works program where new infrastructure can gradually enable renovated sections. Waiting for the entire transformation initiative to complete before starting migration is unwise. Instead, as soon as feasible, you should endeavor to put into production the transformation elements that can deliver value. By doing this you are providing life support to the transformation initiative.

Some might argue that this approach carries the risk of the company being tempted to halt the remainder of the

300

transformation after a few of its main benefits have been enjoyed. But, if management is going to stop a project, they are going to stop it regardless. At least, by following this approach, the transformation will be seen as producing value. If the program is stopped under these conditions, you will be in a good position to defend the outcome. Also, if the initial value represents a significant percentage of the total value of the transformation, then it actually makes sense to give the company a chance to amortize its investment.

A more serious argument against the approach of accelerated migrations is that most transformation initiatives require heavy work on revamped infrastructure before they are able to deliver actual user-perceived value. This is a true conundrum and one that is very difficult to explain to business customers eagerly awaiting actual functionality. Again, it all goes back to how the project was planned, and how well you segmented the various infrastructure deliverables to accomplish a quick return in value. Ideally, you should have segmented the transformation into sub-systems. The horizontal layers provided by the infrastructure should have been segmented along levels of service and functional subsets that can be scoped independently. For example, perhaps you can deliver those data analysis results sooner by relying on a simple data repository that does not have the entire resiliency in place.

In general, it's best to avoid designing the program by first building the entire infrastructure and then delivering the applications. The end user does not care how nice the infrastructure is but only that the functionality and expected services are in place.

o **_Non-disruptiveness._** Regardless, your migration effort should never impact the day to day business. You should focus on reducing risks and minimizing the impact to business every step of the way. Furthermore, ensure that the migration meets the committed SLAs, otherwise you will likely earn a bad reputation from the users. There is nothing worse than having a newly introduced piece of technology fail, causing the credibility of your entire program to suffer. It's best to avoid "Big-Bang" migrations that require switching off the old system in order to introduce the new. Through millions of years of evolution, nature has given us the best example of a proper migration plan in the way a caterpillar transforms into a butterfly.

o **Efficiency and Cost Effectiveness**. The migration effort must not force excessive use of resources, whether human or material. Also, a migration effort that's too expensive is not going to be well received. Therefore, you should try to reuse as much of the existing capabilities as possible. Remember, most of the tools and resources needed for migration will, in most cases, be used only once. Migration is one of those cases where it makes sense to tap into external resources on an outsourcing basis. Finally, don't forget to make the required training a core part of the migration plan.

o **Timeliness.** Although I have stated that, if possible, migration should take place sooner rather than later, don't make the mistake of speeding up migration for the sake of political expediency. A migration has to be done in accordance with an overall timeline that properly balances the risks, the benefits and the application of resources. Migrate too soon, before the system is placed into operation, and you will have a recipe for failure. Migrate too late, and you're going to face a situation where any room for failure is effectively shut down

Avoid expedited migrations just to meet a deadline or for purely PR reasons. It's not worth it. Migration for migration's sake is going to leave your executive sponsors and the business people scratching their heads. There will be those times, however, when migration must take place at a purely infrastructure level that will not be apparent to the end users. When doing so I recommend keeping the PR at a minimum. The last thing you need is a disappointed sponsor wondering what all the brouhaha was about. Think about it, when was the last time your municipal government bragged about replacing those aging sewage lines?

The key thing to remember here is that migration timelines, how you manage the expectations for each migration step, and the degree of exposure you apply (PR), must align with the business requirements in order to accomplish your transformation goals. Accomplishing this requires defining a migration strategy that includes the tenets and principles to be observed.

Migration Tenets & Principles

The transition from the existing system to the target system is where the success or failure of the effort will ultimately be determined. Too often, wrong beliefs about the solidity of the target system encourage risky migration moves. Other times, people forget that the migration strategy must be adapted to the type of systems they are migrating from.

For example, while most of the current, enterprise-based legacy environments are based on Mainframe technology, it is also true that there are several legacy environments that are remnants of the "distributed" PC trends of the eighties and the "mini-computer" architectures of the nineties. The way you migrate from a Mainframe environment is likely to be very different from the way you migrate from a distributed Novell server farm. Already, any company that launched its technology base with first generation Web technologies is now facing the challenge of migration to more current technologies.

Not all migrations are equal. In general, the migration strategy you'll adopt will be a compromise of business requirements, technical capabilities, budgetary constraints, and cultural style. The outcome will define how aggressive or moderate the migration strategy must be and the detailed transition steps you must follow.

Pursuing general "sanity-proven" principles should help you in deciding on the specific migration strategy. This strategy will include more narrowly defined tenets and standards. At a minimum, the following migration principles must be considered:

- Make the migration a planned and controlled exercise. Ideally, make the migration in phases. Each migration step should have a clearly delineated objective. Avoid Big-Bang migrations as much as possible. You can minimize migration risks by making transition steps as granular and manageable as possible.

- A corollary to the previous tenet is that you shouldn't force an all-or-nothing migration scheme. The migration plan must be as flexible as possible, even if this flexibility adds cost or latency to the migration process.
- Be pragmatic. You don't have to throw away the baby with the bathwater. If you can, leverage technology capabilities from an existing system whenever possible.
- Decouple the migration process from specific infrastructure dependencies as much as possible. Use middleware layers or service encapsulation to minimize risk.
- While the end state will comprise novel technology elements and functions, from a functionality point of view, the process should follow a migrate-then-extend precept. In other words, don't try to solve world hunger in a single step. Oftentimes, a migration step is needed simply as a tactical scaffolding process for, say, data access and system management in preparation for future migration moves.
- Whenever possible, avoid disruption to components not being migrated. The two previous tenets should help you achieve this.
- Without a doubt, there will be new subsystems created by the IT Transformation that can be introduced without the need to migrate something old. These new subsystems can be introduced to the environment as soon as available and can be integrated to the legacy as needed via services. However, their introduction does not preclude the need for appropriate regression testing.
- Extract-Transform-Load (ETL) existing data as much as possible, but don't forget that a new system requires clean, well-structured taxonomies. A migration is a cleaning house exercise, and this is a step where you should focus on doing all necessary data cleansing and normalization work. Migrating old content can sometimes be more painful and ultimately more unfeasible than simply creating or acquiring new content from scratch. Data that is unreliable or incomprehensive must be re-entered as part of the migration plan.

- Ensure the migration process is complete and comprehensive in replacing all the appropriate legacy components and data elements. Remember that the end system will only be as strong as its weakest link. If you fail to migrate a key component that then becomes a bottleneck or causes some of the newly promised functionality to not be implemented, then the migration will have failed.

Finally, don't make "Falling Forward" a strategy . . .

<Rant>
The Myth of "Falling Forward"

Once, while planning for a migration, I suggested allocating some extra time as a cushion for migration fallback and other contingencies. Committed to a fixed deadline, the project leaders looked at me with worried frowns that indicated they weren't keen on the idea. "If we encounter a problem we'll fall forward. That's the strategy," a leader stated reassuringly. Everyone else nodded as if "falling forward" really was, in fact, a valid strategy.

Let me say this in no uncertain terms, when it comes to mission-critical projects, there is no such option as "falling forward." Falling forward is a sure way to break your jaw or lose your teeth. Perhaps when dealing with simple, non mission critical projects, we can "fall-forward", but when dealing with IT transformation of mission critical systems there's absolutely no way to "fall forward".

Mind you, during the life of a project there comes the inevitable time when one has to cut the umbilical cord of safety and make the new project final. That moment, when we finally cross the Rubicon, will come with its natural nervous uneasiness. However, we should be confident that the new project will work at least as well as the legacy it's replacing, and that we are comfortable in the belief we are not risking the life of the business. Even if one acknowledges that it is not feasible to expect absolute perfection prior to turning off the legacy system, it is paramount to cover the "derriere" of the migration by including well-planned contingencies and remediation actions. Then, and only then, can you abide by the Evel Knievel style of "falling forward".

</Rant>

Migration Strategies

IT transformation is a perilous business, and regardless of the emphasis you place on the quality of the product and the testing, failures will occur. It therefore makes sense to plan for failure.

The key elements to ensure controlled migration are:

- Doing the migration in phases
- Ensuring migration is fully reversible, at least during the initial phases
- Defining safe fall back points when doing a migration in the more advanced phases
- Allowing accelerated end run migration

You must ensure that, while attempting the migration, you don't leave any orphans behind—missing functionality, legacy processes and systems, etc. This validation is not trivial given that, in most instances, the new system will not be formally equivalent to the old. That is, the old system may have data bases, reports, process tools, and other features that aren't needed in the new system or that are being covered via different means. Ensure you leave nothing fundamental behind by assessing, on a case-by-case basis, the way the old system functionality will be provided in the new system. That is, map the system functionality as opposed to its components.

Additionally, you will need to keep a strong focus on data. If you are performing database conversions from the old system to the new, you should double-check that the new databases maintain all the needed index keys and metadata information. Perhaps the old system uses data that is a result of processes that are to be sunset, but you must also do a referential integrity check to ensure you don't end up neglecting important information, such as historical files or exception logs.

In order to achieve a flexible migration, you'll need to identify the various subsystems that can be moved without affecting each other. Also leverage the power provided by the new system's SOA capabilities to wrap and encapsulate old business logic and infrastructure as a process-step for a controlled migration.

In general, if you have a migration plan that allows for module-by-module migration, the greater the chances of ultimate success.

In addition to staggering the migration of components, you can reduce migration risks by automating key processes required during the migration. By now, you should see a trend: Migration planning may require a certain amount of extra development. Like the scaffolding work needed to create building structures, this work may support only the creation of the new system and may be disposed of once the new system is in place. Many project plans fail to account for the need to develop these migration support elements; thereby forcing delays or affecting the quality and viability of the process. No one likes to spend time and effort on work that may ultimately be thrown away. However, I have been pleasantly surprised to find automated processes, originally envisioned as merely assisting specific migration steps, become part of the reusable toolset for ongoing operations.

Having said this, the next question is how to best migrate a complex system? In particular, if we are following a 3-Tier architecture model, the logical question to ask is whether one should migrate everything at once or focus first on migrating the data? Some suggest it is best to first migrate to the new user interface; others disagree. Which is best?

Evaluating the SOA System Migration Alternatives

Even with traditional systems designs you have an array of options in which to approach your system's migration. The ultimate migration strategy will be driven by the specific business requirements and characteristics of your system. For example, you can do a so-called Big-Bang approach, or you can migrate on a functionality basis. SOA gives you the additional option of migrating on a layer-by-layer basis (Presentation, Process and Data layers).

A system wide Big-Bang migration should be avoided at all costs. However, if you are able to segment the target audience so that you can deploy the system with a series of coverage based "mini-big-bangs", you'll have a great option. For example, if you can "big bang" a particular region or country to the new system (the smaller, the better, as you are using them as guinea pigs), and then gradually add new regions as you grow in confidence, this can be a winning strategy.

Unfortunately, this type of coverage-based migration is not typically possible in transformed systems. After all, IT Transformation programs tend to be enterprise-wide and holistic in nature. In this case, you'll need to check whether it is possible to graduate the migration on a function by function basis.

In functional-based migrations, you gradually introduce specific parts of the presentation, process and data layers for each functional subset identified. An example of a functional based migration would be one in which you first introduce the new CRM system and then add additional functional blocks, gradually sun-setting the legacy environment.

In order to identify whether functional-based migrations are feasible, I suggest preparing a dependency map, and then list the specific subsystems that support each autonomous function. This dependency map will identify the services and subsystems in each SOA layer that can be deployed as standalone deliverables.

As you may imagine, functional-based migrations will demand integration of the legacy to the new function—at least for the duration of the migration. The good news is that you can leverage SOA's ability to integrate legacy systems to new systems via the service encapsulation (i.e. service wrappers) of old functions. The bad news is that this type of integration can quickly become so onerous or complex that functional based migration becomes unmanageable.

Another approach is to take advantage of the fact that well-designed SOA systems facilitate layer-by-layer migrations. This additional level of granularity is another tool in your arsenal. Segments of the new functionality are introduced gradually, via stepwise introduction of the new SOA layers. The question then is which layers to introduce first and how. In this case you will be faced with an array of choices. What you choose to do, once again, will depend upon the specific characteristics of your project. Following are sample pros and cons of each approach:

Migrating the Interface first.

This implies mounting the new GUI and interfaces against the legacy environment.

Pros

o   Technically this is a low risk approach, provided the new interfaces easily replicate the functionality of the legacy interfaces.
o   If the new GUI is friendlier and provides some GUI-specific functionality enhancements, you will be able to benefit from this early on.
o   It can be helpful in expediting the training of users on the new system interfaces.

Cons

o   The business team could be disappointed and confused by this approach as they will naturally expect improved functionality that might not be yet available due to the continued use of the old backend systems during the migration.

o You will need to train the staff prior to completing migration. Depending on needed future refactoring for processing and data layers, this training could become outdated.

o You will need to develop an encapsulated SOA layer so that the new GUI can access the legacy. This is essentially throw-away work.

Combining GUI and Processing Layers First

While theoretically you could first introduce just the processing layer, setting aside the legacy and data layers till a later time, this approach is usually not feasible. You would need to decouple your legacy presentation logic from business logic, and chances are that this would not be trivial. Accessing legacy data from a new processing layer is perhaps easier, but the new functionality will then be severely constrained by the legacy data schemas. A more practical approach is to move the processing *and* the GUI layers together as a unit. You will then have to take into account these considerations:

Pros

o You can introduce enhanced functionality that does not depend on the data layer. For example, new validations or user workflows can be added without changing the data model.

o Since data migration is usually the trickiest part, first migrate the combined GUI and processing layers and you will then be able to replicate existing functionality with minimum risk.

o You will more easily be able to fallback the system, if needed.

Cons

o The business areas will expect more functionality than you can provide: e.g. "Where is the internationalization?" This might not be feasible as long as you continue using ancient DBMS schemas!

Processing and Data Layers First

This is equivalent to a city building infrastructure (water mains, electrical wiring, sewage)s done in such a way that the population remains unaware of the changes happening below ground.

Pros

- o You can do the heavy lifting without troubling the users.
- o Easy to fallback migration since you are making the change in a transparent fashion to the user

Cons

- o You will need to emulate the legacy interface processes and, depending on the legacy system, this might not be doable. Note that I am not recommending that you modify the legacy presentation layer so that it can talk to the new system! This would entail too much throw away work.
- o Lots of work that nobody will notice at first. Management will be asking, "Where's the beef?"

Data Layer First

Frankly, the idea that your legacy processes will be modifiable to use new data schemas is not a practical one. At best, you can expect to do a pure data replication and transformation as an initial stage in what will become a Processing *plus* Data migration. Migrating only data is not a step I recommend.

In any case, any data migration effort should endeavor to create a Y-split that will ensure that legacy and the new data can coexist, at least for the duration of the migration. When migrating processes plus data, you should ideally create process switches that will allow Y processing (parallel processing) of transactions between legacy and the new system. It would be a trial run for the new system, with the plan being to eventually refresh the new system and start from scratch.

Under any scenario, make sure to use appropriate monitoring and control switches and to plan for fallback options. Place the appropriate switches to turn the new elements on and off as needed, and include the necessary logging to ensure you know what's going on.

The best migrations are those that get you to that brave new world in one piece; with satisfied business users and your sanity intact!

IT TRANSFORMATION LIFECYCLE. A WRAP UP.

To sum up, this book has suggested an IT Transformation life cycle that roughly has these steps:

1. Identifying the business needs
2. Defining the drivers for transformation and developing the business case
3. Evaluating the future
4. Understanding the scope and requirements
5. Defining the technology strategy
6. Making the Business Case
7. Applying SOA as a Solution Architecture
8. Defining the Services Taxonomy and the SOA Framework
9. Applying the right SOA approaches & techniques
10. Engineering the solution
11. Establishing the right governance and team
12. Executing on the project via appropriate Project Management techniques
13. Migrating to the new system

The diagram below summarizes this life cycle in terms of the purpose for each step:

We have now reached the end of the cycle. Upon successful migration, you and your team are entitled to celebrate and reward key performers. There is a lot to be happy and grateful for. However, you'd be wise to keep your cell phone active even as you celebrate. Initially at least, there is the likelihood that you will be receiving a large number of calls regarding deployment problems. Truth is, it will take some time before the system becomes truly stable. Indeed, it is a well know fact that all systems follow the so-called "bathtub shape" when it comes to failure rates:

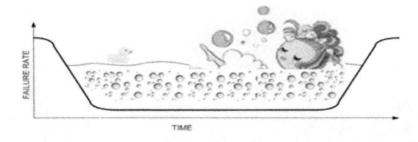

A new system starts with a high failure rate that will (hopefully) diminish in time until it eventually becomes stable. True, failures will never go away during the system's productive years (the "Rubber Ducky years", I call them), but the failure rate should remain reasonably low and under control. However, after cumulative changes and stresses of continued improvements are applied throughout the years, you will notice that, with the passage of time, natural entropy eventually takes its toll, making the system more and more unstable. Problems will arise; changes will become more difficult. This means that, in time, the system will become sufficiently stiffened and inflexible and ripe for yet another IT transformation!

That's right folks. From the moment you cut that ribbon debuting your new system, the system becomes "legacy". So, what is actually accomplished after all the effort and millions of dollars in investment to create a new solution? Well, if more things were done right than were done wrong during the transformation, the "length" of the bathtub will hopefully extend for many years. That's right you'll end up with an Olympic-size swimming pool! Also, the functionality of the new system will have been much improved. All in all, a good IT Transformation effort should be something to delight in, like a good swim!

A new cycle does not imply repetition or more of the same. IT Transformation is about progress. The true shape of progress resembles the picture below, an upward cyclic progression towards new solutions.

In the meantime, it's time to assess the success of the transformation. As the Y2K experience shows, this is not always easy to do.

Y2K and the Fuzzy Nature of Success

Ten years ago the world was abuzz with concern, holding its collective breath and waiting to see if the turn of the millennium, with its much touted Y2K bug, would usher in an end to civilization (now we find that predicted end has been bumped up to 2012!).

The so-called "Millennium Bug" was not actually a bug. Rather, it was a side effect of legacy applications written during a time when storing one character cost about ten million times more than it does today. Storing only the last two digits of the year did save tons of money for everyone using that super-expensive disk storage. The problem arose when legacy applications over-extended their welcome (as they are prone to do). Avoiding a negative impact on the information systems with the coming of the year 2000 became a critical imperative[52].

With a total worldwide estimated cost of $200B, the industry faced the challenge generated by the hype associated with this problem. In the end, the only firework displays arose from the beautiful millennial ceremonies held around the world. January 1, 2000 came and went with barely a hiccup.

Soon a narrative of how we had all been duped by the IT people with their "Y2K fear mongering" began to take shape. During a CNN interview, a U.S. senator who was opposing a new budget request stated, "Let's not have another Y2K project where we spent so much money and then . . . nothing happened!" I was thunderstruck. Leave it to a politician. His line of reasoning was akin to this, "I paid all that money in life insurance to cover me this year and nothing happened! What a bad investment that was!"

---

[52] I like to joke that if moving from the year 1999 to the year 2000 was tough, can you imagine the pain the Chinese had to undergo to move from the year of the Rabbit to the year of the Dragon? (No more millennium jokes, I promise)

All this got me to thinking about the fuzzy nature of success. For the most part, failure is easy to recognize (although good spin doctors can be masters at hiding it!), but success is not. Even endeavors that were clearly successful in terms of having accomplished their stated goals ("send a man to the moon and bring him back safely") have had their detractors: "The project was over-budget", "Astronauts died in the process", "The whole mission was a fool's-errand", "That money could have been used to solve world-hunger", et cetera, et cetera.

Typically, a project that succeeds in each and every one of its dimensions is either a chimera or something that was not ambitious enough to begin with. Every successful project will always have areas were things do not perform perfectly. This is especially true with complex transformation projects!

If the objective of a project is to deliver something tangible, you can at least make a compelling argument for its success. However, projects intended to avoid risks will always be more difficult to defend.

As far as that U.S. senator was concerned, the Y2K intervention had been a failure because he was looking only at the cost involved in the effort. He was unable to understand that "nothing should happen" was actually the criteria for success. The hundreds of billions of dollars spent to avert the Y2K bug was money that had been well spent, precisely because "nothing happened". There's also anecdotal evidence that the Y2K remediation efforts also drove beneficial application makeovers. The Y2K catastrophe was avoided, but sadly, I still hear many who should know better (CFOs. CEOs, TV pundits) making comments similar to that of the senator's.

I have witnessed many projects deprived of recognition simply because they provided a quiet success without drama. It is a sign of our times that projects that first fail and then eventually get fixed (usually at the cost of extra expense and time) are the ones that tend to get credited and celebrated the most (Hubble Space telescope anyone?). However, projects that deliver their promise right off the bat; especially when the promise is one of risk aversion, receive little or no recognition. I have witnessed projects that delivered and even exceeded their key goals, but because they failed to meet one hundred percent the original expectations (and I believe no serious project ever does!), they ended up being perceived as failures. This is particularly true for large projects where the magnifying lens of politically-driven critiques, from those keen on shooting down a successful effort or casting a bad light on other's accomplishments, happily point out missed milestones or highlight wrinkles in the delivery.

Still, it's worth remembering that lack of recognition is one of the main reasons seasoned professionals search for greener pastures. Success should always be assessed fairly and realistically and then celebrated. Every successful milestone and accomplishment should be recognized and used as a foundation for the next step up the ladder. And for every successful step we should also give thanks.

SECTION V
THE FUTURE

More than any other time in history, mankind faces a crossroads. One path leads to despair and utter hopelessness. The other, to total extinction. Let us pray we have the wisdom to choose correctly.

- Woody Allen, comedian and writer.

Trials

The first trial is to figure out what happens next? ✦ The world is now undrgoing major economic upheaval, and the question will be how to best identify the winning technologies of the future.

Techniques

New techniques are being created, and there is no question that the future will see more of what has traditionally been referred to as "Artificial Intelligence". However, it will not be known as AI, but rather by another name. After all, AI will forever be an invention of the future!

Tribulations

Let's live one day at a time, my friend. Facing and overcoming tribulations is what makes this adventure so interesting!

EMERGING BUSINESS MODELS IN IT

Until recently, the traditional IT revenue model landscape was a rather trivial one. You had your vendors—the companies that developed software or hardware products for use by other companies— and then you had your clients who consumed those products through straightforward purchasing or licensing; along with yearly recurrent maintenance payments. On the side you had consulting companies that served as honest brokers who helped define high level strategies. Add to this the providers of ancillary services, and you end up with most of the IT world of yesteryear.

This simple scenario is no more.

Emerging IT technologies and solutions are now being offered under a cornucopia of models; many of which are only now beginning to be fully understood. Beyond the "pay-if-you-can" models spawned by the availability of Freeware, Shareware and Open Systems, the future will see the delivery of software under a variety of revenue models, including Software as a Service, Software as a Function and, ultimately, the probable disappearance of software as a standalone product. Software-under-the-Hood represents a mindset shift wherein consumers are no longer buying software but rather the things that software can do. Companies providing these services will use a variety of revenue models: free plus maintenance, one-off purchasing, subscription, advertisement, charge per utilization and on demand, among others.

Google, for instance, makes the bulk of its revenue from advertisement; not from selling search software. Likewise, eBay's revenue model is based on its auction facilitation and commissions. Facebook's revenue model has flipped the world from what was originally the customer (i.e. Facebook friends) into the actual product sold to advertisers (i.e. you, my friend, are the product!). The generalization of SOA and the emergence of more sophisticated technologies will facilitate the drive to offer services rather than software. After all, subscribing to WebEx may give you a chance to download a client-side software module, but what you are ultimately paying for is the ability to schedule meetings on demand.

Make this recipe: Pour a liter of globalized Internet, season it with Cloud Computing, add a cup of SOA facilitated Software as a Service and a spoonful of Business Process Outsourcing, heat it all up with mobility technologies, and add some spice with the growing success of social networking as the new killer-app. What you'll have is a dish representing the transformative emergence of new players providing yet unheard of business services. Already it is difficult to categorize Facebook or Google under traditional definitions. In the future, the roles played by Microsoft or IBM will still exist, but even traditional software companies realize the need to reinvent their product and business models if they are to better compete under a continually changing landscape. The future will also see the disappearance of some of the typical roles in the value-chain (witness the demise of brick-and-mortar electronic companies such as Circuit City and CompuUSA). More importantly, it will see the emergence of newer models, redefined to better fit the changes in information economy. This type of change can only be ignored at the risk of the company's survival. If you doubt this, recall Wang Laboratories and its word processing flagship product as it faced the PC revolution, Polaroid as it confronted the digital photography revolution, or Blockbuster in the process of being busted by Netflix (pun intended!).

Just as earlier software models were based on the "a computer on every desk" idea, or the importance of search, or some other insightful tenet, the next Bill Gates, Larry Page, or Mark Zuckerberg will most likely be a child of what has been referred to as "The Infosphere[53]". The Infosphere is the paradigm in which all informational elements will be accessible from the electromagnetic digital media around us. You can think of the Infosphere as 3G or WiFi coverage on steroids: ubiquitous, always available and transparent. It will be the natural result of the pervasive advent of Cloud Computing and the continued decoupling from specific access devices[54].

Recall some of my earlier observations about how technology usually "evolves" from hype to invisibility as it becomes pervasive. Unlike Wired Magazine's recent claim that the Web is dead (at least from the perspective of the Web Browser as a universal client), I believe that the Web is very much alive. It's just that it is evolving into invisibility.

While the Web Browser is now embedded in the hidden fabric of technology, the delivery of new applications and content for new mobile devices on a demand basis, anytime, anywhere, is also becoming an assumed capability. There is an umbilical cord being formed between most of the world and the emerging Infosphere.

Already the rapid adoption of technologies such as Apple's iPhone and other Smartphones can be seen as earlier examples of this Infosphere. Mobile devices are today's equivalents to the PC's of yore, computers that you can carry with you at all times—prosthesis for the brain. Using these devices to interact with the

---

[53] Even though the term "Infosphere" has been around for a while (according to Wikipedia, since the 60's), it should be noted that IBM has recently created an Infosphere brand for one of their Information Management software products.

[54] A more esoteric term "Noosphere" has been used to describe a future global sphere of shared human thought—a sort of collective consciousness of human beings. I suppose some nice essays could be written on how the evolution and use of the Infosphere could be the technological enabler for a future Noosphere!

Infosphere from anywhere, anytime, is no longer a technology question but a commercial one. If only phone carriers did the smart thing and lowered those outrageous data roaming charges!

The key now is for someone to figure out the right revenue models to apply in the future Infosphere. Data roaming has got to go, ads on Smartphones might be fine, but I doubt the revenues they generate will help pay for the totality of the mobile services. Subscription or membership fees to social communities may emerge but, in the end, much will depend on what will become of the killer apps and services in the next few years. Figuring that out is the key.

How to do this? Remember the suggestion I made about how best to predict the future of technology? The secret is to find the synergy. That is, visualize the usually unforeseen ways parallel advances will combine to form a new game changing event.

Find the synergy, especially as it relates to how the future may impact either your business or your IT strategy, and you will be on the road to defining your follow-up transformation strategy. If you agree that we are in the midst of an accelerated transition to an Infosphere paradigm, then it makes sense to try to imagine what the likely future business opportunities of such a transition will be.

SOFTWARE AS A SERVICE (SAAS)

True, the traditional view of software commercialization may go the way of the slide rule and the typewriter, but there will always be a need for the services that software provides. However, the ability to access software services depends heavily upon the enabling of shared infrastructure by companies providing hosting, data storage, and networking and telecommunication services. This infrastructure should continue to move towards standardization to facilitate the kind of "plug-and-play" flexibility the market demands. The ongoing standardization of emerging "middleware" technologies, supporting distribution, and access of services via service interfaces, will have an impact comparable to that of the world-wide-web.

Software as a Service (SaaS) is exploding nowadays. Google's application suite is an instance of SaaS providing generic horizontal services. Function specific products such as GoTo Meeting and WebEx for meetings along with Sales Force Automation, a more focused horizontal SaaS tool, have been gaining significant market share over traditional competitors. This explosion also includes vertical industry applications. Thousands of hotels use TravelClick for reservations; the health care industry has hundreds of SaaS applications for patient management, ambulance services, etc. Plus remember, ultimately, Facebook and Twitter are nothing more than social media SaaS environments.

Despite all this, SaaS is not a panacea—at least not yet. The model has to mature and, as a result, the range of options, costs and enrollment mechanisms is still too varied and complex. Most significantly, SaaS systems need to find the right balance between functionality and flexibility; plus the model presents a list of new security considerations. Are you comfortable having your company's most sensitive data out there, somewhere in a cloud?

Take heart though, standardization breeds commoditization and, as a result of standardization, in the future there will be a consolidation of service models and expected features. This consolidation is also being facilitated by the emergence of the "Cloud Computing" model that essentially makes the infrastructure services supporting SaaS invisible to the user. Large vendors are already introducing sophisticated virtualization, security, and management tools that will enable SaaS providers to offer an expanded range of configuration and portioning models to their clients.

But SaaS does not necessarily need to be wholly based on a centralized service delivery. The paradigm also applies to distributed services such as those provided to smart-phones. Already the paradigm for the booming smart-phone market is that of downloadable "apps" with modules providing functions. Some apps run entirely standalone, but others provide a front-end that can access powerful backend systems. Google is making available a suite of shopping apps that instantaneously leverage the powerful Google server environment, displaying reviews, alternative pricing and so on. The popular Shazam App is a complex application that tracks and recognizes tunes being played. There are also a myriad of widgets for all sorts of things. The user, particularly the younger user, no longer views these apps as software. The kid downloading a ring tone is not buying software or data but an experience. The fact is that many apps providers are now moving away from straight purchase models toward service subscription or ad revenue models.

Now, I've already stated that the SaaS paradigm appears to be a consumer of services. The question is how will your company fit into the upcoming Infosphere economy, and how will this impact your very own IT strategy. What kind of SaaS is your company planning to offer, if any? When you envision the IT system of the future, you need to ascertain how you are going to play in this brave new world: as a provider of software services, a user or both. This includes defining the manner in which you will make your IT services accessible to users. When doing this, you will be happy you followed a comprehensive SOA strategy as the baseline for the IT transformation.

In a way, SOA is a necessary (although not sufficient) element for the habilitation of SaaS. SOA systems intrinsically create services that can be selectively commercialized under SaaS. The SOA services become SaaS services. In other words, the concept of Software as a Service will evolve into the more prosaic "Service as a Service." This statement seems obvious, but it has deeper implications. SOA systems usually consist of a complex interplay of components. For example, Provider #1 of service S1, may access a second service, S2, from provider #2, who may depend on service, S3, from Provider #3, and so on. The user need only see the integrated service provided by provider #1 and can be oblivious to the value chain behind the original service request. In essence, SOA enables the replication of the way traditional value chains operate, but by using digital means instead. Just like real markets, SOA systems can become incredibly complex. Their support has to be structured to allow quick resolution of issues presented by complex, intertwined value chains. There has to be clear accountability lines.

Having said this, I am doubtful that mission-critical IT systems should ever rely entirely on external SaaS services. I firmly believe that technology (some technology anyway) will always be used as a weapon to attain commercial advantage and to enhance one's competitiveness. Don't buy into the idea that *all* software will become so commoditized that it will be something you can always provision externally—a simple utility provided by SaaS. What about using general purpose business software, such as ERP systems? Use them as a commodity. These systems do what they say they do. Being able to process payroll or accounts receivable internally is not going to give your company a competitive advantage (I'm sure though that there are exceptions to this!) But there will always be that little extra function, or cost cutting algorithm, or automated innovative process that will not be available externally. This is either because it represents a core intellectual property asset of the company, or because the cost or risk of placing it in an external environment is not acceptable.

The question then is, "What services should you endeavor to create rather than purchase?" The answer to this question depends on an analysis of what you are trying to get out the service: data, content, or wisdom?

Data, Taxonomies, and the Road to Wisdom

In earlier days, computing was all about "Data Processing". However, with the progressive sophistication of hardware and software, the term "Information Systems" became more prevalent. Initially the platonic ideal was to eventually have computers process the world's information the way humans do, except much faster. This goal was known as AI (Artificial Intelligence), and during the eighties there was a strong attempt to applying this objective to narrow domains of expertise under the guise of "Expert Systems". Expert Systems underwent a hype phase, only to fade away as we came to learn that the heuristics needed to replicate the way humans process and organize knowledge is dependent on contextual and even subjective information rules. In other words, we humans process knowledge in a way that is often inaccurate, biased and intuitive, but which we find acceptable for our normal existential needs. Automating our style of "fuzzy" logic will give us computers with the capability to err the same as humans do. Computer results that are at times inaccurate would not be a desirable outcome for someone spending millions of dollars on a system. No, information interpretation and expert understanding will remain a human chore for decades to come even as computers continue to better facilitate the rapid analysis of data.

You have probably noticed that I have been using the term "Information" in its most generic sense. Information can often be "misinformation". Yet, misinformation or even lack of information is, ironically, a form of information (a dog that failed to bark was a clue Sherlock Holmes used to solve a crime). When implementing information systems it does help to classify the type of information we are dealing with. We should be able to define the most appropriate ways to acquire it, handle it, and interpret it. In order to do so, we can make a distinction between the concepts of Data, Content, Knowledge, Understanding, and Wisdom. Each of these concepts represents a progressive evolution in the quality of the information and is on the road to Wisdom:

1. **Data** is primarily raw figures and "facts". By nature it is voluminous and difficult to cope with and so is best stored and communicated in a mechanical way. There is nothing implicit in the concept of data that makes it right. It can be completely wrong. The old GIGO adage (Garbage In/Garbage Out) captures what ought to be the highest priority in the automation of data: ensuring that the data inputted into the system is correct.

2. **Content** is data that has been collated, ordered and classified. That is, Content is Data plus its Taxonomy. As such, content possesses a higher level of value than raw data, particularly as the relationship between different sets of information is leveraged for increased quality and ease of maintenance.

   A note of clarification, Ontology is a specification of the characteristics of a domain:

   o   Things that begin with the letter D
   o   Animals that have four legs
   o   Things that are used to write with
   o   Children toys

   Ontology is what you apply when defining your data sets or when identifying the database schemas you plan to create. Taxonomy, on the other hand, is the categorization or classification of entities within a domain. Consider the following taxonomies used to describe the animal kingdom.

   Linnaeus Taxonomy:

   • Kingdom: Animals, Plants, Single Cells, etc.
   • Phylum: For Animals: Chordatas, Nematoda (worms), etc.
   • Class; mammals, amphibians, aves. . .
   • Order: Carnivorus, cetaceous. . .
   • Family: Ursidae (Bears), Felidae (cats), Canidae (Cats). . .

- Genus...
- Species...

In "The Analytical Language of John Wilkins," Jorge Luis Borges, the famed Argentinean writer who belongs to the ontological set of writers who deserved to win the Nobel Prize but didn't, describes 'a certain Chinese Encyclopedia,' the *Celestial Emporium of Benevolent Knowledge*, in which is written a taxonomy in which animals are divided into:

- those that belong to the Emperor
- embalmed ones
- those that are trained
- suckling pigs
- mermaids
- fabulous ones
- stray dogs
- those included in the present classification
- those that tremble as if they were mad
- innumerable ones
- those drawn with a very fine camelhair brush
- those that have just broken a flower vase
- those that from a long way off look like flies
- others

As you can see, there are many ways to define taxonomies. It is the responsibility of your Information Architect (you do have someone in this role, don't you?) to ensure the agreed taxonomy relates to your line of business. Once you define and apply the taxonomy to your data, you have Content. With the advent of the Web, we have moved from the Age of Data to the Age of Content. "Content is King" is more than a cliché. Content was the engine that generated the fortunes of companies such as Yahoo and Google.

Until recently, the key differentiator between a popular and less popular web site has been its availability of content. But Content requires skilled use or the expenditure of considerable time to extract this value. It is an area that most companies would do well to handle in a structured manner. Dedicated content management groups should be part of the modern governance supporting your company's information systems today.

3. **Knowledge** is what is produced when the information is placed in context, and the resulting significance of relationships within the data is realized. The addition of contextual information requires some element of human input; so the progression to this stage will probably never be possible with the use of computers alone. If you want to see the difference between Content and Knowledge, I suggest you try this exercise: Go to **google.com** and enter "**IBM Apple**". You will get content listing all sites where IBM and Apple are discussed. Now, go to **wolframalpha.com** and enter, "**IBM Apple**". You will get a digested and structured response comparing these two companies to each other. The former is content, the latter is distilled knowledge.

Production and discovery of knowledge are part and parcel of many industries today. Organizations, such as Gallup, exist to mine data and content; producing knowledge on a variety of topics. Voting trends, consumer preferences, etc. are examples of mined knowledge. Business Intelligence, associated Data Mining technologies, and the more recent Internet-driven "Collective Intelligence" applications are examples of the more recent trends in the automation of knowledge acquisition. We are on the verge of moving from the Age of Content to the Age of Knowledge.

4. **Understanding** is realizing the significance of relationships between two or more sets of knowledge and deriving prime

causes and effects from this knowledge. While Gallup may unearth the knowledge that 33% of voters are likely to vote for a particular candidate, the understanding of why they lean that way is something that information systems today can only hint at. Understanding remains an endeavor only humans are adept at. Understanding cannot yet be performed by computers. Understanding is how pundits and large consulting/advisory outfits make their money. Companies like Gartner, your typical TV pundit, or writers of popular science or "How To" books are giving you distilled understanding.

5. **Wisdom** is the ability to distinguish between good understanding and faulty understanding. The fact is that understanding can be the result of wrongly extracted knowledge, which may come from bad Content or Data. In his mind, Hitler "understood" that he had a "Jewish problem". Needless to say, his understanding was the result of bias, prejudice, and cooked up analyses. For all his earthly power he was the most unwise of men.

Wisdom represents the highest level of value in the information progression. Wisdom is not always objective or static. It can be subjective or dependent on the cultural environment or on transitory circumstances. That's why it's unlikely that we will ever be able to codify wisdom within computers and why the idea that these future computers can act as judges is just not feasible.

Wisdom can be applied for material or spiritual benefit. Yes, Wisdom can be applied for profit and business advantage. However, just because something is understood correctly, does not dictate whether it is right or wrong. Beyond wisdom we enter into the realm of morality and philosophy. What might be considered a wise choice by some, might be considered immoral by others.

But I digress. . .

Whether in the future computers will be capable of Understanding (much less Wisdom), is open to debate. There is much we do not yet know about how we humans think or about the nature of our cognitive processes. What's certain, on a more pedestrian context, is that you can use the taxonomy of information to help you distinguish between what is data and what is content, in order to better map the specific goals and governance of your information systems. It's a start.

INFORMATION DISTILLERS & AGGREGATORS

As we move toward the enabling of understanding and wisdom in the years ahead, we should expect an increase in the commercially available services leveraging these new automation models. For example, consulting is already an embedded part of services provided by professionals. However, in the future, consulting will evolve into a set of online services provided via moderated access to human experts or via access to software-based expert systems. Whether they are made of flesh or metal, these bona-fide Information distillers will be ready to augment your thirst for information at the push of the button and the opening of your Pay-Pal wallet.

Emerging Information Distillers will successfully locate and turn the required information into "understandable bits" which can be digested by customers under several revenue models. While, in principle, these services are not fundamentally different from those provided by traditional consulting entities such as the Gartner Group or your corner H&R Block, the difference is that they will be democratized and available to individuals and companies alike. For example, in travel, distillers will not only publish travel magazines (electronically or via hard-copy), but will also package tours and offer special negotiated travel deals. (Tripadvisor.com can be seen as a first generation distiller leveraging the power of social networking.) However, information distillers in the future will be able to provide personalized advice either from paid human experts or from next generation expert mining tools.

As electronic commerce becomes more pervasive, and the speed and specialization of business increases, proxies or electronic avatars will become more prevalent. Functionally, an avatar will not be much different from today's travel agency role when booking travel for a client. However, whereas today's agencies do not represent the interest of the traveler (agencies, in principle, represent the interest of the supplier), future avatars will act as your proxies—your electronic "mini-mes"—working automatically under business and engagement rules that you'll define so as to be presented with the best deal.

As artificial intelligence becomes more mainstream and as technical standards, facilitating electronic brokering, are implemented, these avatars will become virtual software entities capable of representing you, the consumer. Eventually, avatars will completely broker and execute the best possible arrangements for you.

This type of avatar is already a reality in the hectic world of electronic trading, wherein complex software algorithms make nanosecond decisions on whether to buy or sell stock assets. It's best to be forewarned that, as proxies become more commonplace, we must be prepared to face the consequences of relying too heavily on software avatars endowed with automated decision making permits. On September 7, 2008, in an already volatile and jittery financial setting, a Florida newspaper *accidentally* entered an old web article detailing United Airline's 2002 bankruptcy. Google, all-obligingly, indexed the article and distributed it to e-mail subscribers who had requested alerts on news regarding this airline. This is where automated software proxies took over. The stock trading software scanned the article and found the keywords "bankruptcy" and "United Airlines" and automatically ordered sales of UAL's stock portfolio. Other software robots, responsible for monitoring unusually large trade volumes in the stock market, quickly took notice of the sudden sale of UAL stock and proceeded to sell their stock. The outcome was a selling frenzy that resulted in more than a one billion dollar loss for UAL stockholders. The Securities and Exchange Commission began an investigation to determine responsibility. After all, who was at fault? Was it the Florida newspaper? Google? The developers of the software? The companies that transact stock in such a perilous manner?

Clearly, we are entering a brave new world that requires added protocols to safeguard software agents from going rogue and to answer the myriad concerns related to protection of privacy; not to mention the expected security issues related to fraud and software impersonators, with the logical progression to identity theft. In the meantime, if you are on the supplier's side, you can start designing your systems to enable this future "Electronic Mini-Me" concept. Define and be prepared to have the appropriate services and architecture layers that can leverage the deployment automated selling brokers.

As you define this architecture, you will have to rely heavily on the implementation of publish/subscribe systems and asynchronous response patterns. You will also need to focus on implementing a sophisticated combination of Business Rules and Business Process Management based systems that can allow your business team to easily configure and define the automated way broker services will be made available to your customers. For example, these brokers could be configurable to making distressed inventories available electronically. They would also be able to dynamically price on-line offers with available inventory, via dynamic revenue management rules, as applicable. Think of how an electronic auction process on eBay.com works but on steroids.

Just as the electronic avatars discussed here are a practical instantiation of the move towards cyber-understanding, future systems applying basic rules-of-wisdom will emerge. True, wisdom will always be a purview of humans and not computers. However, following the precepts of "Wisdom of the Masses", we are now experiencing the benefits of the wisdom provided by virtual communities; areas where we find reviews on a broad range of areas, "How-To" tips, and better deals. A case can be made that this wisdom is an emergent property, resulting from the aggregation of large catalogues and information, and the associated tie-in of user areas and access to content. These areas are best represented by "Virtual Malls" such as Yahoo.com, Overstock.com and Amazon.com, but they are also expected to rapidly merge with social networking sites in the so-called Web 2.0 world.

There is already a linkage between merchandiser sites and places such as Linkedin.com, MySpace.com, and Facebook.com. This integration will ultimately occur via business partnerships or mergers, but it will be initially accelerated by automation known as Collective Intelligence, the process that combines the behavior, preferences or ideas of a group of people or sites to gain new insights[55].

Analogously, it is to be expected that, as this vertical industry matures, we will continue to see the emergence of portals specialized according to industry. That is, we will see "electronic virtual malls" integrating offerings, on the one hand, and acting as "aggregators", dealing with the specific industry groupings. The aggregators will be able to convert the volumes of data found on the Internet into useful information. This information will be presented in a form that will be customized for information seekers as a consolidated package of knowledge. The automated assembly of related knowledge, designed to fulfill the "seeker's" goals, can be related to the area of specialization of the site. This trend will be evident first in consumer-facing verticals such as travel sites Expedia.com, TripAdvisor.com, Travelocity.com and various other special-domain sites such as MusiciansFriend.com and WebMD.com. The question you'll need to answer is: how can you make your company a part of this new world.

---

[55] Programming Collective Intelligence—Toby Segaran

AND IN THE END . . .

One of my favorite treats, as a young child growing up in Mexico City, was a candy known as "Suertes" ("luckies"). This was a paper roll containing little round candies (known as "chochitos") and a hidden, plastic toy (the toy was the lucky surprise). The plastic toy was usually a cheap spin top or a soldier figurine, and the chochitos could be consumed in a single bite. It was a cheap treat—think of it as a third-world version of the British Kinder Eggs. Less third-world was the way these "Suertes" were wrapped. The roll was made with discarded IBM punch cards wrapped in wax paper so as to prevent the diminutive, round chochitos from falling through the holes formed by the used card's EBCDIC encodings. (Of course, as a child I did not know of the existence of punch cards and so always thought how stupid it was to wrap the chochitos with cards full of holes!)

After I discovered the cards were really eighty column data encoders, I came to this realization: Data is very fungible. It can even be used to wrap candies!

Enter the new millennium...

Forecasters tell us that human population reached the seven billion mark at the end October/2011—during Halloween, which is appropriate. Even if you find it somewhat frightening that the world population doubled from my chochito candy days, the fact remains that data storage capability has grown exponentially during the same period. While 80 byte punch cards were the norm in the late 1960's, nowadays you can purchase an 8 GB thumb drive for ten bucks.

This is the second lesson: Storage capacity is on its way to far outstripping the maximum information content humanity might be able to generate.

Not only has digital storage become a dirt-cheap commodity, but advances in compression and search algorithms have turned storage into a dynamically accessible asset—a true online source of information. The advent of the Cloud is likely to cause a major flip in the way we envision data storage and how we access information.

Arthur C. Clarke's famed third law states that any sufficiently advanced technology is indistinguishable from magic. I would add a fourth law: *The best indication that a technology has matured is when it has become invisible.*

Think of electricity, the water supply, or even the internal workings of an automobile. In all these cases, we operate these technologies almost obliviously in a Switch On/Switch Off basis.

For the most part, technologies follow a well-defined life-cycle that takes them from inception in a lab all the way to invisibility. The time spent within a cycle is technology-dependent, but the average time to maturity can span decades.

Many futurists believe that one of the main evolutionary aspects of computing in the future is to also make it invisible—embedded in the fabric of the thing we call "reality". Instead of screens, keyboards and mouses, users will interface with computers in a seamless manner.

The ultimate interface achievement will be to hide the fact that a user is accessing, or even programming, a computer. This later attribute is often confused with the famed Turing Test of Artificial Intelligence (AI). However, the Turing Test establishes that Artificial Intelligence will only be achieved when a computer is able to hide the fact that it is a computer when communicating with a human in a *broad* domain. AI has been long in coming, and many believe it to be still a century away; others that it is around the corner. But AI requires common-sense and pattern recognition capabilities if it is to work, and progress has been fairly slow on these two fronts. I tend to agree that AI as originally envisioned will take a long time to be achieved. However once it does happen, AI will not appear as an overnight invention;

instead, we will see continual improvements in computer systems that gradually appear to make them smarter and smarter.

Think about your car's navigation system, which already appears quite smart, and of the novel capabilities of your digital camera, such as face recognition. Pseudo-AI behavior in narrow knowledge domains is arriving thanks to the growing computer power made possible by Moore's Law. Consider that in the beginning it was assumed that a chess program, capable of beating a chess grandmaster, would require a full-fledged AI system. However, this feat has been achieved thanks to the use of the brute-force represented by massive parallel processors and the ingenuity of sophisticated heuristics; not by the invention of a human mind emulator. In May, 1997 an IBM computer nicknamed, Deep Blue, beat World Chess champion Garry Kasparov much to the chagrin of the Grand Master who found it difficult to accept he had been beaten by a computer! To all intents and purposes, playing against a chess computer does convey the eerie feeling of competing against an "intelligent" device. The machine behaves like AI, but it is actually based on the narrow domain of chess-playing, making the computer an "idiot-savant" of sorts.

As discussed earlier, most transformative technologies are the result of synergistic combinations of various evolutionary advances. To the degree that we see continued advances in user interface paradigms as represented by gestures ala iPhone or voice recognition, combined with improved algorithms and availability of ultra-fast communication bandwidths, we will see a wealth of interesting applications; many of them with true transformative effects. For example, enhanced user interfaces in the future, combined with more advanced artificial intelligence heuristics and the merging social networking paradigms, can deliver a suite of Virtual Sidekick capabilities:

- Attaining complete knowledge of your preferences. In fact, complete knowledge of you as a person.

- Exercise controlled empowerment to take independent action.

- Have immediate access to all sources of information available electronically. The ability to alert you to those specific developments that interest you, such as breaking news or TV specials.

- Adopt different service personalities based on context.

- Monitor actions performed on your behalf in a non-obtrusive manner. Certain events will automatically initiate pre-approved actions. For example, a calendar event schedule change will automatically trigger an action from your Virtual Sidekick to initiate a flight change.

This type of automated avatar will spawn new industries just as the Internet has spawned the multi-billion dollar Google. The Virtual Sidekick is but one example of a concept that should be propelling your R&D efforts. There are others. For example, it's logical to imagine a future in which web access devices will have become so small and non-intrusive that they can be implanted into our bodies. In a world permeated with wireless access to the Web (the" Infosphere" I discussed earlier), imagine a scenario where you can search and access the Internet by simply thinking about it; where you can "Skype" your wife and talk to her using your own embedded phone. You won't even need to speak to communicate. A microprocessor embedded in your brain will convert your brain waves into speech. Think of this scenario as technology-enabled telepathy! These and other interesting possibilities can be extrapolated from the intriguing technology forecasts by author, Ray Kurzweil[56].

There can be no doubt that the transformative effect of such future inventions will generate heated debates about the ethics

---

[56] "The Singularity is Near: When Humans Transcend Biology" by Ray Kurzweill.

and dangers associated with their use, but that's a subject for another book.

This section has the same title as the last song from history's best pop/rock group for a reason. In the end, I want to close this book with an optimist note regarding the future. I firmly believe that technology is the Noah's Ark of the twenty first century, and that humanity will continue to advance in its relentless march toward the stars (possibly using an evolved form of SOA!). No one knows what the future holds. The only certainty is that we will survive and will continue to encounter a common human cause. Along the way there are sure to be new business opportunities amenable to emergent IT capabilities and, along with them, new challenges in the process. So, continue on with your IT Transformation projects. Do position yourself and your company for that next cycle, and by the way, feel free to drop me an email to let me know about that great money-making idea of yours!

APPENDIX A
EXAMPLES OF TENETS & STANDARDS

Defining tenets and standards is ultimately a process that should be consistent with your company's higher level directives. For example, if the technology strategy is to ultimately outsource everything because your company does not see technology as a mission-critical component, then it doesn't make sense to have tenets that push for obscure nonstandard technologies.

The power of tenets is that they will define the framework under which your multi-year, multi-departmental, multi-disciplinary effort will operate. To achieve a high degree of congruency without spending a great deal of money on the creation of a "Tenet-Enforcement-Police", you will need to structure the communication of the tenets around well-defined categories. This classification will ensure that your team is "burdened" only with those tenets that are relevant to them.

The tenets and standards you will ultimately choose must be aligned with the specific strategies in your organization. The following tenets are given as examples only.

GENERAL TENETS

Protect and use Legacy as appropriate	Replace old systems as quickly as possible
Revamp infrastructure first; then look at applications	Focus only on applications
Buy all best-of-breed components, if possible.	Build at the application layer and purchase integrated vendor solutions for systems
Do all development using internal resources and augment with contractors only as necessary	Off-shore all development
Preserve as many legacy components as possible	Do all new
Buying an end-to-end solution is preferable to buying multiple functional solutions or building from scratch	Buy best-of-breed and perform in house integration
Move new business applications and services into off-loaded application processors.	Build new components on top of existing infrastructure first. Re-write business applications in existing platforms

DATA TENETS

Provide a single central data base repository with a "single view of the truth" for all applications and users, regardless of location or the channel used for access.	Provide a set of federated data bases, customized and configured for different purposes/users
Establish business unit "ownership" for each data item.	Create a centralized governance for all data
Ensure the data is primarily portioned according to business function	Partition data primarily on geography
Establish a centralized Operational Data Store system for fast transactional responses, and a separate OLAP data base for analytics	Establish a group of Operational Data systems providing online and analytical capabilities on a segmented basis

Services Tenets

Leverage legacy investments by exposing the content through services, and ensure that legacy applications are pushed to deliver new and compelling functions for the enterprise and its customers.	Enable services for new applications only
Application development APIs will become business-oriented as opposed to functionality oriented. Expose coarsely granular XML	Expose services only as coarse SOAP services
Will use J2EE Containers with Java Beans as the base OOP paradigm	Will use Plain java Objects (POJOs)

FOUNDATIONAL TENETS

Use message queuing as the strategic middleware standard. Mapping to other middleware will be supported as required, but the canonical service distribution protocol will be XML based.	Use federated middleware backbones, integrated via an Enterprise Service Bus
Unify connectivity protocols and communications interfaces end-to-end. Use open, off-the-shelf protocols and systems.	Allow multiple protocols, but convert protocols at the boundary.
Optimize negotiated contracts with the suppliers of network products and services to reduce network costs.	Allow best-pricing contracts on a regional basis
Support currently installed hardware base, but ensure a suitable hardware upgrade path.	Replace all old hardware

PRESENTATION TENETS

Use interfaces that run as thin client in all major web browsers	Use Ajax Rich Client technology with focus on supporting the Microsoft Explorer browser for all internal applications, and Firefox and IE for external applications
Will seamlessly support multiple content delivery mechanisms (email, pub/sub, etc.)	Use different interface gateways for email, publish/subscribe, and wireless distribution.
Approach presentation needs according to market and product segmentation.	Develop a separate interface handler for each independent user channel.
For all interface functions provide a keyboard shortcut and an escape path to command line mode	Minimize the need for keyboards. Standardize the user interface around the use of the mouse for desk based applications and the touch-screen for all self-serve applications.

THE STANDARDS

The standards portion of the "Tenets and Standards" document is more straightforward, if not less conflictive. Here you place the stake in the ground to define the key technologies you will be using.

Use Linux and Open Systems as the preferred technology platform	Use of Microsoft's NET technology base is preferred
Oracle is the preferred DBMS	MySQL will be used
Hardware will be Intel based	Will use IBM's p-Series hardware
The preferred development languages are Java and/or C++.	Will use Python with wrapped C functions when needed
Will use IBM's Websphere J2EE as the standard operational environment	Will use JBoss as the standard J2EE platform
Use the Struts Framework for development	Use the Django Framework

BIBLIOGRAPHY

Armour, Philip G. "The Laws of Software Process"—Auerbach Publications. Boca Raton, Fl. 2004

Barabasi Albert-Laszio. "Linked" — Plume Printing. Cambridge, MA. 2003

Bernstein Philip A. & Newcomer, Eric. "Principles of Transaction Processing"— Morgan Kaufmann Publishers Inc. San Francisco, CA. 1997

Boehm, Barry, and Turner, Richard. "Balancing Agility and Discipline"— Addison-Wesley. Boston, M. 2004

Bosch, Jan. "Design & Use of Software Architectures"— Addison-Wesley. London, England.2000

Britton, Chris." IT Architectures and Middleware"— Addison-Wesley. Indianapolis, IN. 2001

Brooks, Jr. Frederick P. "The Mythical man-Month" — Addison-Wesley. Chapel Hill, NC. 2002

Carter, Sandy. "The New Language of Business, SOA & Web 2.0"— IBM Press. Ipper Saddle River, NJ. 2007

Chorafas, Dimitris N. "Enterprise Architecture and New Generation Information Systems"— St Lucie Press. Boca Raton, Fl. 2002

Chou, Timothy. "Seven—Software Business Models" — Active Book Press. Los Angeles, CA. 2008

Chou, Timothy. "The End of Software" — Sams Publishing Indianapolis, IN. 2005

Enriquez, Juan. "As the Future Catches You"— Crown Business. New York, NY. 2001

Gabriel P. Richard. "Patterns of Software"— Oxford University Press. New York, NY. 1998

Gladwell, Malcom. "Blink, then power of thinking without thinking"—Little, Brown and Co. New York, NY. 2005

Glass, Robert L. "Facts and Fallacies of Software Engineering"— Addison-Wesley. Boston. MA. 2004

Hurtwitz, Judith. Bloor, Robin. Baroudi, Carol. Kaufman, Marcia. "Service Oriented Architecture for Dummies"—Wiley Publsihing, Inc. Indianapolis, IN. 2007

Kaku, Michiu. Visions. How Science Will Revolutionize the 21st Century. Anchor. New York, NY. 1998

Kurzweil, Ray. "The Singularity is Near"—Penguin Books, New York, NY. 2005

Lane, Dean. "CIO Wisdom"— Prentice Hall Inc. Upper Saddle River, NJ. 2004

Merholz, Peter, Schauer, Brandon. "Subject to Change"— O'Reilly Media Inc. Sebastopol, CA 95472

McConnell. "Software Estimation"—Microsoft Press. Redmont, WA. 2006

Rosenberg Scott. "Dreaming in Code"—Three Rivers Press, NY. 2008

Satndage Tom, "The Victorian Internet" the Remarkable Story of the Telegraph"— Walker & Company, New York, NY. 2005

Segaran, Toby. "Programming Collective Intelligence"— O'Reilly Media Inc. Sebastopol, CA. 2007

Shuen, Amy. "Web 2.0: A Strategy Guide"—O'Reilly Media Inc. Sebastopol, Ca. 2008

Spewak, Steven H, with Steven C. Hill. "Enterprise Architecture Planning. Developing a Blueprint for Data, Applications and Technology" —A Wiley-QED Publication, John Wiley & Sons, Inc. Princeton, NJ. 1992.

Spewak, Steven H. "Enterprise Architecture Planning"—John Wiley & Sons Inc. Princeton, NJ. 1992

Spolsky, Joel. "Joel on Software"—Apress. New Your, NY. 2004

Spolsky, Joel. "More Joel on Software"—Apress. New Your, NY. 2008

Sunstein, Cass R. "Infotopia"— Oxford University Press. New York, NY.2006

Stutzke, Richard D. "Estimating Software-Intensive Systems"— Addison-Wesley. Upper Saddle River, NJ. 2005.

Thrasher, Harwell. "Boiling the IT Frog""— MakingITClear, Inc. Duluth, GA. 2007

Younker, Jeff. "Foundations of Agile Python Development"— Apress. New York, NY. 2008

INDEX

A

Architecture **A**
Architecture
Abstraction · iii, iv
Business Process Modeling · 151, 207
Cloud · xiii, xiv, 155, 157, 164, 174,
  197, 204, 371, 372, 375, 389
CORBA · 191
Distributed Processing · vi, 159, 161
Fabric · vii, 115, 116, 197, 209, 210,
  269
Integration · 140, 203, 211, 338
Level I · 101, 102, 103, 104, 106, 107,
  108, 118, 123, 140, 143, 144, 217,
  219
Level II · 102, 103, 106, 107, 118,
  140, 143, 144, 217
Level III · 102, 103, 106, 107, 140,
  217
Membrane · vii, 196, 203
Object Oriented · 144
ODS · 228
Open Systems Interconnect · 114,
  115, 116, 141
Orchestrator · 197, 206
Presentation Layer · x, 142, 159, 195,
  356, 398
Reference Model · vi, 115, 117, 119,
  120, 121, 122
RMI · 174, 191, 192
SOA · i, iii, iv, vi, vii, viii, ix, xiii, xiv,
  xvi, xvii, xviii, xx, 31, 36, 39, 78,
  79, 101, 106, 116, 118, 121, 126,
  134, 140, 142, 143, 144, 145, 146,

147, 148, 150, 151, 155, 157, 158,
  159, 161, 163, 165, 167, 168, 170,
  171, 172, 173, 174, 176, 177,
  180,182, 186, 188, 189, 191, 192,
  194, 195, 196, 197, 198, 203, 206,
  207, 208, 209, 210, 211, 212, 214,
  215, 217, 218, 219, 220, 221, 222,
  224, 226, 227, 230, 234, 238, 240,
  241, 243, 244, 245, 246, 247, 248,
  249, 252, 255, 256, 258, 264, 265,
  266, 269, 271, 276, 279, 286, 287,
  288, 330, 336, 337, 338, 339, 340,
  341, 342, 355, 356, 357, 358, 361,
  371, 376, 392, 403
Standards · vi, ix, x, 105, 114, 123,
  124, 332, 393, 400
Systems Management · viii, 209, 215,
  242, 254, 264, 265, 266, 269, 270
Tenets · vi, ix, x, 123, 124, 125, 126,
  128, 129, 130, 131, 137, 138, 140,
  142, 143, 350, 393, 394, 395, 397,
  398, 400
Transaction Integrity · 225, 227, 229,
  260
Transactions · 225, 227
Transparency · 156, 157
Availability & Performance
Caching · vii, 221, 236, 238, 242, 244
Performance · vii, 107, 139, 217, 243,
  246, 337
Prophesy · 250
Reliability · viii, 254, 255
Service Level Agreement · 76
Systems Management · viii, 254, 264,
  266

B

Business Case · 361

Competitive Set · v, 38, 41, 50

Innovation · v, 80, 81

Requirements · v, 86

Return on Investment · 28, 53, 74

Business Process Re-engineering · 23

C

Computer Languages

Algol · 135

Basic · 68, 135, 154, 302

C · 35, 46, 135, 167, 206, 389, 400, 405

C++ · 135, 400

COBOL · xiii, xv, 32, 135, 292, 293

Dynamic Link Libraries · 153

Eiffel · 135

Java · 127, 135, 191, 199, 200, 292, 293, 396, 400

LISP · 135

Object Oriented · 144

PL/I · 135

Python · 136, 400, 405

Ruby · 136

Computer Reservation Systems · xi

Concept Simulation · 247

CRM · 55, 357

Loyalty · 122

D

Data

CICS · 227

Data Keeper · 197

Data Modeling · vii, ix, x, 122, 142, 152, 160, 180, 195, 197, 204, 213, 214, 215, 220, 221, 227, 228, 230, 231, 232, 240, 286, 352, 356, 359, 360, 373, 378, 379, 381, 382, 388, 395, 405

Databases · 122, 216

Enterprise Application Integration · 211

Extract/Transform/Load · 228, 296, 351

Information Aggregators · ix, 384

Information Distillers · ix, 384

MapReduce · 230

Matching and Integration · vii, 230

Operational Data Store · 228

Relational Database · 226

Sentinel · vii, 213, 214, 215, 220, 227, 228, 230

Visibility Exceptions · vii, 228

Detailed Simulation · 247

E

Engineering · viii, 107, 252, 253, 361, 404

I

Interactive Voice Recognition · 29, 94

L

Legacy · 27, 394

M

Moore's Law · 30, 48, 68, 148, 390

N

NASA · 37, 123, 264, 266

Network

Bell Labs · 68

DECNet · 114

DMZ · 121, 178, 203, 262

Internet · xvi, 26, 31, 36, 38, 44, 47, 48, 49, 50, 52, 56, 58, 59, 61, 66, 71, 72, 112, 128, 164, 259, 371, 381, 387, 391, 404

OSI · 114, 115, 116, 141

Simulation · 250

SNA · 114, 141

TCP/IP · 114, 116, 139, 141

Virtual Private Network · 122, 204

Web · 27, 31, 35, 38, 48, 51, 59, 70, 121, 135, 190, 200, 213, 250, 350, 372, 380, 387, 391, 403, 405

O

Operating Systems

Android · 50

Linux · 155, 164, 318, 400

MS/DOS · 92, 109

Windows · 83, 109, 153, 154, 155, 200, 201, 250

Organization

Culture · viii, 307

Dealing with Politics · ix, 310

Engineering · viii, 252

Governance · viii, 276

Leadership · viii, 300, 303, 304

Skills and Training · ix, 343, 345

Team · viii, 283

P

Project Management · viii, ix, 88, 279, 280, 281, 288, 325, 326, 332, 361

Documentation · ix, 332, 334, 336

Migration · ix, 156, 281, 346, 348, 349, 350, 354, 355, 356

Milestones · ix, 325, 328, 329

Requirements · v, 39, 43, 86

Trade Offs · 86, 87

Y2K Example · ix, 213, 364, 365, 366

Prophesy

Characteristics · 248

Q

Quality Assurance · 272, 340

Documentation · ix, 332, 334, 336

Testing · ix, 210, 337, 338, 340, 341

R

Rapid Modeling · 247

S

Project Management · v, vi, 86, 108, 109, 113

Security · viii, 209, 215, 254, 260, 267

DMZ · 121, 178, 203, 262

Service Oriented Architecture

Architectures · 104, 144, 156, 403

SaaS · ix, xiv, 44, 370, 371, 374, 376

SOA · i, iii, iv, vi, vii, viii, ix, xiii, xiv, xvi, xvii, xviii, xx, 31, 36, 39, 78, 79, 101, 106, 116, 118, 121, 126, 134, 140, 142, 143, 144, 145, 146, 147, 148, 150, 151, 155, 157, 158,

159, 161, 163, 165, 167, 168, 170, 171, 172, 173, 174, 176, 177, 180,182, 186, 188, 189, 191, 192, 194, 195, 196, 197, 198, 203, 206, 207, 208, 209, 210, 211, 212, 214, 215, 217, 218, 219, 220, 221, 222, 224, 226, 227, 230, 234, 238, 240, 241, 243, 244, 245, 246, 247, 248, 249, 252, 255, 256, 258, 264, 265, 266, 269, 271, 276, 279, 286, 287, 288, 330, 336, 337, 338, 339, 340, 341, 342, 355, 356, 357, 358, 361, 371, 376, 392, 403

Services · vi, vii, x, 43, 122, 154, 170, 172, 177, 178, 179, 180, 184, 190, 215, 220, 225, 277, 286, 287, 361, 396

Asynchronous · 182, 209

Business Services · 178, 179

Event Driven · 183, 209

Interface · 139, 190, 192, 238, 396

Interfaces · vi, 190, 192, 286

Lifecycle · ix, 361

Query/Reply · 182, 186, 243

Service Granularity · vi, 187

Taxonomy · vi, 168, 361, 379

Transactional · vii, 220, 225

WSDL · 190, 286

Simulation · vii, 246, 247

Prophesy · 250

Types of · 246

single queue · 247

SOA

Control Layer · vii, 241, 269

Enterprise Service Bus · vii, 116, 171, 186, 209, 210, 211, 212, 241

Framework · vii, 100, 104, 170, 194, 196, 198, 242, 361, 401

Managing · vii, viii, 88, 165, 167, 222, 241, 266, 273, 303

Service Repository · 266, 287

Services · vi, vii, x, 43, 122, 154, 170, 172, 177, 178, 179, 180, 184, 190, 215, 220, 225, 277, 286, 287, 361, 396

Testing · 209, 337, 338, 340, 341

Social Media

Facebook · 70, 196, 370, 371, 374, 387

Google · 27, 50, 61, 199, 213, 234, 258, 259, 312, 370, 371, 374, 375, 381, 385, 391

Twitter · 70, 374

Strategy

Architecture · vi, viii, xiii, xiv, xvi, xvii, 24, 35, 36, 75, 79, 85, 98, 99, 100, 103, 104, 105, 106, 107, 108, 109, 114, 117, 118, 131, 133, 134, 143, 144, 145, 146, 160, 190, 191, 245, 253, 279, 283, 284, 286, 361, 403, 404, 405

Business process Reengineering · 23

CASE Methodology · 34, 144

Complexity · v, 91, 92, 222

Enterprise Resource Planning · 24, 51, 52, 95, 109, 132, 377

Gartner Hype Chart · xiii, 27, 29, 382, 384

Migration · ix, 156, 281, 346, 348, 349, 350, 354, 355, 356

Open Systems · xiv, 75, 113, 370, 400

Outsourcing · viii, 295, 371

Security · viii, 209, 215, 254, 260, 267

Systems Management · viii, 254, 264, 266

Technology · v, vi, ix, xvii, xx, 25, 37, 38, 40, 43, 46, 48, 51, 55, 57, 64, 73, 74, 95, 99, 126, 157, 167, 186, 315, 317, 318, 405

T

Technologies

Emerging · v, 46

Transformation · iv, v, vii, viii, ix, xix, xx, xxi, 23, 24, 25, 26, 37, 73, 74, 80, 86, 88, 91, 106, 109, 140, 201, 220, 232, 273, 275, 279, 331, 343, 346, 351, 356, 361, 363, 364, 392

Technology

Artificial Intelligence · 207, 369, 378, 389

Blackberry · 45

Cloud · xiii, xiv, 155, 157, 164, 174, 197, 204, 371, 372, 375, 389

HTML · 200

Infrastructure · 170

Innovation · v, 80, 81

Internet · xvi, 26, 31, 36, 38, 44, 47, 48, 49, 50, 52, 56, 58, 59, 61, 66, 71, 72, 112, 128, 164, 259, 371, 381, 387, 391, 404

iPod · 45, 61, 196

IVR · 29, 94

J2EE · 136, 396, 400

Kindle · 71

Mobile · 373

Skype · 72, 391

Smartphones · 373

Social Media · 35, 48, 70, 387, 403, 405

Telepresence · 65, 66, 67, 69, 71, 72

Thin Clients · 200

Transformation · iv, v, vii, viii, ix, xix, xx, xxi, 23, 24, 25, 26, 37, 73, 74, 80, 86, 88, 91, 106, 109, 140, 201, 220, 232, 273, 275, 279, 331, 343, 346, 351, 356, 361, 363, 364, 392

Virtual Machine · 199, 250

Visicalc · 40, 150

XML · 142, 178, 190, 191, 192, 234, 238, 396, 397

Tenets

Category I · vi, 125, 126, 128, 129, 130, 131, 134, 137, 138, 140, 142, 143

Category II · vi, 125, 128, 129, 134, 137, 138, 140, 142, 143

Category III · vi, 125, 129, 140, 142, 143

V

Vendors

Apple · 29, 50, 59, 61, 71, 92, 335, 373, 381

DEC · 30, 56, 59, 60

Hewlett Packard · 30

IBM · xi, 27, 30, 31, 40, 59, 60, 93, 135, 186, 321, 371, 372, 381, 388, 390, 400, 403

Abstraction · iii, iv

Business Process Modeling · 170, 229

Cloud · xiii, xiv, 174, 176, 183, 194, 218, 225, 410, 411, 415, 431

CORBA · 212

Distributed Processing · vi, 178, 181

Fabric · vii, 126, 218, 232, 233, 298

Integration · 157, 224, 235, 373

Level I · 111, 112, 114, 116, 117, 118, 130, 135, 158, 161, 162, 163, 241, 243

Level II · 111, 112, 116, 117, 130, 158, 161, 162, 163, 241

Level III · 111, 112, 116, 117, 158, 241

Membrane · vii, 217, 224

Object Oriented · 162

ODS · 254

Open Systems Interconnect · 124, 125, 127, 158, 159

Orchestrator · 218, 228

Presentation Layer · x, 126, 160, 179, 216, 394, 440

Linux · 155, 164, 318, 400

Microsoft · 27, 50, 60, 87, 109, 164, 199, 250, 318, 321, 371, 398, 400, 404

MS/Windows · 83, 109, 153, 154, 155, 200, 201, 250

Open Systems · xiv, 75, 113, 370, 400

PeopleSoft · 132

Philips · 30

Prime Computers · 30, 59

Request for Proposals · 95, 321, 322

Reference Model · vi, 126, 128, 130, 131, 132, 133

RMI · 194, 212, 213, 214

SOA · i, iii, iv, vi, vii, viii, ix, xiii, xiv, xvi, xvii, xviii, xx, 33, 37, 40, 83, 85, 110, 116, 126, 127, 129, 133, 138, 149, 157, 160, 161, 162, 163, 165, 166, 167, 169, 170, 174, 176, 177, 178, 180, 181, 182, 184, 185, 187, 189, 190, 192, 193, 194, 196,197, 200, 202, 205, 208, 209, 212, 213, 214, 215, 216, 217, 219, 224, 228, 229, 230, 232, 233, 234, 235, 236, 238, 239, 240, 241, 242, 243, 244, 245, 247, 249, 252, 253, 256, 257, 260, 264, 267, 268, 270, 272, 273, 274, 275, 276, 277, 281, 284, 285, 287, 293, 294, 295, 298, 300, 305, 308, 316, 317, 365, 371, 372, 373, 374, 375, 376, 377, 392, 394, 395, 396, 400, 410, 416, 434, 444

Standards · vi, ix, x, 114, 124, 134, 135, 367, 436, 442

Systems Management · viii, 233, 239, 269, 283, 293, 294, 295, 298, 299, 300

Tenets · vi, ix, x, 134, 135, 136,
137, 138, 141, 142, 143, 144,
153, 154, 157, 158, 160, 161,
387, 436, 437, 440, 442
Transaction Integrity · 251, 253,
255, 289, 290
Transactions · 251, 253
Transparency · 174, 175
Availability & Performance
Caching · vii, 245, 263, 264, 269,
272
Performance · vii, 117, 156, 241,
270, 274, 372
Prophesy · 279
Reliability · viii, 283, 284
Service Level Agreement · 82
Systems Management · viii, 283,
293, 295

B

Business Case · 400
Competitive Set · v, 39, 43, 53
Innovation · v, 86, 87
Requirements · v, 92
Return on Investment · 30, 56, 80
Business Process Re-engineering · 23

C

Computer Languages
Algol · 151
Basic · 73, 151, 173, 332
C · 36, 50, 151, 185, 228, 431, 442,
445
C++ · 151, 442
COBOL · xiii, xv, 34, 150, 322, 323
Dynamic Link Libraries · 172
Eiffel · 151

Java · 127, 140, 151, 213, 221,
322, 324, 439, 442
LISP · 151
Object Oriented · 162
PL/I · 150
Python · 151, 442, 446
Ruby · 151
Computer Reservation Systems · xi
Concept Simulation · 275
CRM · 58, 395
Loyalty · 133

D

Data
CICS · 253
Data Keeper · 219
Data Modeling · vii, ix, x, 133, 160,
171, 179, 180, 200, 216, 219,
225, 237, 238, 239, 240, 245,
253, 254, 256, 257, 258, 266,
316, 389, 394, 397, 398, 412,
418, 419, 421, 422, 423, 430,
437, 446
Databases · 133, 240
Enterprise Application Integration
· 235
Extract/Transform/Load · 255,
326, 389
Information Aggregators · ix, 425
Information Distillers · ix, 425
MapReduce · 256
Matching and Integration · vii, 256
Operational Data Store · 254
Relational Database · 253
Sentinel · vii, 237, 238, 239, 240,
245, 253, 254, 256
Visibility Exceptions · vii, 254
Detailed Simulation · 276

E

Engineering · viii, 117, 281, 282, 400, 445

I

Interactive Voice Recognition · 30, 102

L

Legacy · 28, 437

M

Moore's Law · 31, 51, 73, 167, 432

N

NASA · 38, 135, 293, 295
Network
  Bell Labs · 72
  DECNet · 124
  DMZ · 133, 198, 225, 291
  Internet · xvi, 27, 32, 37, 39, 47, 50, 51, 52, 53, 56, 59, 62, 65, 70, 76, 122, 140, 183, 288, 410, 422, 429, 433, 445
  OSI · 124, 125, 127, 158, 159
  Simulation · 279
  SNA · 124, 158
  TCP/IP · 124, 125, 126, 155, 158, 159
  Virtual Private Network · 133, 225
  Web · 28, 32, 36, 39, 52, 54, 62, 74, 127, 132, 150, 211, 221, 237, 279, 387, 412, 421, 428, 434, 444, 445

O

Operating Systems
  Android · 53
  Linux · 173, 183, 351, 442
  MS/DOS · 99, 119
  Windows · 90, 119, 172, 173, 221, 222, 279
Organization
  Culture · viii, 338
  Dealing with Politics · ix, 342
  Engineering · viii, 281
  Governance · viii, 305
  Leadership · viii, 330, 334, 335
  Skills and Training · ix, 378, 381
  Team · viii, 313

P

Project Management · viii, ix, 94, 308, 309, 310, 311, 318, 358, 360, 367, 401
  Documentation · ix, 367, 369, 371
  Migration · ix, 175, 310, 382, 385, 387, 391, 392, 394
  Milestones · ix, 358, 362, 363
  Requirements · v, 40, 46, 92
  Trade Offs · 92, 93, 94
  Y2K Example · ix, 237, 403, 404, 405
Prophesy
  Characteristics · 277

Q

Quality Assurance · 301, 375
  Documentation · ix, 367, 369, 371

Testing · ix, 233, 372, 373, 375, 376

R

Rapid Modeling · 275

S

Project Management · v, vi, 92, 118, 119, 123
Security · viii, 233, 239, 283, 289, 296
DMZ · 133, 198, 225, 291
Service Oriented Architecture
Architectures · 113, 162, 174, 444
SaaS · ix, xiv, 47, 409, 410, 414, 416
SOA · i, iii, iv, vi, vii, viii, ix, xiii, xiv, xvi, xvii, xviii, xx, 33, 37, 40, 83, 85, 110, 116, 126, 127, 129, 133, 138, 149, 157, 160, 161, 162, 163, 165, 166, 167, 169, 170, 174, 176, 177, 178, 180, 181, 182, 184, 185, 187, 189, 190, 192, 193, 194, 196,197, 200, 202, 206, 208, 209, 212, 213, 214, 215, 216, 217, 219, 224, 228, 229, 230, 232, 233, 234, 235, 236, 238, 239, 240, 241, 242, 243, 244, 245, 247, 249, 252, 253, 256, 257, 260, 264, 267, 268, 270, 272, 273, 274, 275, 276, 277, 281, 284, 285, 287, 293, 294, 295, 298, 300, 305, 308, 316, 317, 365, 371, 372, 373, 374, 375, 376, 377, 392, 394, 395, 396, 400, 410, 416, 434, 444
Services · vi, vii, x, 46, 133, 173, 189, 192, 197, 198, 199, 200, 204, 211,

240, 244, 251, 306, 316, 317, 400, 439
Asynchronous · 202, 233
Business Services · 198
Event Driven · 203, 233
Interface · 155, 211, 213, 264, 439
Interfaces · vi, 211, 214, 316
Lifecycle · ix, 400
Query/Reply · 202, 205, 271
Service Granularity · vi, 207
Taxonomy · vi, 187, 400, 419, 420
Transactional · vii, 244, 251
WSDL · 211, 316
Simulation · vii, 274, 276
Prophesy · 279
Types of · 275
single queue · 275
SOA
Control Layer · vii, 268, 298
Enterprise Service Bus · vii, 126, 190, 206, 232, 233, 234, 235, 236, 268
Framework · vii, 110, 113, 189, 215, 217, 219, 270, 400, 442
Managing · vii, viii, 94, 184, 185, 247, 268, 295, 302, 333
Service Repository · 295, 317
Services · vi, vii, x, 46, 133, 173, 189, 192, 197, 198, 199, 200, 204, 211, 240, 244, 251, 305, 316, 317, 400, 439
Testing · 233, 372, 373, 375, 376
Social Media
Facebook · 74, 217, 410, 414, 428
Google · 28, 53, 65, 220, 237, 260, 287, 344, 409, 410, 414, 415, 421, 426, 434
Twitter · 74, 414
Strategy
Architecture · vi, viii, xiii, xiv, xvi, xvii, 24, 36, 37, 80, 85, 90, 107, 108, 110, 112, 113, 114, 116,

117, 118, 119, 124, 128, 130,
145, 147, 148, 161, 162, 163,
165, 179, 211, 212, 273, 282,
308, 313, 314, 316, 400, 444,
445, 446
Business process Reengineering ·
23
CASE Methodology · 35, 162
Complexity · v, 98, 99, 247
Enterprise Resource Planning · 24,
54, 55, 103, 119, 120, 145, 417
Gartner Hype Chart · xiii, 29, 30,
422, 425
Migration · ix, 175, 310, 382, 385,
387, 391, 392, 394
Open Systems · xiv, 81, 124, 409,
442
Outsourcing · viii, 325, 410
Security · viii, 233, 239, 283, 289,
296
Systems Management · viii, 283,
293, 295
Technology · v, vi, ix, xvii, xx, 25,
38, 39, 41, 46, 49, 51, 54, 58,
60, 68, 77, 79, 103, 108, 139,
175, 185, 206, 347, 349, 350,
446

T

Technologies
  Emerging · v, 49
  Transformation · iv, v, vii, viii, ix,
  xix, xx, xxi, 23, 24, 25, 27, 38,
  77, 79, 86, 87, 92, 94, 98, 116,
  119, 157, 222, 223, 245, 258,
  302, 304, 308, 365, 378, 382,
  383, 388, 394, 400, 402, 403,
  435
Technology

Artificial Intelligence · 229, 408,
  418, 431
Blackberry · 48
Cloud · xiii, xiv, 173, 176, 183,
  194, 218, 225, 410, 411, 415,
  431
HTML · 221
Infrastructure · 189
Innovation · v, 86, 87
Internet · xvi, 28, 32, 37, 39, 47,
  50, 51, 52, 53, 56, 59, 62, 65,
  70, 76, 122, 140, 183, 288, 410,
  422, 429, 433, 445
iPod · 48, 64, 217
IVR · 30, 102
J2EE · 152, 439, 442
Kindle · 75
Mobile · 412
Skype · 76, 434
Smartphones · 412
Social Media · 36, 52, 74, 428,
  444, 445
Telepresence · 69, 70, 71, 73, 75,
  76, 77
Thin Clients · 221
Transformation · iv, v, vii, viii, ix,
  xix, xx, xxi, 23, 24, 25, 27, 38,
  77, 79, 86, 92, 94, 98, 116, 119,
  157, 222, 223, 245, 258, 302,
  304, 308, 365, 378, 382, 383,
  388, 394, 400, 402, 403, 435
Virtual Machine · 221, 279
Visicalc · 42, 169
XML · 160, 198, 211, 212, 213,
  260, 264, 439, 440
Tenets
  Category I · vi, 136, 137, 138, 141,
  142, 143, 144, 149, 153, 154,
  157, 158, 159, 160
  Category II · vi, 137, 141, 149,
  153, 154, 157, 158, 159, 160,
  161

Category III · vi, 137, 142, 157,
159, 160, 161

V

Vendors
Apple · 30, 53, 62, 64, 75, 99, 370,
412, 422
DEC · 31, 59, 62, 64
Hewlett Packard · 31
IBM · xi, 28, 32, 42, 62, 63, 100,
150, 206, 353, 410, 411, 422,
430, 432, 442, 444
Linux · 173, 183, 351, 442
Microsoft · 28, 53, 64, 93, 119,
183, 220, 279, 351, 353, 410,
440, 442, 445
MS/Windows · 90, 119, 172, 173,
221, 222, 279
Object Management Group · 126
Open Systems · xiv, 81, 124, 409,
442
PeopleSoft · 145
Philips · 31
Prime Computers · 31, 62
Request for Proposals · 104, 353,
354, 355

www.ingramcontent.com/pod-product-compliance
Lightning Source LLC
Chambersburg PA
CBHW071359050326
40689CB00010B/1699